Danny Johnson

Best Wishes!

Joe Brightwell Ernsall

Merry Christmas Dewey
from
Don & Pat Bishop
1964

The Best of True West

THE BEST OF
TRUE
WEST

edited by
Joe Austell Small

Julian Messner, Inc.
New York

Published by Julian Messner, Inc.
8 West 40 Street, New York 18

© Copyright 1964, by Julian Messner, Inc.

FIRST EDITION

Printed in the United States of America

Library of Congress Catalog Card No. 64-23117

In memory of Dr. Walter Prescott Webb

FOREWORD

I doubt if you have ever read a collection of stories on Western Americana quite like this. For the most part, it has been taken from the first five years of *True West*. These issues, long out of print, are now collector's items. The material, much in demand and not generally available, created the need for this book.

We have selected stories that represent the very *heart* of a fantastic era. Included are the gunfighters, lawmen and Indians—long portrayed as the *only* West—as well as stories about the little men and women who were BIG in building our West, and whose experiences were every bit as dramatic and colorful as those of the Sitting Bulls and Billy-the-Kids.

I believe you will value this book because it affords a glimpse into those rowdy days *as they really were*. This era has been so grossly distorted that the words "western" and "fiction" are almost synonymous. It is a pity that the romantic part of our history has been presented in such complete fantasy for so long a time. I discovered years ago that the truth about the West was much more fascinating than the "cloppity-clop, bang, bang!" version. Unfortunately, few people were doing anything to correct the distortion.

Back in 1933 while I was interviewing the president of a large bank for a magazine article, he reached into the bottom drawer of his desk, pulled out a "pulp" western and demanded angrily, "When is someone going to publish a magazine about the West that a man can leave *on top* of his desk?"

Even after that bank president had planted the idea for a new type of Western magazine, I hesitated to attempt such an "experiment." I was no historian. Who was I to present the unvarnished truth about the West?

Twenty years later, when I launched my career as a publisher, it was with an outdoor magazine: *Western Sportsman*. Soon after it started, I decided that perhaps a collection of pieces on our better known outlaws wouldn't be entirely amiss. When our new BAD MAN series began to bring in 80% of the magazine's fan mail, I knew it was time to quit dreaming and act! That's when *True West* was born.

Simple as it may sound, the title came at two o'clock one morning; the outlines, plans, and a continual fluttery feeling in the pit of my stomach came night and day thereafter until the first issue appeared on the newsstands in August of 1953.

It took long, grueling months before we received much critical attention. When we finally were noticed, it became apparent that people were taking us seriously, referring to *True West* as "a new type of western journalism."

Our brand of writing was created by combining the accuracy of the dry, historical journals with the swift movement of fiction. Fact plus entertainment. We proved that a "Western" magazine could be successful without distortion. We proved that a popular, *authentic* approach could and would keep all age groups interested.

In presenting our magazine about the ways of the Old West, we decided there would be no holds barred when it came to the truth. Every sentence would be as authentic as the testimony of eye-witnesses and skillful research by top authorities could make it. This was, and is, *True West*. The most important element of the magazine and of this book is truth—all too rare a quality in the world today.

What *is* the truth? The question is not always easy to answer. We all have a point of view, a different perspective. We don't all see the same event in exactly the same way.

Foreword

Was the Dalton-Doolin gang good or bad? They robbed, they stole, and they killed. Society today would consider them thoroughly bad. But you could not have convinced a good many people in the town of Ingalls, Oklahoma, and much of the surrounding territory that these boys were evil men. They were "good old cowboys that got off on the wrong path" to some, and knights in armor to others. Compared to several of the marshals of that period, they were downright heroes!

In 1954, when we published the "accepted," thoroughly documented version of "Rose of Cimarron," we raised a major controversy. One of the complainers was an old man who walked into my office three days after the magazine hit the stands. He told me an amazing story. Insofar as he saw it, *he* was telling the truth.

The old fellow claimed the Dalton-Doolin boys were loved by people throughout their part of the country. He had personally ridden down the streets of Ingalls on the shoulders of Bill Doolin while Doolin fired his gun into the air, raised good-natured Cain, and bought every kid in sight anything he wanted. This man asked me, "Do you remember the two little boys in the story who were playing in the street when the first bullet was fired and one of them got nicked on the left heel?" I told him that I did. "Well," he replied, "I was that *other* little boy!"

The Dalton-Doolin gang overpaid for services, room and board; gave loans; and helped people in a hundred different ways, the old man told me. Between these outlaws and the marshals there was no comparison. For some, the outlaws were good, the marshals were bad.

What *is* the truth? We are not always absolutely sure, but we try to be fair and factual. I sincerely believe people are fascinated by an accurate presentation of what happened in the Old West to the railroad worker, the sod-buster, the little cowman, the not-so-barbarous Indian and even the poor fellow who *didn't* find gold. I think readers are more interested in some of the happy, heart-rending and often incredible things that happened to these

9

people than they are in the fantasies which have given the world a lopsided view of the West.

The magazine had been struggling along for years and, then, came the realization that it was a success. A good friend, one of the great historians of our day, came into my office and announced with a grin, "Joe, you've got it made! Today I saw a copy of *True West* on a bank president's desk." He never knew how much that meant to me.

If my magazine has only served to take Western Americana out of the bottom drawer and put it in plain view with other "respectable" periodicals, that is reward enough for me. As it turns out, however, perhaps the biggest contribution *True West* has made (and one which I did not anticipate) was to unearth primary source material which otherwise might have been destroyed or overlooked.

We are only a generation or two away from the people and events that made up the Old West. Men and women are still living who knew the frontier intimately. Our magazine stimulated their interest and restored their pride in those bygone days—and the treasure hunt was on!

From the number of priceless, first-hand accounts of the old pioneering days that we have published, it is clear *True West* has made its greatest contribution in preserving authentic details of our western movement that might otherwise have been lost forever.

With the help of Pat Wagner and Cathie Wilson, I have chosen the stories in this collection because, in my estimation, they are the best we have published and most worthy of being preserved in permanent book form. I hope you will agree.

JOE AUSTELL SMALL

Table of Contents

The Best of True West

Asthan-Dat-Sah-Ie, The Dead Woman

by Marietta Wetherill as told to Mabel C. Wright

You are surprised that I speak of a medicine woman? There are a few of them. In all my years with the Navajos, I knew of but one—*Asthan-Dat-Sah-Ie,* The Dead Woman. This is her story:

Pretty One and Younger Sister lived with their mother, Blanket Weaver, at the head of Yellow Bird Canyon, a narrow defile leading into the great Chaco Canyon in New Mexico. It was a beautiful spot; the hogans were half hidden among the greasewood brush; here and there was a splotch of vivid green grass; and always, day and night, you heard the song of birds.

15

The two girls often came down to our trading post, close to the ruins of Pueblo Bonito, to visit me. At the end of the last century, when these events took place, my husband Richard Wetherill was directing excavations for the Hyde Exploring Expedition. In that section of Navajoland, Anglos were still a novelty, though Mexican sheepherders had been filtering in for some decades. Our trading post, which was set up to care for the needs of the scientific work, with its Indian laborers, was quite the social center.

It was not my first contact, however, with Navajos. In fact I was truly one of them. I had been initiated into the Che Clan when a young girl traveling through the Southwest with my archeologically curious father, Sidney Palmer. Navajo was a second language to me, and I could appreciate Pretty One's pride in the long turquoise earrings which told her world that she was now a woman. The girls felt, then, that they could confide in me; and in the tragedies that so soon followed, perhaps I was closer to them than any one else.

But now the problems were only those of teen-agers. Younger Sister, for example, could have no identity of her own, not even a name, until Pretty One, the first-born and a year older, was married. Not that it appeared there would be any great delay. Both were very attractive. Pretty One was gentle with a shy smile. She was industrious and obedient, and we all liked to have her around. Younger Sister was unquestionably the smarter of the two and had a gift for mimicry which she used with the cruelty of youth.

She was the pet clown of her clan. When you heard roaring laughter coming from the group of Indian youths gathered outside the trading post, you could be sure that Younger Sister was doing one of her imitations. It might be Old Badger in a fit of temper being tossed off his horse, or even funnier, an impersonation of Cats' Mother. This aged squaw lived up in the hills and was shunned by the Navajos as demented. As far as I could see, her only peculiarity was an intense love for cats. She sheltered at least a dozen in her little hogan. When Younger Sister imitated Cats' Mother, her chin and nose would actually seem to grow together, as she mumbled her gums and limped rapidly along. Then her eyes would roll wildly under wisps of hair which she pulled over her forehead. In the next minute, with a whoop, she would transform herself into a gang of cats, yowling and spitting.

Only her mother did not laugh. Blanket Weaver would catch Younger Sister by the arm and shake her. "The Great Spirit will surely punish you for mocking the old." But for all that, Blanket Weaver was proud of this second daughter. When a visiting medicine man came to the Chaco and held a *Bejing* to examine the children, it was Younger Sister who won all the prizes, while Pretty One was severely chastised for forgetting what she had been so carefully taught.

Gradually the medicine man began to take notice of Younger Sister. With no written language the Navajos depend on the brighter of their pupils to remember and pass on the history and tradition of the *Diné,* (The People). They saw promise in this girl. But that did not save her from punishment.

One day, as usual, Younger Sister had excelled all the other children and received her prize, a silver concho button, from the medicine man. He turned to make the next award. Younger Sister turned too, nose high, chest puffed out and arm stiffly extended, in his exact gesture. Unfortunately he looked back and caught her!

As I have said Pretty One was wearing the long turquoise earrings that August, and their length and quality indicated that her mother was expecting a good price for her. By Navajo law the price for a virgin was fixed—fourteen horses, no more, no less; but Pretty One was so charming that her mother intended to hold out for four-year-old geldings, well broken.

The whole business was in the hands of the Marriage Arranger and his first wife. It was to their interest to get the best possible offer, for then they could collect a fee from the successful bidder as well as from the mother. A Navajo could have as many wives as he could afford but alas, it was the old men who had the fat purses. The chances for love matches were few indeed!

Every day the two girls drove the sheep up onto the mesa overlooking the Great Canyon and occupied themselves until dusk, herding. I doubt if Pretty One ever knew that her mother had already gone to the Marriage Arranger with gifts of coffee and flour for the first wife and instructions to start looking for a husband. It was unbearably hot on one of these days and the sheep stretched out in the scant shade of the cedars. The girls wandered over to the edge of the cliff and scrambled down, where they knew there were ruins of the Ancient People. Younger Sister found a bit of pottery and an arrowhead. They amused themselves hunting for more and did not see a horseman riding up the trail until he was almost upon them.

As a well brought up Navajo girl should, Pretty One at once drew her blanket about her head and lowered her eyes, but not so Younger Sister. She just stood barefaced and stared. Anyway she had not yet reached woman's estate, so what did it matter? The young Navajo rode on.

"Oh, Little Friend, he was so handsome," Pretty One told me later. "Never have I seen one so handsome, with huge turquoise beads and a gorgeous silver bridle for his fat horse. Who do you think he could be?"

Direct questions are a serious breach of etiquette, but I soon learned by keeping my ears open that Slender Pine, the young stranger in our midst, was a boy from The Mountain. He had been away for several years with his uncle, up on the San Juan River.

The day following their first meeting, he rode again to the mesa where the girls were herding. This time Pretty One neglected to pull her blanket over her head and returned his greeting.

As the sisters were driving the flock home that evening, Pretty One took off a fine turquoise ring and gave it to Younger Sister. Not a word was said, but Younger Sister grinned and accepted the bribe. It meant that there was to be no mention to their mother of Slender Pine's trips to the mesa. For there were daily ones after that, and soon all of Pretty One's possessions had been transferred to Younger Sister. At first all three young people chatted together, but before long Younger Sister found that she alone was guarding the sheep. She gibed and jeered mercilessly, but every night she added a nickel or a bead to her collection.

So matters stood, when a rain ceremonial was held. There had been no welcoming relief that hot summer, and the Great Spirit must be invoked to send his people rain clouds. A cave in the wall of the canyon was chosen for the sand painting of the medicine man. This was a favorable spot because, even in very dry years, a trickle of water could usually be found trying to reach the parched lands below.

The sand painting was a long time in the making, as are all good prayers. In the center was a frog, the messenger who would tell the earth spirits of the clan's needs. At the four corners were placed the four points of the compass. On one side a small stone figure of a deer was placed, for animals, too, were thirsty. Opposite was an image of a bird who could be trusted to fly to the sky above with these human longings carried on his wings. All around the sand painting were wands of willow and cedar boughs, tipped with the feathers of Rain Crows. When it was finished the medicine man sat for a long time in contemplation, and a reverent hush settled over the canyon until the sun had set.

Then everyone was ready for a little relaxation and gathered around the hogan of a head man for boiled meat, wheat bread and coffee until the dancing started. First the performers were only men, shuffling to the low beat of the drum, resplendent in ceremonial dress. Later came the real fun of the evening—a squaw dance. Any girl could go over to the line of braves and take one of her choosing by the arm. If willing to dance with her, well and good; if not, he could buy freedom with a coin. There was a great deal of giggling and hanging back, but suddenly I saw Younger Sister break from the group of girls. As she ran past me I was surprised to notice a small blue bead in each of her ears. No long turquoise earrings could be hers until Pretty One was taken, but the touch of blue told her people that she was no longer a child. Slender Pine looked embarrassed as she grabbed his arm; but he danced with her, not just then but several times, for she kept coming back. Pretty One remained with the other girls, but for once she was not smiling. I wondered what she would have to say to Younger Sister the next morning!

I heard a piece of gossip that same evening. Old Badger had made an offer for Pretty One. He was so rich and his proposition so good, it looked hopeless for any other suitor.

A few days later I found Pretty One standing at the door of our house. "Oh, Little Friend," she sobbed, "you must help me. My mother has found out how I feel toward Slender Pine."

"Who told her?" I asked.

"I don't know. I am sure it was not Younger Sister."

I was not so sure. I had seen Younger Sister's expression as she danced with Slender Pine.

"The Marriage Arranger has already promised me to Old Badger; and when my mother heard about this other one she sent for Old Badger, and he brought the betrothal gift. Half a buckskin, it was!"

This was no mean gift. A buckskin has many uses and is highly valued.

"What did you do?" I asked.

"I threw it at him!"

Certainly love had worked an amazing transformation in a gentle little girl.

She went on: "My mother could not believe what I had done, and so terrible was her rage that I was scared. So at last, at her command, I picked up the buckskin." Her eyes filled with tears. We both knew that in accepting Old Badger's gift, she had accepted Old Badger.

"And Younger Sister," she continued, lips quivering, "hid in the brush and laughed, and when he had gone she made herself into a picture of Old Badger—all puffed up, so!"

It seemed that when Slender Pine came to the mesa the next

20

morning and heard the story, he rode at once to his father on The Mountain. The father proved understanding and offered to provide the required fourteen horses.

But the Marriage Arranger only laughed when he was approached. He knew that Old Badger could outbid anyone else. However, he saw a chance to make a little extra on the side, so he warned Old Badger of the new bidder. Now Old Badger desired Pretty One more than ever and raised his offer to fourteen cows, and for the Marriage Arranger there would be three fine geldings. The situation looked bad. Slender Pine tried to persuade Pretty One to run away, but as she said, "Where could we go? We have no land, no horses, no silver. It would be against all the laws of the tribe, and we would only be found and brought back. Slender Pine would be punished and I would be sold to Old Badger. My mother would get fourteen horses instead of fourteen cows and would take it out on me. Little Friend, what shall we do? You must tell us."

I thought it all over for quite a while and then hit on a possible solution. Though a Navajo girl has no rights whatsoever in the selection of a husband, she has one right which cannot be taken from her. She can refuse marriage. It is a step seldom resorted to, as it amounts to taking the veil. She loses all privileges in the clan and is little better than a slave. "Go to your mother," I told Pretty One, "and declare that unless you can wed Slender Pine, you will publicly announce that you are refusing marriage. You will see, if you stand firm, that your mother will realize that the fourteen horses of Slender Pine's father, even if they are old and skinny, are better than no horses at all."

"But they are *good* horses, Little Friend," said loyal Pretty One, "and I promise you, I will stand firm."

There must have been a lively row in Yellow Bird Canyon that night. In fact I heard it lasted almost a week. The medicine man was called in to reinforce the angry but helpless mother. In the end the two of them had to give in. Slender Pine was accepted as Pretty One's betrothed.

Immediately preparations for the wedding were started. Slender Pine built a new hogan for his bride a mile away from the hogan of Blanket Weaver. A Navajo must never look at his mother-in-law, a taboo which carries with it a great deal of inconvenience; but in this case, as in many others, it had its good points. When the hogan was finished Slender Pine led his fourteen horses to the Marriage Arranger, who, the following day, drove them around to the corral of Blanket Weaver. Often the acceptance or rejection of horses took days of argument; but between Slender Pine's fear of losing Pretty One and Blanket Weaver's fear of getting no horses at all, negotiations were speedily concluded.

Only one more ceremony remained before the wedding. In his finest clothes and blankets, bedecked with silver and turquoise jewelry, Slender Pine rode slowly up the canyon, on both sides of which were clustered hogans. This was so that all might see that he went proudly to the home of his betrothed. If, at the last minute, he was to be rejected, Blanket Weaver would stand in front of her hogan and look him squarely in the eye, a sign of her refusal to consider him as a son-in-law. Slender Pine's relief was great when he saw no one there and the blanket hanging down over the opening. He was riding past, rejoicing that all was well, when a swift figure darted out and stopped in his horse's path. Younger Sister clutched at his bridle. By then he must have been pretty much annoyed with the child who he never doubted had betrayed her sister; so without a glance at her upturned face and with a mere twist of his bridle hand, he rode on.

Now followed a great bustle in Yellow Bird Canyon. In a few hours the wedding guests would arrive, and there was bread to bake in the ashes, sheep to be roasted and a dozen other things to be done, all at once. Blanket Weaver, seeing Younger Sister standing idle, gazing off down the trail, sent her to the cornfield to gather pollen needed in the wedding ceremony. It was some time before it was noticed that she had not returned from this errand. A couple of the children ran off to search for her.

We had as a guest at that time, Dr. T. Mitchell Prudden, an

eminent physician from New York. He was eager to see all he could of Indian life, and we had promised to take him to this wedding. We were just getting ready to go when we heard the pounding of horses' hoofs outside. In the next instant a Navajo hurried into the house. "Blanket Weaver says to come—come quick! Younger Sister is dead."

Dr. Prudden snatched his medicine bag. In no time the team was hitched, and we were off at full gallop.

As we drew near to Yellow Bird Canyon, we could hear wailing. Everything there was in the wildest confusion. Stunned Navajos stood around the edge of the cornfield, and Blanket Weaver and Pretty One crouched side by side on the ground, their blankets drawn over their heads. One of the men guided us a short distance into the cornfield, pointed, turned and ran.

Younger Sister lay among the stalks, just as she had fallen. No one had dared touch her, for death is the Awful Unknown; and this one had a special horror. A short time before, Younger Sister had been the pet of the clan; now they all drew off in revulsion. Dr. Prudden bent over her, then looked up.

"She's not dead."

I noticed her ankle. There were five angry spots there, and the leg was beginning to swell.

"She was bitten by a rattler," I said. "She must have stepped on it, for it evidently coiled around her leg."

"I'll try strychnine injections," said the doctor and motioned to some of the Indians to carry her up to her mother's hogan.

They had all vanished! "It's no use, doctor," I told him, "they won't help us. The snake is an underground spirit. No one will come near. We will have to take her ourselves."

For an hour we worked over her, then her eyelids flickered ever so slightly. I went out and called to Blanket Weaver.

"She's alive. Perhaps she can be saved."

The mother's countenance reflected a queer mixture of sorrow and fear. "No," she said, "my daughter is dead."

Of course I should have known that this would be her reaction.

Once a soul has entered the Spirit World, there is no return. There was nothing to do but to take the unconscious girl home with us. Dr. Prudden and I held her while my husband drove. As we lifted her out my husband remarked to me, "This is the first time I recall ever hearing of an Indian stepping on a rattler. Do you find it strange?"

"Yes," I replied, "they always seem to sense them far off."

Was it an accident? I wondered. Younger Sister had been deeply in love!

For three days we fought for the girl's life. No one came from Yellow Bird Canyon even to inquire about her. Finally my husband rode over. There he learned that after our departure the grief-stricken Navajos had gone completely berserk. They broke one of their most binding laws. Every inch of the cornfield was searched until the rattler was found, and that spot, my husband reported, was mangled and torn as if by plowshares, so furiously had they beaten the snake to death.

After fury followed realization. To kill a snake was inviting upon the clan all sorts of unknown plagues and misfortunes. The snake's spirit would return to the earth and with the aid of every earth spirit would seek vengeance.

Pretty One's wedding was postponed indefinitely. Slender Pine's father would not permit his son to marry into a clan over which hung so ominous a cloud. Of course there would be a snake ceremonial in an effort to appease the snake, but no one could tell until spring if it would be successful. So Pretty One wept, not only for her sister but for her lover.

My husband found Blanket Weaver alone in the hogan.

"I have come to bring you news of your daughter," he said.

Blanket Weaver's face turned gray, and she shivered. "My daughter is dead!"

"No, your daughter lives and, in great pain, calls for her mother."

Tears streamed down her face. "Oh, I hear her, I hear her all the time, but she calls from the Home of the Great Spirit!"

It was useless to try to make her understand that Younger

Sister was alive and with us. It was like asking someone to embrace a ghost and an evil one at that. Blanket Weaver would have given her life for this child, but she would not come to see the pitiful creature we sheltered.

I did not know that anyone could go through such suffering and survive. Younger Sister was swollen to twice her natural size, and one knee was drawn up rigid to her chin. She screamed until she was so hoarse that no sounds came, and I could just see her mouth and throat going through the motions. Dr. Prudden kept her under morphine, and when he had to leave he left a quantity with me; but soon that ran out, and I had to appeal to the medicine man for sedatives. I don't know what he gave me, but by degrees Younger Sister recovered. At the end of three months she was able to hobble a little on a crutch. Her hair had turned white, and from the child-face underneath it looked out eyes so old and tragic that I did not wonder that Indians who came to the trading post avoided her.

At least a dozen times during these three months I had seen, high on the cliffs above us, an Indian woman standing motionless, looking down on our home. We knew it was Blanket Weaver. My husband went up several times to try and bring her in, but before he could get to her she was gone. At last I sent for Pretty One. She would come no farther than the horse corral.

"Pretty One, Younger Sister is here. She asks for you and her heart is sick."

The girl trembled. "No, no, Little Friend, I can not go in. You don't understand. I can not." Exasperated I pulled her along with me. Poor Younger Sister's eyes flashed with joy.

"Pretty One, here is your sister."

Pretty One gave such a violent start of terror that my hold on her arm was broken. "My sister is dead, I have no sister," she gasped, and fled.

That moment must have been as bad as any of her agony for Young Sister. She had hardly spoken during the weeks of convalescence, so I had no way of guessing her feelings; but she spoke now.

25

"Oh, Little Friend, why did you bring me back? Nobody wants me. It would have been better if I had stayed dead."

That winter everything seemed to go wrong. My children were sick and one upset followed another. Though Younger Sister was growing stronger day by day, I knew that it was impossible for me to give her the time and care she needed. In the early spring I went to the hogan in Yellow Bird Canyon.

"Blanket Weaver," I said, "I have more children in my home than I can take care of. One of them is a poor little girl with white hair and a crippled leg. I believe that if she were somewhere where she could ride a horse every day she would improve. I want to ask you to care for this child for me."

Blanket Weaver did not answer at once. She stood very still and expressionless while she pondered the matter from this new angle. At last she said, "You want me to care for *your* child?"

"Yes," I answered meekly.

"If I were to care for *your* child I would wish everyone to know it was *your* child and why I take it. I would wish also that the spirits be told. Will you make a ceremony and tell in the presence of all that it is *your* child?"

Again I agreed. There was nothing else to do. The requested announcements were made, and Younger Sister went home. She went silently and was received silently. They took her in and cared for her physically, but she was treated like a stranger whom they must through necessity tolerate.

Pretty One had not had a very happy winter either, but as spring came she began to take heart. There was no scourge of diseases, the corn came up as usual, the sheep did not sicken and strangely enough there were no snakes seen that spring. The snake ceremonial had accomplished its purpose; the curse was lifted. So one May morning Slender Pine's fourteen horses were again led into Blanket Weaver's corral, and the interrupted ceremonies of the previous year were concluded. Early in the day, with painful effort, Younger Sister had struggled up the path onto the mesa, presumably to herd her mother's sheep. She never returned to the hogan in Yellow Bird Canyon.

Asthan-Dat-Sah-Ie, The Dead Woman

It was several days before I got word of her whereabouts. She had gone to Cats' Mother, the same old squaw who, in the days of her young gaiety, she had so often mocked. It was there I found her and begged her to return with me.

"Why did you come here, of all places?" I asked.

"All the animals take refuge with Cats' Mother," she answered. "Since I am no longer a person, it may be that I am an animal."

My pleadings fell on deaf ears.

It looked as if she would spend the rest of a wretched existence with her fellow outcast, but I was mistaken. I had not counted on the medicine men. They remembered their promising pupil, and now that she had returned from the dead, she had unusual prestige. They taught her all they could, and in a few years she had built up a great reputation and the trail to Cats' Mother's hogan was worn smooth with moccasined feet. She made no mistakes, she had no failures, and she placed a proportionate price on her services. At last she had even achieved a name of her own. She was known throughout Navajoland as *Asthan-Dat-Sah-Ie,* The Dead Woman.

Years later I went up to see her again. I found her outside the hogan, leaning on a greasewood stick to ease her withered leg. She pointed down the trail, up which a great flock of sheep was being herded. "They are all mine," she intoned. "I have done well, done well!" Her turquoise and silver necklace contrasted with her brown, wrinkled skin, her black eyes, her dead white hair. White hair is unusual on an Indian and is striking.

"You have certainly prospered, Asthan-Dat-Sah-Ie," I agreed, "but you are alone and have little use for your wealth. Do you know that your sister, Pretty One, has many children, and Slender Pine has little to give to so many? They are happy in that hogan, but sometimes they are hungry. Could you not help your sister?"

For one fleeting instant I had the illusion that I was again looking at Younger Sister, the mocking little clown of her clan. The thin bitter lips had sketched a sardonic grin. Then they stiffened into their usual impassive line.

She said, "I have no sister."

Avenger of Skeleton Canyon

by Nell Murbarger

From his place of concealment on the canyon rim, the dark-eyed youth watched, tensely alert, while the trail camp below stirred into life.

As the first man quit his blankets, the boy's forefinger curled nervously about the trigger of his rifle.

But this was not his man. This *vaquero* he might kill later. Old Devil Face, the man with the whiskers, must be first to die. . . .

Another rider, likewise beardless, emerged from back of the chuckwagon. In his arms was a bundle of desert brush. Together the pair kindled a crackling cookfire, set a battered coffeepot to boil.

To the half-frozen boy on the rimrock, nothing could have carried more appeal than that leaping blaze and the hot coffee. He was wet, cold and hungry.

Again his frame grew tense. Stiffened fingers tightened convulsively upon the gunstock held hard against his right shoulder. In the chuckwagon a man had tossed aside his blankets and was getting to his feet. He was a mountain of a man, broad, tall and obviously old. His leathery face, furrowed and checked like a strip of malpais, was nearly hidden behind a great, brushy white beard. About his shoulders cascaded a mop of unkempt white hair.

There could be no mistaking that beard and hair! This was Old Devil Face, the man whom this youth had sought for so many months, across so many weary miles.

While the boy watched, transfixed with anticipation, the old man flexed stiff muscles, ran stubby fingers through tobacco-stained beard. Yawning, he turned to survey a clear, red glow over the eastern hills. It looked like a good day after the storm. . . .

Slowly the youth raised his rifle. Deliberately he lined his sights upon the broad, woolen-clad chest. Grimly, exultantly, he squeezed the trigger.

With the single, sharp crack that reverberated across a rain-soaked desert, the old man crumpled over the wagon tailgate. For a long moment his body hung head downward, motionless; then, slowly, grudgingly, it slipped to the ground to pile itself in a huddled heap. From the canyon rim it appeared strangely like an empty suit of castaway clothing.

The ruthless old he-wolf of the frontier had howled his last howl. . . .

Details of Clanton's boyhood are apparently unrecorded. The first history knows of him he was bull-whacking from Texas to California during the Gold Rush. Later he married and drifted back to Arizona Territory, there to establish a cattle ranch near Fort Thomas, about twenty-seven miles northwest of the present town of Safford.

Several years later when young Mrs. Clanton succumbed to the rigors of frontier life, she bequeathed to her husband a legacy of potential gallows fodder—three wild hellions, Finn, Ike and Billy. There was also a daughter, Mary, a quiet, decent girl, who married at an early age and moved to her husband's ranch on the Little Colorado.

Soon after his wife's death, Clanton disposed of his Fort Thomas holdings and migrated south to a new location in the San Pedro Valley, of Cochise country. With the passage of time Clanton the rancher became "Old Man" Clanton—a fiery, cold-blooded old gunslinger whose utter ruthlessness was masked by a benign appearance. With his great white beard and billowing white hair, his blue eyes and ruddy, wrinkled cheeks, he lacked but a red suit and a few span of reindeer to have been the living counterpart of Santa Claus.

The heart that beat under Clanton's woolen shirt, however, would have sent cold shivers through the soul of jolly St. Nick.

The Clanton ranch, near Charleston, became a gun-bristling no-man's land where every cattle rustler, horse thief, stage robber and fugitive murderer of the border country was welcomed and given sanctuary.

As soon as this hideout was well established, Old Man Clanton relinquished its management to his wildling sons and in the latter part of 1880 moved to the Animas Valley—then, possibly, the most lawless region in the United States. There he established a second ranch, although only by courtesy was it accorded such title.

Cattle fattening on its grasslands were sought by a dozen different owners from both sides of the border. Hard-bitten punchers who lounged around the Clanton corral by day and rode by night were renegades of the first water.

For ordinary cattle-rustling activities Old Man Clanton headed his own band of cutthroats, but more important raids found him and his men aligned behind Curly Bill Brocius, Arizona's outlaw baron. Thus it was that the gory massacre in Skeleton Canyon found Clanton playing second fiddle to Curly Bill, yet it was for this secondary part that he ultimately paid with his life. . . .

Advised that a packtrain laden with Mexican silver was proceeding northward from Chihuahua, bound for the San Simon Valley in Arizona, Curly Bill surmised correctly that the wayfarers would pass through Skeleton Canyon—a wild gorge situated in the Peloncillo Mountains a short distance northeast of the present city of Douglas. There he and his men, including Clanton, took up strategic positions and made themselves comfortable.

At a sleepy jog-trot, mule bells jingling joyously, saddle leather creaking and hooves strumming a staccato tune on the rocky trail, Don Miguel Garcia and nineteen of his compatriots rode unsuspectingly into the canyon's welcome shade on that warm July day in 1881.

No snowball in Hades ever had a slimmer chance for survival.

When the last specie-laden packmule and drag rider had single-filed into the narrow passageway, the canyon walls suddenly reverberated to the roar of a dozen hidden rifles, and from a dozen carefully chosen vantage points came whining a rain of leaden death.

None of the western badmen's alleged sporting code entered into that attack. Slain and wounded plunged headlong from their saddles. Horses screamed in pain and terror. Mules bolted wildly, throwing their packs and strewing over the blood-drenched landscape a shower of silver treasure. Riders, set afoot when their mounts were shot from under them, rushed blindly from the scene of carnage, only to be cut down by a hail of bullets from those still unseen attackers. The wounded fared no better. Of nineteen men who had ridden into the canyon behind Don Miguel, only one escaped.

He was a sixteen-year-old boy, a slender, dark-eyed Mexican youth, who had seen his two elder brothers shot from their horses in the melee and who had escaped that same end by what miracle only his patron saint could know. In his precipitous flight from the canyon, a rifle bullet had flattened itself angrily against a rock at his side.

Snapping a terrified glance up toward the missile's evident source, his eyes had fastened upon the face of a man—fastened upon it and photographed it for all time to come. It was the

31

malevolent, fiendish face of a devil—an old man with heavy white beard and long white hair which blew wildly in the canyon wind.

Even if all others of those unseen participants must forever escape earthly punishment for their murderous attack, this man with the devil face and the white beard, vowed the boy, should be made to pay.

Following the massacre Curly Bill, Clanton and the others mercilessly clubbed to death any remaining wounded, and from the slain mules stripped the bulging packs of treasure—$75,000 worth of silver coin. Leaving the unburied bodies of the nineteen murdered men to be clawed and torn by buzzards and coyotes, the gang loaded their loot and headed jubilantly for Cave Creek Canyon in the Chiricahuas, there to divide the spoils and embark upon a prolonged orgy of drinking and gambling.

Meanwhile, by astute inquiry, the stripling youth had learned the identity of the old man with the beard, and from that time forward his shadow lay upon Clanton's trail like the shadow of death.

Slipping through the wild crags of the Peloncillos, combing the ranges of the Animas, skulking silent and wraith-like along the rimrock, prowling the arroyas, his life became circumscribed by a single obsession—to kill this man of the devil face; to shoot him down in cold blood as his brothers and comrades had been shot, without warning and without mercy.

It proved not an easy quest. To approach the well-guarded Clanton ranch without detection was at all times impossible; while Clanton himself, perhaps sensing that cold retribution rode his trail, employed every device of cunning to assure his continued well-being.

Into the life of every fugitive, however, there eventually enters the mistake—the wrong trail, the ill-chosen camp, the misplaced trust. Old Man Clanton was no exception to the rule and vengeance at last found its long-awaited opportunity.

Three hundred head of cattle, stolen from ranges below the

border at the cost of fourteen Mexican lives, were to be driven from Clanton's Animas Valley ranch to Tombstone for market. When the boy learned that Clanton would personally head the drive, he knew that his chance was at hand, for in wild, rough country, a rider cannot be every minute on guard.

Trailherding the three hundred stolen beeves, Clanton and four of his men had halted at nightfall on the first day in the Guadalupes, where they made camp.

It was their last earthly camp, for dawn brought with it the payoff for Skeleton Canyon. . . .

After his first shot had sent the old man tumbling, the slender Mexican youth finished the job, the members of Clanton's evil crew being picked off deliberately, one by one, like fish in a rain barrel. Perhaps not all the men in that camp were guilty of participation in the earlier massacre. Possibly not all deserved to die in such fashion, but Fate has her own way of calling the turn.

Only the nightherder escaped. Being with the cattle a short distance from camp, he was able to make his getaway through the chaparral. Procuring help and horses in Cloverdale, he led the way back to the scene of carnage.

The unseen attacker and his lethal rifle were gone. The stolen cattle were gone. The horses were gone. Only the four dead men remained as they had fallen; Old Man Clanton slumped at the rear of the chuckwagon; the others sprawled about cold embers of the campfire, sightless eyes staring up at a lonely sky and stiff fingers clutching guns still unfired for lack of a target.

Lashed across saddles, their heads, arms and legs flopping loosely, the four were carried to a little mesa bordering Animas Valley, not far from the Clanton stronghold. There they were buried in a sombre row. Over their graves stones were heaped high.

Later the Clanton boys had the body of their father moved to Tombstone's Boothill graveyard, where he lies today among the clan he knew best—the men who lived by violent means and by violence died.

The crude cross which marks his grave carries no birth date and no particulars of death. Only the simple inscription:

OLD MAN CLANTON

Nearby lies his son Billy, shot down at the O. K. Corral in Tombstone by Frontier Marshall Wyatt Earp, and elsewhere in the Southwest two nameless graves hold the bones of Finn and Ike, the last of an unholy crew.

One Against an Army

by Bryce W. Anderson

When they call the roll of the brave at the last great roundup, you can bet they won't forget Nate Champion.

Nate was a rustler—or so the Wyoming Stock Growers Association claimed when it put a price on his head. In fact they called him "King of the Rustlers."

Champion was a Texan by birth. He was born September 29, 1857, in Williamson County, Texas, the sixth son of Jack and Naomi Standifer Champion. His mother died when he was a child, and his father remarried, siring six more sons and six daughters.

Having to shift for himself at a tender age, Nate turned naturally to the cow camps for employment. By the time he was old enough to shave, he was a crack shot and at home in the saddle.

Sometime in the eighties, Nate and his brother Dudley rode north with a Texas trail crew that took a herd into Wyoming Territory. They liked the clear, crisp air of the high plateaus among

35

the Rockies. Both stayed—but not together. Dudley went to work for one of the many cattle outfits. Nate struck out on his own.

In Johnson County, a dog-eared rectangle that sweeps from the crest of the Big Horn west past Powder River, he found what he wanted. Here was a secluded land where no one asked questions of a man so long as he dealt fairly with his neighbors, picked no quarrel but proved he could fight. Here the small ranchers were making a stand against the big cattle companies that laid claim to all the open range. The cattle barons were said to own the state house in Cheyenne, but the little ranchers and nesters elected the officials in Johnson County.

Nesters and small stockmen were allied. They had another ally too: the outlaw band that rode out of the Hole-in-the-Wall, an all but hidden gap in the Red Wall of the Big Horn. Such men as Flat-Nosed George Curry, the Logan brothers and others of their stripe rode with that gang. They brought strange cattle on night drives over secret trails and moved them by circuitous routes to far-off markets—with their brands somehow changing on the way.

The outlaws by tacit agreement left the locally owned herds alone, while they preyed on the big herds of the absentee owners. And the Johnson County folk reciprocated in their own way. They left the Hole-in-the-Wall Gang alone, and when a man was arrested for rustling, their juries somehow always found the evidence unsatisfactory. Of 180 rustling arrests in this period, Johnson County juries brought in only one conviction.

The winter of 1886–87 was one of disaster for the Wyoming cattle industry. The summer had been dry and hot. Then across the starved benchlands, great blizzards swept. The critters could find no grass and died by the dozens, hundreds and thousands beside frozen water holes or in the drift-filled draws. The big absentee owners, accustomed to lush profits and loose bookkeeping, were especially hard hit. Many of the great spreads were forced to the wall. Among these was Morton Frewen's Powder River Cattle Company, the "76" spread which controlled—or claimed—some one hundred thousand acres of mountain and valley lands.

One of the "76" holdings was Nolan's KC Ranch, on the Middle Fork of Powder River, where the town of Kaycee now stands. As the big spread was broken up, Nathan D. Champion set up headquarters in the old Nolan cabin on a barren rise.

Champion was an unprepossessing man of thirty by then. He had a large Roman nose that gave him a "horse-faced" look. He stooped slightly, and his legs were bowed. He was only of medium size and no impressive figure despite flashing black eyes. But his skill as a markman had brought him local fame. And in a country of taciturn men, he was well liked.

To the Nolan cabin rode members of the loose-knit rustler gang. Perhaps Champion had known some of them in his Texas days, for men who had ridden the long trail north were among these riders of the dark ways. Some of them, like him, wore the broad red sash that Texas cowboys had copied from the Mexican *vaqueros*.

Pinkerton men, working as cattle detectives, carried the word that Nate Champion was "king" of the rustler gang. They said the red sash was the outlaw band's insignia, so it became known as the Red Sash Gang. They said Champion's ranch was a handy place to hide stolen livestock and that he had built his own herd with a long loop and a running iron.

The Wyoming cattle country strife was mounting. And the Wyoming Stock Growers Association instituted a blackball list of cowpokes suspected of rustling or being friendly with the stock thieves. These men were denied employment on any ranch of an association member. Some of them stopped for a while with Champion, as employees or partners. One such was Nick Ray, a big, hard-fisted top hand from Missouri. His fate and Champion's were to be linked in tragedy.

On the morning after Halloween of 1891, Champion and Ross Gilbertson lay sleeping in an outlying cabin. Four men spooked the cabin. The sleeping pair awoke in the nick of time and drove

37

the four away with six-gun fire. But their visitors left evidence that they had come to kill—and that they had been sent by the stock growers association.

Two dry gulchings of nesters followed this attempt on Champion and Gilbertson. Johnson County men began carrying their Winchesters wherever they went and watching every unknown visitor with intense suspicion.

No drummer calling on merchants in Buffalo, the county seat, could feel safe that uneasy winter. He would be eyed narrowly everywhere he went as a possible emissary of the hated association. And his suitcase full of samples would be suspected of containing dynamite until he threw it open to display its harmless contents.

Then the small rancher—with Champion as their front man—took an action of calculated defiance of the association. With approval of the county's elected officials, they set an 1892 spring roundup date of their own—one month earlier than that decreed by the association-controlled State Livestock Board.

The gauntlet was cast, and the stock growers association was quick to pick it up. John Clay, Jr., the association president, was abroad at the baronial estate in his ancestral Scotland which he had purchased with his profits from Black Hills beef. But the vice-president, George W. Baxter of Cheyenne, a former governor of Wyoming, called a special membership meeting for April 4. All members, he decreed, must be present or represented by proxies. And H. B. Ijams, the association secretary, prepared to put into operation plans already months in the making.

The meeting was held behind closed doors at the Cheyenne Club. No minute books were kept. The executive minutes of the Wyoming Stock Growers Association state that no meeting was held in 1892. But forty-three members answered the roll call.

While the cattle barons gathered to hear and approve Ijams' plans, some of their hired hands and a few hard cases recruited by the secretary were branding three carloads of horses in the Cheyenne stockyards. The brand they used was A—, an unrecorded iron.

One Against an Army

The day after the meeting a special train arrived over the Union Pacific Railroad from Denver. It consisted of a chair car with curtains tightly drawn, a baggage car, three stock cars, a flat car and caboose.

Onto the stock cars the hired hands loaded the newly branded horses. Onto the flat car they put three wagons and into the baggage car supplies and equipment for an extended outing by half a hundred men. Armed guards patrolled the railroad yards to see that no unauthorized person went near the train.

At dusk the hired hands who had been loading the train were ordered aboard. Behind the drawn curtains they found thirty Texas gunmen, who had been recruited by Ijams' agents with promises of $5 per day plus $50 each for every rustler killed.

Several members of the stock growers association also boarded the train, along with an imported surgeon, Dr. Charles Penrose of Philadelphia, a brother of the noted Boies Penrose; and two newspaper correspondents, Sam T. Clover of the Chicago *Herald* and Ed Towse of The Cheyenne *Sun*. There reportedly were fifty-two men on the train, all told. They styled themselves the "Regulators." Major Frank Walcott, a retired army man who loved a battle, was placed in command.

Through the night the train rolled north and west to Casper, the nearest railroad point to Johnson County. There its passengers, horses and cargo were unloaded. Then the Regulators rode for Powder River. Tom Smith, a former United States Marshal in the Indian Territory, commanded the Texas contingent. Frank M. Canton, who had bossed the fight on rustlers for the association, was in charge of the remainder. One man remained behind to cut the telegraph wires near Casper. Johnson County was to have no advance warning if they could help it.

The first night out, as they camped in open country about twenty miles from Casper, Major Wolcott disclosed to his lieutenants a list of thirty men marked for death. Topping the list were the names of W. G. "Red" Angus, sheriff of Johnson County, and Nathan D. Champion.

The following day the Regulators headed for the ranch of Bob Tisdale on the Johnson County line. Just before they reached it they were met by Mike Shonsey, range foreman for the Western Union Beef Company, of which Vice-President Baxter of the association was general manager. Shonsey had news: Nate Champion was at his headquarters on the KC Ranch.

Leaders of the expedition had been planning to move first on Buffalo to get the sheriff and his deputies. But here was closer quarry—likely to escape if not dealt with at once. And so after resting men and horses at Tisdale's ranch, the Regulators rode north toward the KC Ranch on the night of April 8.

It was a cold night, but there was a roaring fire inside the Nolan cabin; and on a table was a bottle of whiskey to add its inner warmth. Nick Ray, properly warmed with drink, was squeezing out lively country tunes on a squeaky fiddle; Champion was lending a reedy baritone. Their song was interrupted by heavy rapping at the door.

By instinct both men grabbed their guns. Cautiously Champion moved to the door and hallooed the visitors.

He was answered by two trappers, an old man named Ben Jones and a youth named William W. Walker. They asked to spend the night.

Conviviality returned. The horses were put up and the visitors invited in. Champion passed the bottle. For an hour or so he, his partner and the unexpected guests talked, sang and drank. Unknown to them they were watched from a distance by Mike Shonsey and three companions, who had ridden ahead of the main body of Regulators as advance scouts.

Snow fell lightly during the night. It brought a mild, drowsy morning. The four men inside the cabin slept past their usual time, and the sun was nearly two hours high when Champion started making flapjacks for breakfast.

Old Man Jones, arising a few minutes later, picked up a bucket and started toward the river for wash water.

When breakfast was ready, Jones had not returned.

"Seems like it's taking him an awful long time to get that water," said Ray. He and Walker stepped outside to look around. On the way out Ray picked up his Winchester.

The two men scanned yard and skyline closely. Nothing seemed amiss. The trappers' wagon stood in plain view, where they had unhitched the horses the night before. One of the horses whinnied from the stable.

Walker remarked that Jones, who had lived alone for much of his life, sometimes wandered off for hours by himself. The two men returned to the cabin and sat down to the steaming flapjacks.

When breakfast was over, Walker announced he would search further for Jones. He walked out slowly, made a circuit about the cabin, then decided to look in the stable. He disappeared through the stable doorway and did not emerge.

Moments later Nick Ray walked out, picked up an ax and began to cut kindling. After he had broken up some small branches lying on the ground, he began to hew a limb from a big cottonwood tree in the dooryard.

For perhaps ten minutes Ray swung his ax. Then a rifle barrel poked through a little window in the stable wall—a window used for throwing out manure. The gun barked once.

Ray whirled. As he did so nearly half a hundred men who were concealed in the stable, among the low growth along the river bank and in a gully that skirted the rise on which stood the cabin, opened fire simultaneously. Ray staggered and fell.

The big man lay still only a moment, then raised himself by inches to his hands and knees. Slowly he began to crawl toward the cabin door. He left a trail of blood across the snow.

The door flew open. Nate Champion leaped out, rifle in hand. He sent a rapid volley of shots toward the stable, then ducked indoors. A moment later he was out again, his gun again leaping against his shoulder.

The Regulators divided their fire. Some shot at the figure which darted in and out of the doorway. Others fired again at the man crawling across the yard more and more slowly. Several times

41

Ray was hit. Each time he collapsed for a few seconds, then doggedly started on again.

When the crawling figure was within a few steps of the doorway, Champion again leaped out. This time he ran to Ray's side, lifted the big man and lugged him into the cabin amid a hail of bullets.

Inside he laid Ray on the bed, turned to fire several times through the windows, then examined his partner's wounds. They were many. Champion took such first-aid measures as he knew, but broke off frequently to fire at the hidden men surrounding the house—and each time drew a volley in reply.

As he alternately nursed and shot, the man in the red sash considered his situation. He was alone now. No telling what had happened to the two trappers. Probably they had been captured. Anyhow they were of no further use to him. Nick Ray was done for. And Nate Champion was surrounded by an army bent on his destruction. He could only guess at how many men crouched in concealment outside. But he felt he did not need to guess as to who had sent them.

From a shelf he took down a pocket memorandum book and a stub of lead pencil. He concentrated for a moment to arrange the words in his mind, then began to write.

"Me and Nick was getting breakfast when the attack took place," he wrote. "Two men here with us—Ben Jones and another man. The old man went after water and did not come back. Nick started out and I told him to look out, that I thought that there was someone at the stable that would not let them come back. Nick is shot, but not dead yet. He is awful sick. I must go and wait on him."

He shoved notebook and pencil into a pocket. He worked briefly with Ray, who was moaning now in agony. Then again he moved from window to window, watching for a target, firing now and then, to draw answering fire. He must keep watch on all sides. He mustn't let them get too close.

The log cabin was well constructed for defense. Champion knew

42

these men dreaded his accurate shooting. He doubted they would try to rush him. Still the siege could have but one end, unless help came.

Some time later he paused to take out his notebook and pencil again. He wrote:

"It is now about two hours since the first shot. Nick is still alive; they are still shooting and are all around the house."

He broke off quickly as the fusillade from outside increased. Perhaps they were trying to storm his fortress. He ran from window to window, firing here, and there. Behind him the moans of the dying man ended in a rattling gasp.

It seemed to Champion a very long time before he paused to write again. His blue shirt was stuck to his broad, bent back with sweat from his exertions. He crouched against the wall, and to the bark of guns and whine of bullets, he wrote:

"Boys, there is bullets coming in like hail. Them fellows is in such shape I can't get at them. They are shooting from the stable and river and back of the house. Nick is dead, he died about 9 o'clock."

Then: "I see a smoke down at the stable. I think they have fired it. I don't think they intend to let me get away this time."

The fire in the stable had been started by accident. Walcott, in charge there, put a half dozen Regulators to work beating it out. He ordered the rest to keep up their fusillade.

Perhaps never have so many shots been fired in the attempt to kill one man. But Champions, as yet unscathed, found time to write another brief entry:

"It is now about noon. There is someone at the stable yet; they are throwing a rope out at the door and drawing it back. I guess it is to draw me out. I wish that duck would get out further so I could get a shot at him."

Two of the "ducks" surrounding the house had been wounded by Champion's fire. But he could not know that. And now a note of despondency crept into his penciling in the notebook:

"Boys, I don't know what they have done with them two fellows that staid here last night. Boys, I feel pretty lonesome just now. I wish there was someone here with me so we could watch all sides at once." And then, hopefully: "They may fool around until I get a good shot before they leave."

Shortly before three o'clock, a team drawing the running gears of a wagon, followed by a man on horseback, appeared on the road. The man was Jack Flagg, who combined ranching with editing a weekly newspaper at Buffalo, an organ of the nesters and small ranchers. Driving the team was his seventeen-year-old stepson.

As the wagon drew within about seventy-five yards of the stable, several men leaped out and shouted for it to stop. The boy flicked the team with the reins and sped for a bridge a half mile ahead. One man laid his rifle across a fence corner and sent a shot after the running team, but missed. Some twenty men behind the stable now saw Flagg on his horse. As they grabbed their guns several shouted:

"Stop and throw up your hands!"

The rancher-editor did just the opposite. He spurred his horse alongside the boy as several rifles cracked.

Flagg was unarmed, but his rifle was on the wagon running gears. As he drew beside it he glanced over his shoulder and saw seven men riding after him.

"Hand me the rifle!" he shouted.

The boy complied.

"Now stop and cut one horse free!" shouted Flagg, whirling his mount as he spoke and drawing a bead on his pursuers.

The horsemen reined in. They did not know that Flagg had only three cartridges for his rifle.

The boy quickly cut one horse loose and sprang to its back. He and his stepfather raced away.

Champion wrote in his notebook:

"It's about 3 o'clock now. There was a man in a buckboard and one on horseback just passed. They fired on them as they went by. I don't know if they killed them or not. I seen lots of men come out on horses on the other side of the river and take after them.

I shot at the men in the stable just now; don't know if I got any or not. I must go and look again."

Major Walcott, Canton, and Smith, the leaders of the Regulators, realized they must act quickly. The man and boy would arouse the countryside.

The three leaders held a brief conference. Then at their orders several of the men rode to where Flagg's stepson had left the running gears and horse. They wheeled the vehicle behind the stable. There they unhitched the horse and loaded the running gears with hay and shavings. Meanwhile other Regulators kept up their firing at the cabin.

Champion could not see what the men were doing with the running gears. But he saw more movement outside—beyond effective rifle range. Sensing a break in the pattern of the siege, he wrote:

"It don't look as if there is much show of my getting away. I see twelve or fifteen men. One looks like ————. I don't know whether it is or not. I hope they did not catch them fellows that run over the bridge toward Smith's. They are shooting at the house now. If I had a pair of glasses, I believe I would know some of the men. They are coming back. I've got to look out."

The men behind the stable ripped boards from that structure and logs from the fence to pile upon the hay and shavings on the wagon gears. They heaped in brush and pitch pine. Walcott and Smith passed orders for the rest to step up their fire to keep their prisoner pinned down.

During one brief break in the shooting, Champion scrawled hurriedly in his notebook:

"Well, they have just got through shelling the house like hail. I heard them splitting wood. I guess they are going to fire the house tonight. I think I will make a break when night comes. Shooting again."

The wagon gears were now loaded high with inflammables. A group of Regulators pushed them around the stable. Then Major Walcott, Tom Smith, Bob Tisdale, A. B. Clark and James Dudley

45

began to push the contraption toward the cabin, keeping behind the load so that it shielded them from Champion's shots.

The vehicle's purpose was plain to Champion. He fired helplessly at it. Then while bullets zinged through window apertures, splintered doors and thudded into the thick walls, he dropped close to the floor, took out his notebook and wrote:

"Shooting again. I think they will fire the house this time. It's not night yet."

The five men drove the loaded wagon gears hard against the cabin. Someone darted up behind with a flaming brand, thrust it again and again into the brush, hay and shavings.

The flames licked from the wagon onto the cabin. Its dry logs first smoldered slowly, sending clouds of smoke within. Champion was driven slowly across the house, dragging the body of Nick Ray with him to try to keep his dead comrade from the roasting fire.

Tongues of flame began to shoot upward from the cabin roof. There was loud cheering among the Regulators. Gradually they moved their circle closer.

The north wall now was a sheet of flame. Champion's warning shots became fewer and fewer, then ceased altogether.

The word went around the circle: "Reckon he's burned up in there or shot himself. No fellow could stay in that hole a minute and be alive."

But Nate Champion was writing a final entry in the log of his last stand:

"The house is all fired. Goodbye, boys, if I never see you again. Nathan D. Champion."

Then, rifle in hand and loaded six-gun in his belt, he burst through the doorway on the south side of the house.

There was a ravine some fifty yards south of the cabin. He ran for it—head-on toward a line of Texas gunmen.

"There he goes!" shouted someone. There was a volley of perhaps fifty shots. Still Champion ran on. He raised his Winchester to reply to the fire, but before he could squeeze the trigger, a second volley roared.

Champion spun like a wobbly top, then fell, face up.

The Regulators were taking no chance. They fired shot after shot into the inert body. The undertaker later found twenty-eight slugs in the corpse.

Finally they crowded around. One of the gang took the six-shooter and gun belt from the corpse as trophies. Tom Smith went through the dead man's pockets. He found the notebook, drenched in blood and drilled by a bullet. He read the entries and scratched out the name of the man Champion had recognized.

Clover, the Chicago *Herald* correspondent, lettered "Cattle Thieves Beware" on a sheet of paper and buttoned it to Champion's vest.

The supply wagons had drawn up to the creek during the siege. Now, with the cabin still burning in the background, the Regulators ate a long delayed meal. Then they rode on toward Buffalo.

Flagg and others had spread word of the invasion. Sheriff Angus was leading a posse of twelve men from Buffalo to the relief of the KC Ranch—little realizing how his posse was outnumbered. Flagg, his stepson and three men from Grabing also headed back. They were joined by another dozen at Carr's Ranch.

When they reached the scene they found only the riddled body of Champion and the smoldering cabin with the charred remains of Nick Ray on the blackened floor within.

Back in Buffalo, Arapahoe Brown and E. U. Snider were heading up another posse in the absense of the sheriff. By now they realized they had to deal with a sizable force. They deputized some two hundred men and rode out to intercept the invaders.

The Regulators got word of the defending army's advance and holed up at the TA Ranch. They now became the besieged, their foes, the besiegers. On the second day of this battle, the Buffalo men sought to complete the turnabout. They rigged up a "go devil," loaded it with dynamite captured from the Regulators' wagons, and were wheeling it toward the ranch house when three troops of cavalry from Fort McKinney rode up to stop the battle.

An emissary from the Regulators had ridden at breakneck speed to Casper, past the cut in the telegraph line, to flash the word to Acting Governor Amos W. Barber to call out the troops.

Forty-five of the Regulators surrendered to the cavalry. Eventually they were turned over to the civil authorities, but to be lodged in Cheyenne instead of jailed in Buffalo. After long delay in bringing them to trial, they were released on the pretext that Johnson County could no longer bear the expense of their incarceration.

Jones and Walker, the two trappers who had witnessed the KC siege as prisoners of the invaders, were spirited out of the state.

But even while Johnson County's own "army" was besieging the Regulators at the TA Ranch, a vacant store building in Buffalo was packed with men and women come for the funeral of Nick Ray and Nathan Champion.

The Rev. M. A. Raden, a fire-eating Methodist preacher who had proved his worth on the frontier by soundly thrashing a cattleman in a street fight preached the funeral sermon.

"These men have been sent to eternity; we know not why," he said. "They were not criminals. They were of Christian parents."

One hundred and fifty mounted men rode in the funeral procession to the cemetery. There the bodies were lowered and earth mounded over each grave. And at the head of each was placed a little board, its only monument.

Cowboy!

by Milt Hinkle

Why that word? Where did it come from?

Back in the days before the coming of the white man there weren't any cattle roaming the broad reaches of what is now the western portion of the United States. It was not until the Spaniards pushed northward out of Mexico in search of more gold that cattle were seen by startled Indians. Extremely poor hunters, these foreign treasure seekers drove herds of cattle with them to be slaughtered for food when needed.

Many Spanish companies died before the arrows and war spears of outraged Indians. Heat, lack of water and illness struck down many more. The cattle, left without herders, wandered off to multiply and become wild and fat on the bountiful grass. Some the Indians domesticated. Many fell prey to wild animals; but nature has a way of caring for her own, so by the early 1800's, there were many great herds of wild cattle roaming the lush valleys and prairies, then covered with rich, nourishing Buffalo grass. By this time many bold settlers had arrived in the West.

Because the land was free and broad, stretching away for miles beyond the horizon, men laid claim to vast reaches and built themselves veritable empires where their word was the only law. Thus the first cattle ranches came into being. Wild cattle were rounded up and mixed with domestic breeds. Some of those early ranches numbered their cattle by thousands and tens of thousands. A "spread" of several hundred was considered too small for notice.

To care for these big herds roaming the unfenced ranges, the owners hired men who became known as *cow boys*. The words *cow men* were applied to the owners. There was no room for a weakling in that rough business of cattle care. Those fellows had to be men and endowed not only with physical strength but a certain amount of stubborn courage. In other words they had to have "guts" as well as a body as resilient as a tempered steel spring.

It was the duty of the cowboys to ride swift and tough horses from twelve to twenty-four hours every day, with rarely a day of rest. They had to guard those cattle at all hours. Hard and bitter work it was. Only the man who has lived the life of those early ranching days can say just how hard and bitter. The vast distances of the country, the loneliness, the days and nights of solitude were hard but by no means the worst of their difficulties.

Much of the land was dry. Streams and springs were few and far between, yet it was the duty of these men to see that the cattle got ample water. They undertook to keep them on good grass at all times and protect the herds from marauding wild beasts, such as wolves and mountain lions. They had the hardest kind of work at branding time; and on the slow, tedious drives overland to distant railroads, they were always vigilant to prevent a catastrophic stampede. A stampede could be caused by such a simple thing as a loud laugh, the flare of a match or a flash of lightning after the animals had bedded down for the night.

Thousands of cattle have been known to get to their feet and run senselessly until they dropped dead because of these simple things. Men have died under their pounding hoofs while trying to guide them into a great circle, to calm and save them. All honor to those brave men, giving their lives simply because of a loyal sense of duty and for wages that would seem ridiculous now.

Yes, of such stuff were the early-day cowboys made. They never knew four walls and a roof except for the few days and nights of fun after the herd had arrived at a railroad town. They slept in bedrolls composed of several blankets, and quilts encased in waterproof, heavy canvas were used in all kinds of weather. Their food was always from the ever-present "chuckwagon," which followed the herds.

These chuckwagons were under the complete supervision of the camp cook. He could fry steaks to equal the product of the finest French cook. In his long-handled iron pans with their heavy rimmed lids he could make sourdough bread and dried fruit pies that were mouth-watering and filling. His coffee was strong and heartwarming and always ready on a pothook placed between heavy iron, prong-tipped posts over a "cow chip" or "buffalo chip" fire.

The chips were simply the sun-dried dung of the aforementioned animals, and they burned with a clean, hot flame. There were always plenty of chips picked up and sacked by the "wrangler" or "wagon boy."

Young boys loved the life of the ranges, and many good cowboys got their start as helpers around the camps. There was always a *remuda* boy. His job was to look after the cowboy's string of private saddle horses, to keep them on good grazing when not in use and to have them in camp before daylight, watered and ready to be caught and saddled for the work to come.

After the cowboys, squatting on boot heels, had finished their meals, scraped off plates and carried them to a wash tub of hot water, these boys washed the tin plates, cups and cutlery. No person even so much as hinted any dissatisfaction with the food within hearing of the cook, who was usually an old cowboy unable to ride much. The men humored and respected him with good-natured tolerance. It was a dark day when the cook "blew up" and rode stiffly away into the distance.

Cowboys of the Old West!

As I muse over my past life it occurs to me that possibly more has been written about the American cowboy, more has been said, more moving pictures made of and about him, than any other character in American history. I am proud to have been one of these early-day cowboys, proud to have lived the life of those times in the great West. He has been, and is now, the idol of millions. He has been glorified to the stars. He is the most romantic, most glamorized and most misunderstood figure ever to ride across the pages of our history.

Yes, it was my privilege in the long ago to live and work with these lean, bronzed men, to share their loneliness, hard work, laughter and fun, and also their loyal friendships, heartaches and joys. I have slept with them around a flickering campfire, in the rain and under the bright western stars, as well as in sleet and snow. I have shared their hasty meals of beef, sourdough bread and beans in the frosty predawn as well as in the dusty, dry camps with heat burning and dust shimmering in clouds around us.

I can see these cowboys now in my mind's eye. They were booted and spurred as I was, with broad-brimmed hats at a jaunty angle. Colored neckerchiefs were loosely knotted around their throats, and heavy Colt six-guns swung low at their thighs. Broad belts were strapped around their middle, bullets agleam in the light.

Their talk ("lingo" as they called it) has left its mark on our American language—such words as *lariat, latigo, roundup, remuda, dogie, dingbat, wrangler, chounce, stomper, ramrod, chuck, and flash riders,* to mention only a few.

Cowboy!

And these men are not legendary figures at all. Many of the younger generation live much the same today as we old fellows did. Warm-hearted, hard working, rough-and-ready for a fight or a good time, these younger men are important today in the over-all scheme of our American economy, and everyone should know them better.

These youngsters rope and brand the calf crop each year, watch out for and doctor for "screw worms" and dip cattle for ticks and scabs. Like we did, they burn in summer and freeze in winter while attending to the unending duties of their jobs. In my day we did all these things and many more besides, and did it for twenty dollars to thirty dollars a month and found. Yes, it was a hard life, but a full one and not without its satisfaction.

In the midsummer during my cowboy days, it was customary for all ranchers to unite forces, then to round up the cattle from the open range and brand them. Any calf following a branded cow received the same brand, thereby establishing true ownership. This was truly a time of hard and grueling labor. Then came the "fiesta." Cowboys dressed in their best polished boots and gleaming regalia mounted their finest horses and rode, sometimes many miles, to display their skill as top hands.

They vied with each other with complete sportsmanship for the coveted title of all-round top hand of the range and in the arena contests. These get-togethers were "cowboy reunions," the forerunners of our modern-day rodeo. There wild horses were broken to ride and steers were roped in the shortest possible time. Rules and points were kept religiously, and when a man won the contests, the fun broke up.

In the fall came the rounding up of thousands of head of cattle, and everyone made ready for the long, long drive overland to the railroads and market. I have followed the dusty, plodding way along the famous old Chisholm Trail, the Blocker Trail and many others. Now a person can rarely hear the weird song of the lonesome coyote from the mesas or glimpse the far distant flicker of an antelope's white rump as he signals to his timid band.

The old longhorn has vanished. I recall watching heat lightning jump from tip to tip of those wide horns now gone forever. Where the city of Clovis, New Mexico, now stands was the roundup grounds of the big Green Igo, Buckle G Ranch. There was a windmill there and plenty of water. Many times I was one of the weary bunch of cowboys who rode night herd at that spot. I rode restless, wiry, mustang cow ponies. Now the wiry mustang I rode has been replaced by the marvelous quarter horse.

Yes, methods are more in keeping with modern times, more scientific. The cowboy of today works with his automobile. His horse moves in a trailer. His bunkhouse is a very modern ranch house and his meals are cooked with gas. Yet at heart, the character of these cowboys is the same as in my time. The broad Stetson hat, the high-heeled boots and spurs are still seen in the West as working attire. Famous brands are still seared into the hides of many cattle but are now worked with the new invention—the branding chutes.

While these present-day cowboys never have known the long overland trails and other discomforts of my time, they do understand the handling of cattle. They can swing a catch rope with astonishing speed and skill. They can ride an outlaw horse just as easily as any of us old-timers ever could. Their calf-roping speed and skill outclasses the old-timers' two to one. All honor to these boys, the best of whom may be seen in rodeos from Madison Square Garden in New York to Cheyenne, Wyoming; Pendleton, Oregon; and points elsewhere all over the United States and Canada.

No, the American cowboy is not a forgotten man, for he is still with us. He is real, warm-hearted, steel-muscled and reckless in gambling or fighting or flirting, and his play time is as much enjoyed as mine ever was.

Do not forsake me when I am old.

The Man Who Found $85,000,000!

by Tom Bailey

It was going on noon when Ed Schieffelin and his old burro Cactus came onto the tortuous stretch of the Indian trail leading down to the San Pedro River. The trail, just a dim trace in the hard earth, was full of steep pitches and sharp turns with jumping cholla and greasewood growing on both sides of it. From the summit, where it plunged steeply toward the valley clear down to the valley itself almost, were a series of switchbacks where the path doubled back below itself so sharply that Schieffelin and the burro found themselves passing each other, going in opposite directions. When this happened the prospector could reach out and almost touch Cactus on the nose when she thrust it toward him, as she did occasionally, as if to say imagine meeting you here.

He liked to think that when she thrust her nose out like that it was to show affection for him, though there had been times during her more selfish moments when he seriously doubted she cared anything for him at all. Like when they were forty miles from nowhere and she ate his only sack of smoking tobacco, and again when he came in from a hard day scratching around in the hills to find the flour sack empty and part of its contents strewn over the ground. That time he swore he was going to trade her for a mule, but he never did.

When the light tapping of the burro's hoofs behind him stopped suddenly, he stopped too and turned around to see what was up. Old Cactus not only had a nose for Indians, but sometimes she could see them farther away than he could. It was really their shaggy ponies that she disliked, more than the Indians themselves.

It wasn't Indians she saw this time, however; it was something a few yards off the trail that gleamed snow-white in the midday sun.

He walked over to see what it was, and there in the bear grass lay two human skeletons. The sparse grass had grown up around them and up between the ribs. A hardy desert vine crawled across the breastbone of one skeleton, while inside the rib cage of the other a family of mice had built a nest. The disjointed bones, bleached by many suns to a ghastly whiteness, were but slightly out of place here and there. They lay skull to skull, the leg bones pointing in opposite directions, as if they had gone to sleep in that position. There was no clothing, guns, cooking utensils or anything else to suggest how long they had lain there. Near the two heads was a small pile of ore, perhaps a foot high, the dissevered arm bones almost encircling it. Directly overhead, as though to mark the spot well, a tall yucca lifted a great cluster of drooping lily-white blossoms that swayed gently in the breeze.

It was not too difficult for Ed Schieffelin, who was not unaccustomed to coming upon desert tragedies, to picture in his own mind what manner of thing had happened at this spot. The two prospectors—and prospectors he was certain they had been—had stopped here to take stock of the ore they had found, or perhaps they had even camped there. They had become so absorbed in their own affairs of the moment that they'd forgotten to watch for Apaches, and the inevitable had happened. The Chiricahua Apaches took no scalps, so the bodies had not been disturbed. Only guns, tools, and equipment had been carried off.

Kneeling beside the pile of ore, the prospector examined it piece by piece, as was his habit when he came upon any kind of ore. Each time he scrutinized a hunk of it through the little magnifying glass he carried, his excitement grew, for each piece was heavily shot through with silver! Finally his hands were shaking so badly that he could no longer hold the glass steady. For the first time in his life, he was to say later, he had the prospector's ague, a sort of malarial fever attended by the shakes that came on a man when he suddenly struck it rich.

Leaping to his feet like a small boy after finding a whole silver dollar in the street, he began shouting crazily at the burro. "It's the same ore, old girl! No doubt about it!" He dug into his shirt pocket for a piece of ore he had carried there for many months and compared it with the ore on the ground. "Danged if it ain't! They found it! They found it!" He was so excited he did not know what he was saying, and old Cactus stood drowsing through it all, grateful for the opportunity to catch a wink or two while she could. "But where, for Pete's sake? Where'd they come from?'

That was a good question, and Ed Schieffelin looked down at the ground, as if hopeful there might still be a footprint or two after all the intervening months or even years to indicate whence the two prospectors came. But tracks in the hard desert didn't last forever, and you couldn't back-track a pair of ghosts.

The piece of silver ore that matched the stuff on the ground, both in texture and composition, had been Ed Schieffelin's inspiration for months, the driving force that had sent him roaming across much of this wild land, looking for its source. Into this wilderness of cactus, yucca, Chiricahua Apaches, diamondback rattlers and instant death, he had come at the age of twenty-two as a civilian scout for a column of dragoons under the command of Al Sieber. They had established an army post at Camp Huachuca and fanned out from there in search of marauding Apaches. That had been back in 1870, and now it was the spring of 1877.

One day when Scout Schieffelin had ridden into this very same tier of hills, his eye had caught the gleam of deep mineral stains on a stone that in the prospector's terminology was called *float*. He dismounted and examined it carefully. And he would always remember the thrill he felt upon recognizing the rock for what it was.

He turned to a companion and said: "Silver ore!"

"Ah, go on!" the man said. "Who'd be findin' silver in a country like this?"

Schieffelin dropped the float into his pocket and rode on, but his find went to his head like potent wine. That night he could think of nothing else.

The next morning he resigned as an army scout and bought old Cactus, already seven and in the prime of life, for only seven dollars, and it had been the best investment of his life.

For a few months he had lived frugally at the cabin of George Woolfolk on Barbarcomari Creek, sleeping there nights and going out every day into the hills. He found the spot where he had picked up the float but had never been able to trace the ore to its source. He later fell in with Bill Griffith, who came down from Tucson to do assessment work on the Bruncko Mine; Schieffelin's principal function at the mine had been to stand guard against Indian attacks while Griffith did the necessary work. For this chore he received a dollar a day and board.

One day as he stood around, up rode Al Sieber with a party of Indian fighters.

"Watcha doin' here, Ed?" Sieber inquired.

"Prospectin' mostly," Ed replied.

"Whar?"

"Over yonder a ways." He waved a hand toward the hills.

"Thar ain't nothin' over yonder," scoffed Sieber.

"I've picked up some mighty nice-lookin' float."

"All you'll ever find in them thar hills is your tombstone," Sieber warned. "Geronimo'll get you if you don't watch out."

"I'll take a chance on that," Ed told him.

For more long months the search had gone on, the poverty-stricken Schieffelin living on beans most of the time. He never had in his pocket more than five or six dollars at any one time, and most of the time his pockets were empty.

And now at last his wanderings had brought him to this spot, where a couple of prospectors who had found the bonanza of his dreams had died for lack of caution.

Just then he happened to look at old Cactus, and her ears were slanted forward in the characteristic pose she assumed when she saw something in the distance. He followed her gaze with his eyes, and there in the sky, directly over the long ridge behind him, were three puffs of black smoke.

Injun signals! Somewhere up there an Apache was manipulating a blanket over a fire of greasewood, sending a message to a war party in the valley likely.

Leaving Cactus tied to a mesquite, well out of sight of anyone above them, he worked his way up the hills through the brush, and finally he saw the Apache he thought had made the signals, standing with a rifle cradled in his arms, peering into the shadows beginning to veil the mesa. The Indian made a fine picture there against the copper sky, but he made a better target, Schieffelin thought. He was about to pull the trigger of his old .40-.82 when a second warrior appeared, then a third. Two more rose ghostlike against the sky from the nether shadow.

It began to look as if Al Sieber's prophecy might come true. One Indian a man could take care of, but not five at that range. Glancing back at the valley he saw about twenty Apaches heading toward him, riding at a fast clip. This, he decided quickly, was no place for a lone white man. He headed back to where he'd left Cactus.

The Apaches charged up the steep trail, apparently to join their

59

brothers above, and Schieffelin breathed easier. Obviously there was something going on back there to the west that interested them. He hoped they wouldn't see his footprints in the trail and change their minds.

Darkness came on swiftly, lowering its curtain on the scene, and he stole away like a thief in the night. But high above the darkened valley, an intense golden light, almost liquid, fanned out from the peaks and reached eastward, lighting his way. Cactus followed dutifully behind, threading her way through the thorny bushes with hardly a sound.

Every time the clicking of her hoofs behind him stopped, he stopped too and turned around. But now with hunger gnawing at her innards, the burro was not smelling Indian horses; she was stopping frequently to grab at tufts of wild rye grass.

"Come on, Cactus," he said patiently each time she stopped, and she would dutifully start forward again, but not before grabbing a last mouthful, her nose working feverishly as she chewed it, the ends of the grass standing out from each side of her mouth like whiskers on a walrus.

They began to climb the next ridge, avoiding the trail, and an hour later Schieffelin made camp on a little knoll where he had a commanding view of the valley.

It had been a long time since he had come that close to a run-in with the Apaches. Always he avoided them like poison by maintaining a sharp lookout for them, and frequently it was Cactus who warned him when they were near.

With the excitement that surged through him like a swollen stream going over its banks, he had little room in his mind for the Indians just now, except to maintain the usual surveillance that had become a habit with him. He kept thinking of the pile of ore that matched the piece in his pocket, final proof at last that somewhere within the area a great bonanza was waiting to be rediscovered. With ore as rich as that it would be a whale of a strike, something to make the country sit up and take notice. You didn't find ore as rich as that in very many places. It would have to be a whopper.

He had made many a start in his long quest for the source of the float. He could still remember vividly his finding the float and how it had set him on edge, and now it seemed like a long time ago. It had been seven years to be exact, and part of that time he had gone hungry. Most of the time as a matter of fact. There had been times when he started out on prospecting trips with only enough flour to see him through and a little baking powder, counting on killing enough meat to live on. Antelope and deer were plentiful but difficult to approach.

Toward morning there was a change in the wind. It no longer was a wind born in the near mountains, cold with night and altitude, but a wind from far places, full of damp chill that crept through his ragged blankets and into his bones. Trouble was, he didn't have enough blankets to keep a bedbug warm. In Arizona blankets were not always essential to a man's comfort and winds from far places were rare, but tonight it was freezing cold. A spring snow, he thought, would just about do it. The Apaches would get him for sure. Even Cactus, hardy as she was, was thumping about protestingly, rattling her hobbles.

He tried to go back to sleep but couldn't. All he could think of were piles and piles of silver ore. He would almost drop off to sleep, and then the pile would grow and grow until it was higher than his head. By then he was too excited to sleep.

At last he got up and made a fire. Because of his limited supply he had rationed himself down to coffee only once a week. He wasn't due for coffee again until Sunday and this was only Thursday, but this was a special occasion. He made coffee.

Cactus had wandered off a distance to browse. He did not disturb her until the first faint hint of dawn, then he put the pack on her and headed back for the country he had crossed last night to get away from the Indians. As cold as it was it would be unusual to find an Apache anywhere except in his teepee.

Starting at a place well above the spot where he had found the float seven long years back, he struck out north, intending to go higher this time than he ever had before. He reasoned that ore thrown off from a ledge or pocket would travel downhill for quite a piece during a millennium, or ten millenniums for that matter, no telling how long.

This trip was a little different from most, though it had started the same as usual. He recalled that never before on any of his trips had he taken his long-handled shovel or his drill and hammer. For some reason he could not now recall, he had put them in the pack. The long-handled shovel was a handicap really, for the handle sticking out of the pack had caught on bushes so that Cactus had to stop and back up many times to free it before making a new start. He couldn't think of any real reason for bringing it along, unless a kind providence, an all-wise providence, had nudged him into it. Maybe the power that moved men to perform unusual feats had planned it that way. If he made a strike he would need the shovel, and the hammer and drill no doubt.

The chilling wind of the night had now passed, and the overcast was breaking up as it frequently did when the sun came out. The Apaches had gone with the night, apparently, for he saw no sign of them.

Three miles west of him lay the hills that had so long intrigued and baffled him. Before him the wide wash led up to the heights now bathed in sunlight. He had never ranged that high before, and therefore it was virgin territory to him.

Though the chill had gone from the lower ridges, the higher he climbed the more he felt the cold. His corduroy britches, threadbare at the knees, and the old buckskin jacket that had a big hole burned in the back were little protection in that higher altitude. His grimy slouch hat that was five years old had a worn brim that flopped over his eyes when the wind pushed against it and an old boot that was run down at the heels started a blister on his right little toe. His red flannel shirt afforded him little comfort in the biting wind. His face was half hidden by a heavy, curly brown beard, and a mass of dark, tangled, unkempt hair with burrs in it fell to his shoulders. His appearance, he was to confess later under more luxurious circumstances, would have frightened crows out of a cornfield. But there was something about him that touched his rags with a certain nobility. His serious, deep gray eyes reflected the courage of a vivid personality. A man of destiny, about to set the world agog with one of the most fabulous discoveries since Columbus, had stepped out of a dinghy and onto a new world.

He had climbed no more than a quarter of a mile into the unexplored area when he spotted a piece of float. Along a seam that shot through it from end to end, he detected the unmistakable presence of pure silver. It matched the ore he carried in his shirt pocket, and it was not unlike that he had found by the skeletons.

He raised his voice in song:

> Darling, I am growing old,
> Silver threads among the gold,
> Shine upon my brow today,
> Life is fading fast away . . .

This was more like it; he was getting somewhere. No telling how long ago some terrific upheaval of the earth had cast off shattered pieces of a main ledge and sent them on their downhill journey. It might be very high up, near the summit.

At last he came to where the wash divided. He was uncertain as to which branch he should follow. He would have to try one side, and if he found no more float, he would try the other.

As he stood contemplating his next move, a jackrabbit popped out of a clump of mountain cedar and scurried away—up the right-hand branch.

That was good enough for Ed Schieffelin. He'd been following hunches all his life and if a rabbit wanted to give him a nudge, that was just fine.

He unloaded the pack and put the hobbles on Cactus, who gave him a grateful push with her cold nose. She always did that when relieved of her burden.

"All right, old girl, go find your breakfast."

Above there the hillside flattened out into a tiny plateau before it again rose to the heights, with little tables and hollow saddles where float might collect.

He found several pieces of ore, some heavy with silver, and his spirits soared. He felt like singing again but was afraid the Apaches might hear him.

Higher toward the summit where the wind came over the ridge and chilled him to the bone, he saw something in the distance that looked like a streak along the hillside.

He climbed faster now, watching it. It appeared to be of grayish rock of an irregular shape, with reddish-yellow streaks through it. He estimated it was about fifty feet long and a foot wide.

He had to fight his way through thickets of catclaw and wild pear that tore at his threadbare britches, but he didn't mind. He felt something tear and saw that one leg of his pants had a rip a foot long; the catclaw had brought blood, but this he did not mind either. Nothing mattered now, for this indeed might be it! This could be the end of the trail for him.

At last, breathless and soaked with sweat, he stood before the ledge. He could see the streaks of pure silver, and he let out a whoop that could have brought all of Apacheland down upon him. It was the most thrilling moment of his life.

He drove his prospector's pick into the vein, and a small avalanche of brittle lumps came crashing down at his feet. He picked up a piece and examined it with feverish eye. One didn't have to know much about minerals to realize that this was it. The piece was so heavy with pure silver that it felt like lead in his hands.

The ague was upon him again, the fever that made his hands shake like leaves in a stiff breeze. His fingers shook so violently that he dropped the specimen at his feet, unable to hold onto it.

For a moment or two he thought he was going to pass out from sheer joy. He felt dizzy and had to rest a minute.

He picked up another hunk of the stuff, and his brain reeled with the richness of it. Was he having a dream, or could this be true?

Suddenly he was babbling like a fool. "This is it, boy! This is what you've been looking for all these years, you old sonofab——! You found it at last." He wasn't old, really; he was just turning thirty.

He thought he could see where another pick had been plunged into the vein. Maybe those men whose skeletons he'd found. Who else? Had someone been there before, the country would have heard of the discovery long before this. It had to be them.

He was alone to enjoy this moment. Only a bluejay, he recalled later, shared the glory. It had perched on a limb above him and scolded raucously in protest of his presence there. It had a nest nearby.

It was a moment in history, as things turned out. No one but Ed Schieffelin knew the thrill and romance of it. Not even his faithful burro, now knee-deep in luscious grass, had been there to witness it.

The silver in the vein was so pure and soft that when he pressed a twenty-five-cent piece against it real hard, it left the imprint so clearly defined that he was able to decipher the national motto, "E Pluribus Unum."

The quarter happened to be the last cent Ed Schieffelin had to his name. It represented his next sack of plug-cut.

He thought of Al Sieber's gibe—"all you'll find in them thar hills is your tombstone."

Well, he'd found his tombstone all right—a whole mountain of silver, it looked like. He could see outcroppings of the same vein farther along and again where it broke over the ridge.

"By golly," he said, "I'll call her Tombstone, that's what I'll do. The Tombstone Mine."

He didn't know it at the time, but he had christened not only the mine but the hills as well, a whole silver field, and an unborn town whose story was to become one of the West's most picturesque and dramatic chronicles—a story that for nearly a hundred years has entertained millions of readers, movie fans and TV audiences; and it probably will go on entertaining them for another hundred years or so.

But it was not the end of the story for Ed Schieffelin, not by a long shot. There was more to come, some of it rather heartbreaking.

Filling a sack with as much of the ore as he could carry, Schieffelin erected a rock monument to mark his claim, then went back to collect his burro and pack.

Striking out across the hills and with an eye out for Injun signs, he headed for Tucson, living on game he shot along the way, for his larder consisted of a small bag of salt, some pepper, an ounce or two of coffee and some baking powder. His flour had petered out several days before.

He arrived in Tucson while the Mexican population was celebrating one of its several fiesta days and filed his claim, spotting it on the crude map the recorder kept for that purpose. There had been no survey of the region as yet; and a claim could not be located by sections and townships, but it had to be described accurately.

Schieffelin had to borrow the filing fee from a friend, and while he was about it he borrowed enough for stage fare to Globe, up in the northern part of the state. He wanted to contact his brother Al and cut him in on the find, if he'd finance the development of the vein. Al was working and had a little money.

Cactus was put out to pasture in a field near Fort Lowell while her master was away. Finding herself free of her hobbles at last, she kicked up her heels and ran off into the cactus and greasewood. It was to be the last Schieffelin ever saw of her, for his affairs did not bring him back that way for a while.

In Globe he learned that his brother had moved on to another mine at Signal, and he was almost a week getting there, begging rides with ore wagons and the like.

He found Brother Al's interest in his discovery only lukewarm. Al insisted that Ed show his rocks to the foreman of the mine, a man named Hewelett.

Hewelett looked at the ore briefly. "Mostly lead," he said and handed the pieces back.

During the next two or three days Ed showed his specimens to other mining men who should know silver when they saw it. But none waxed enthusiastic. "Just medium ore," one old pro said. "Not worth bothering with."

"Better forget it and go to work," Brother Al suggested.

Ed went to the door of Al's shack, and one by one he hurled the ore pieces down the hillside as far as he could send them. He saved but two pieces of the stuff and laid them on a shelf.

The next day he went to work in the McCracken mine.

During the next few weeks Ed Schieffelin met the McCracken mine assayer, Dick Gird.

"I got a piece of ore I'd like to have you assay," Ed said. "When you got time."

"Bring it over," Gird said. He was a dour, hard-featured man who had little time for anything but his duties at the mine. But he had been friendly to Ed Schieffelin, and for the remainder of his life he was to be glad he had; for his assay of the specimen gave him goose pimples.

Ed was asleep in the shack when Al burst in one morning and shook him vigorously. "Wake up, Ed! Mr. Gird wants to see you right away in his office."

Ed got over there as fast as he could.

"Where did you say you found this rock?" Gird wanted to know.

"Over on the San Pedro."

"That's not very definite."

"I could make it more definite if you'd tell me what this is all about," Ed said.

"How much money have you?"

"Not much till payday."

"If you'll cut me in on this I'll buy some mules and grubstake an expedition back to where you found this stuff."

"Did you find that rock worth much?" Ed fished, suspiciously.

"It's fabulous, man! You've found a bonanza and I want in on it."

It was finally agreed that all three would be in on it—Ed, Al and Mr. Gird. There was no written agreement, just a handshake all around that was to hold inviolate by the three partners to the end.

"What about your job here at the mine?" Al wanted to know of Gird.

"To hell with the job! With something as big as this, who needs a job?"

When he handed in his resignation, the company offered him the general superintendency, but he refused it with thanks.

Gird bought mules and a wagon, loaded up with guns, ammunition, food, tools, a surveyor's transit and level and his own assaying outfit, ready to pull out; but at the last moment Brother Al lost his nerve. He said he couldn't pull away from a job that paid him $4 a day for something so uncertain as a ledge of rock in a hillside.

"All right," Ed said, "that leaves all the more for Dick and me. Goodbye, Al!" He pulled out without another word.

With a camp finally established just below the discovery, Gird began taking samples and making assays. He found that the rich ore extended for only a few feet, and the vein was not deep. At some time back in the dark ages, most of the vein had been thrown off down the hillside, scattered hell-to-breakfast, and there wasn't enough of it left to make an operation worthwhile.

Unfortunately Brother Al had shown up that very day, having finally thought better of his decision and decided to come along.

"Now look what I've gone and done!" he said with tears in his eyes. "I've quit a good job for nothing. I was afraid of this from the start."

"What about me?" Gird said. "You're not the only one."

But it was small comfort to Al, who stayed up all night pacing back and forth and bemoaning his misfortune.

"There's silver here in this mountain somewhere," Gird said. "It may take a little time to find it."

During the next few weeks the hunt settled down to a systematic routine, directed by Gird, who was after all a mining engineer and knew his stuff.

Gird did the searching; Al, the skeptical one, the cooking; and Ed kept the larder supplied with meat.

One morning Al came upon Ed in the hills.

"Look at this," Ed said, "a rock that's almost pure silver. I think I've found it this time for sure."

Al looked at the rock. "You're a lucky cuss," he said.

"By golly," Ed said, "that's the name of my mine—the Lucky Cuss. What do you know!"

Gird assayed only one piece of the ore, and that was enough. Figuring the ratio in ounces and pounds, it would go pretty close to $10,000 to the ton.

This time Ed had found it!

Three days later a couple of mules belonging to Hank Williams and John Oliver, two prospectors who were in the region but who knew nothing of the Schieffelin find wandered off and while looking for them Williams saw a gleam of metal in the trail that had been gouged out by the dragging halter chains of the vagrant animals. He recognized it as virgin silver and began looking around. Above the trail he found the ledge and named it the Grand Central.

The next day Williams saw smoke and wandered into the Schieffelin camp to reveal his discovery. Gird claimed it was on the Lucky Cuss property and in fact it appeared to be. So as a friendly gesture they divided the new claim, the Schieffelin camp taking half and Williams and Oliver half, which retained the name Grand Central. The Schieffelins and Gird named theirs the

Contention because of Gird's contention that the Grand Central claim infringed on the Lucky Cuss property.

All three—the Lucky Cuss, the Grand Central and the Contention were to become the three richest silver mines ever found on earth.

The two Schieffelins sold out cheaply—for about a million dollars. Gird hung on and amassed a huge fortune. He became so wealthy that at the age of fifty he could not tell within a million dollars what he was worth without consulting his bankers.

Wealthy, famous and still young, Ed Schieffelin wanted to see what the world was like beyond his mountain of silver. He traveled extensively and for a time lived in New York City, where the best restaurants gave him the red-carpet treatment and cabbies knew him by his first name. One Sunday morning when President Rutherford B. Hayes took a walk in Central Park, the police and secret service agents expected a crowd would follow him but were amazed to find the crowd on the other side of the park gawking at the man who had found a mountain worth $85,000,000. Ed Schieffelin had also taken a walk that morning, and a cab driver had pointed him out to the crowd expecting the President. There were only a few scattered cheers for Hayes.

Schieffelin went to Chicago and to Washington. He was not a showman and tried to avoid attention, but wherever he went people turned out to get a look at him. In Washington he was the guest of western senators and men in high places. But society and politics had no appeal. He hated the adulation and the fuss people made over him. Actually there was little change in the original Ed Schieffelin who was by nature a kindly, simple-hearted soul.

"I don't care for all the fuss and feathers," he told Governor John Charles Fremont in the fall of 1879. "Who am I to bend a knee to, anyway? Just a plain old prospector from the hills who's been a little luckier than most, that's all. I wish people would let me enjoy myself."

The Man Who Found $85,000,000!

To get away from it all he had a boat specially built and cruised Alaskan waters with only the crew as company.

Brother Al's death in 1885 left him lonely, and he longed for the hills and solitude where nature provided companionship. He could go for weeks and months on end without seeing a human being and loved it.

He met Mary E. Brown, a comely widow of Alameda, California, and married her. His wife took a keen interest in his welfare and tried to plan his life for him. But it did not work out well. There were too many parties and social events that bored him.

Born in Pennsylvania, he had gone with his parents to the wilds of Oregon while still a small boy, and it was there he wanted to return to try and recapture some of the happiness of his childhood. Oregon had been a wild country and still was, as wild as the deserts he knew, and there he thought he might find the solitude he longed for.

"I will go with you," Mrs. Schieffelin said.

"No," he replied, "You'd better not. You wouldn't like roughing it, my dear. You stay here till I come back."

Before going north he went back to Tucson and Fort Lowell to see if he could find old Cactus, who had been his daily companion for nearly seven years. Now almost fifteen, she would still be a good pack burro.

But Cactus had taken off into the hills long ago, he found. No one knew where she was. Schieffelin made several trips into the hills searching for her, but without success.

In Oregon, Ed Schieffelin dropped from sight. Only a few people knew of the remote cabin in the coastal area where he lived. He was still a young man, only forty-two, and seemed in the best of health; but one day a logger who passed his cabin every day on his way home from work noticed no smoke coming from the chimney. Always at that hour of the day Schieffelin was cooking his supper, and the logger wondered if the recluse might be ill.

He found Ed Stretched out on the floor, dead. He had been

hiking in the woods that day and apparently had overtaxed his heart.

Ed Schieffelin's funeral in Tombstone was the largest ever held in that town. Saloons, stores and county offices closed, and people came from all parts of the territory to take a last look at the man who had found a hill of silver that already had produced $85,000,000. The funeral parlor was crammed with flowers, many of them remembrances from men in high places.

The body was dressed in Schieffelin's old flannel shirt, bright red after its last trip to the laundry, and his prospector's clothes. Beside the coffin rested the pick and shovel and the canteen he had carried the day he made his strike. All that was needed to recall the past was old Cactus, but she was off somewhere, presumably gallivanting around with other creatures of her kind, enjoying a new freedom.

Today a towering monument marks the resting place of this man who, with steadfast faith and courage, followed a dream and won everlasting fame.

Where the Outlaws Hid

by Homer Croy

One reason the Oklahoma outlaws were so hard to bring to their knees was the multitude of hiding places they knew of in which they could tuck themselves away for weeks at a time. Deputies would not have the slightest idea where they were. Sometimes the officers would think the bandits had left the country and gone to Mexico, but all the time they would be comfortably hidden within the confines of Indian Territory.

The owners of many ranches welcomed the saddle boys. In fact some of the owners were just a step above being outlaws themselves. The outlaws were not too much of a nuisance; they helped with the work—a little. That is they helped brand calves and they helped break horses, since both of these activities were classed under the heading of fun. Sometimes one of the outlaws would offer to help build fence; however, in a day or two he usually would develop a lame back and would have to quit.

If a ranch owner had even suggested that these men go out and plow, the outlaws would have shunned him as an Indian would a white man with the smallpox. If a rancher's wife had suggested that the outlaws help do the washing, they would have gone to the husband in alarm and told him that something was wrong with his wife! Sometimes when things were going well, the outlaws paid for their food. When things turned bad they overlooked this item.

On occasion as many as five outlaws would be living at a harboring place. They would sleep in the house when they thought it was safe; when they thought it was dangerous, they would post a guard. Sometimes they would all leave the house and hide in the timber—where they often had fortified huts and could remain until they thought it safe to return to the house.

They not only posted their own lookouts but also had friends who would rush word that officers were in the neighborhood. Most of the dugouts were all concealed and well equipped. The outlaws added to their food supply by hunting wild turkeys, deer and antelope in the thinly populated sections. They would take a ranchman's steer and turn it into meat and sometimes boldly enter a country store to buy additional provisions. Usually the merchant did not find it convenient to report the strangers.

Some dugouts would sleep eight men; usually the number would be four or five. The beds were arranged in tiers, one above the other. The men usually selected one of their number as cook —a sissy job—but he was relieved from guard duty and on the whole didn't fare too badly.

Their relaxation, their sport, their pleasure, was gambling. They would put down a horse blanket out in a cornfield, all squat around it and play for the money they had taken in their last robbery. Sometimes after a series of games, one man would owe another a handsome sum of money. He always paid.

When they felt a ranch or a particular dugout was under suspicion, the outlaws would suddenly fly away like birds from a tree. When too hard pressed, they would divide and get jobs on ranches as cowboys, and rarely did they ever go to a city. They were mostly cowboys or ranch hands and wanted none of the ways of "civilization."

Being the owner of a harboring place was particularly trying. Sometimes the man had to carry water on both shoulders. If he informed on the outlaws, they would return and make it unpleasant for him. If he didn't give up the information, the officers would have him in court. And it was especially hard on the wife of a ranch owner; any day, or any hour, four or five evil-looking men might ride up and, without invitation, become her guests. In many cases she would have a boy of impressionable age who admired these men who didn't have to work.

Here is a listing of some of the main harboring places:

JIM RILEY'S RANCH in the northwestern part of Oklahoma Territory, twenty miles south of Taloga on the South Canadian. In this district, west from Enid, were the Gloss Mountains, where every breeze shifted the sand, covering the tracks of man and horse. Riley was a water carrier; he tried to keep on good terms with both law and outlaw, a difficult balancing feat.

FITZGERALD'S on the Cimarron River at Cowboy Flat, about fifteen miles northeast of Guthrie. Through these doors passed some of the greatest outlaws of Oklahoma.

GEORGE ISAAC'S on the north side of the Washita River, four miles from Chickasha, Indian Territory. Timber came up close to the ranch house; if the outlaws were disturbed at night, they would rush into the timber where no officer would be foolhardy enough to follow.

THE DUNN BROTHERS' ROCK FORT. It was really that —a fort. It was about eighteen miles east of Ingalls. Here Bitter Creek and Charlie Pierce gave up their lives and "The Rose of Cimarron" lived. What a life it was!

THE CASEYS' near the present town of Clinton, five miles south of Arapaho. "Old Man Casey" (as he was called) had seven sons. They were about what you'd think.

AMOS CHAPMAN'S where the town of Seiling is now located. Chapman had a wooden leg and was a squaw man. Sometimes he was a deputy upholding the law; sometimes he wasn't. Anyway he was one of Oklahoma's early picturesque characters.

THE OSAGE HILLS. This was no ranch, no fortified position. It was open country—wild and desolate—near Pawhuska and sixty miles southwest of Coffeyville, Kansas. There was a saying that outlaws were as thick as jackrabbits in the Osage Hills.

THE MILITARY RESERVATION near Fort Sill. The reservation backed up into the Wichita Mountains, and it was wild and unfenced. Here existed the situation of the government's owning land on which were hiding the very men it was looking for. Sometimes home seekers would start across this forbidding stretch of country in covered wagons. Some time later an old wagon wreck would be found in a canyon, and that would be the end of it.

THE BAR-X-BAR RANCH on Turkey Creek near Pawnee. The Dalton-Doolin Gang loved the place.

THE JIM HUGHES RANCH on the Washita River near Fort Cobb, west of Anadarko. The Bert Casey Gang was often in residence.

THE JOHN HOLT RANCH on Bear Creek, about twenty miles southeast of Marlow—a good place for badmen.

THE H-X BAR RANCH on Cowboy Flat, thirteen miles northeast of Guthrie, owned by Oscar D. Halsell.

THE MASHED-O RANCH northeast of Tulsa. The Daltons, tired and weary from robbing, often stopped here to rest and get away from it all.

There were other places where the outlaws got fresh horses and supplies. Sometimes the owners shared in the loot; mostly they didn't share, but were afraid to openly oppose their "visitors."

The ranch owners who harbored men on the run had one protection: it was exceedingly difficult for a prosecuting attorney to prove "intent" on the part of the ranch owners. The ranch owners usually testified they were afraid not to shelter the outlaws, and the juries accepted it that way.

A Plot of Earth

by J. Frank Dobie

On the twenty-sixth day of September, 1888, I was born in a three-room rock house with wooden dining room and kitchen added, on a ranch in Live Oak County, Texas. My father owned the ranch before he and my mother were married. They added to it and added to the house while rearing six children, I being the oldest. As ranches went then it was small, approximately seven thousand acres. My father, a very modest man, sometimes called it a "place." He leased additional acreage and pastured cattle on other ranches. Not long before he died, in 1920, he sold off three thousand acres to an adjoining landholder. My mother kept the remainder until her death, November 22, 1948.

In 1951, as one of six heirs, I signed a piece of paper passing ownership of the inheritance to alien hands. Time with its unending changes may see another human being on this plot of earth with roots into it as deep as mine, but not soon, I think. No one of the six men who bought it has any idea of living upon it. They are oil men, not ranchers; they bought it as a hunting ground and as an investment. It has become a piece of property and little more. In a little while I shall become a clod of earth. Until then no matter who holds title to the ground, my roots into it, invisible and unmaterial, will be ineradicable.

In a way I feel that for a piece of money I have betrayed the soil that nurtured me, though the purchasers, with means and with modern ideas of conservation, will probably do more to restore it than my family did. As a matter of fact, we did absolutely nothing to restore it.

For forty-five years we ourselves were absentee owners. In 1906 my family moved to the town of Beeville, twenty-seven horse miles over a weary road to the east, where we used to trade. That fall I left for college, never to reside again in the region. Nevertheless for years after I left, I spent summers on the ranch and have never ceased returning to it with eagerness. It has been a place where I belonged both in imagination and in reality, a place on which I felt free in the way that one can feel only on a congenial plot of earth that is his own. This plot has said more to me than any person I have known or any writer I have read, though only through association with fine minds and spirits have I come to realize its sayings.

It is not a rich land. *Caliche* hills and thorned brush make a section of it forbidding. The remainder is sandyish. Yet the sweep of hills and valleys, wooded Ramirenia Creek, open prairies and live oak trees scattered singly and clustered into groves make the ranch gracious. One of the live oaks, 18 feet in circumference, has the largest spread in all that part of Texas—120 feet. *Chilipi-*

quines, the little red Mexican peppers, always grow wild under it. It is near what used to be called Alligator Waterhole; alligators lived there before I was born. In a seasonable spring all the land is beautiful with growing grass, fresh leaves on all the trees and brush, wine-burnished hollyhocks in the valleys, pink phlox and Indian paintbrushes on the hillsides, splashes and stretches of the lupines called bluebonnets and scores of other wild flowers everywhere. Some of the mesquites along Ramirenia Creek are noble. One has a circumference of 13 feet.

I did not know it at the time, but I began listening to this piece of land talk while I was the merest child. When my father settled on it Ramirenia Creek ran clear water the year round. When I was a youth it held lasting water holes that supplied the cattle in two pastures with water. Since 1912 or 1915, however, the creek has been bone dry except after rains. Erosion.

Yet I stick up for the old ranch as a ranch. Cattle thrive there if it is not overstocked and if droughts are not too prolonged. As a result of popular ideas on game conservation, it has far more deer and wild turkeys than it had when we left it. A widow and her two sons and daughter lived on a half-section of land joining us. At times they must have subsisted mainly on wild meat and cornbread. One son was a constant hunter, and one year he killed about twenty deer on our ranch. In time almost none was left to kill. When I was not more than six years old, my father rode in one day with a wild gobbler tied to his saddle. He had roped it on a prairie. By the time I was grown no turkeys were left at all, and much of the prairie land had grown up in brush. This taking of the land by brush was going on over tens of millions of acres in southern Texas, a result of grazing off and trampling down the turf.

When my father began ranching he raised horses, traded horses and drove a herd or two to Kansas. I used to hear talk by him and other men about mares, trailed northeastward from our country to Arkansas or some other faraway land, that showed up in the spring to have their colts on ground where they had been raised.

This was before barbed wire fenced the country. The instinct in me is the instinct that was in those homing mares. The difference between them and me is that I can think and use words beyond horse power. For all that, words do not make clear what I feel. I am unable to make the tie clear to myself, much less to others. It is not sentimentality, not even sentiment, that I feel. Something of instinct, strengthened perhaps by cultivated sensitivity, lies beyond rationalization.

I do not wish to go back there to live. The summers are scorching; for six months of the year the air is enervating. Clouds drift up from the Gulf of Mexico, barely fifty miles away and not more than a hundred feet lower, but they seldom bear rain. One can waste his heart out there vainly hoping for rain, and during the frequent droughts the unyielding land is a desolation. If I were wealthy I should buy the ranch, modernize the house and live there during the hunting season with books, typewriter, some pictures and mesquite furniture beside the fireplace in the room where I was born. The fire in that fireplace would talk to me as no other fire in any other fireplace can talk.

The richest days of my life have not been spent on this ranch, not at all. The hymn singing we had on Sundays at home, while my mother played the piano and my father enjoyed his good voice, gives me a depressed feeling to this day. I was afraid of God, prayed Him to help me find a lost pocketknife and in time found that the personal God of my forefathers is for me as mythical as Jupiter and not nearly so plausible as Venus. I believe in a Supreme Law of the Universe.

There were two or three youths in the country with whom I felt congenial, but I remember little from my boy schoolmates but vulgarities and stupidities. Puberty brought wretchedness—the payment of adult Puritan refusal to face physiology. I was too tame.

All ranch work was congenial, even doctoring wormy yearlings by day and skinning dead ones by lantern light after dark, but the year we boys tried raising a bale of cotton remains a dark blot.

A Plot of Earth

Ab Blocker, a noted old trail driver, spoke for me when he said that after he had farmed for a year, "I got down on my knees and promised God Almighty if I ever planted another seed of cotton I'd boil it first for three days so it could never sprout." Picturesque talk and characters like that were not cultivated in our home. Itinerant preachers were favored above all other company. They specialized in eating fried chicken, potato salad and lemon pie, and in long blessings at the table, longer prayers in the evening.

But no play world could have been happier than ours. With pegs, twine and sticks we built big pastures and stocked them with spools from which my mother's sewing machine had used the thread, for horses; with tips of cattle horns sawed off in the branding chute in the ranch corrals, for cattle; and with oak galls for sheep and dried snail shells for goats. The goats could not be branded, but we branded the other stock with pieces of baling wire heated red hot. Trains of empty sardine cans strung together hauled the cattle from ranch to ranch. We sold cattle to each other for dollars molded in the bottoms of round wooden bluing boxes. Our metal was solder melted from tin cans and rifle bullets gouged out of oak trees, into which they had been shot for practice.

I became a knight in the image of Ivanhoe, and with my brother Elrich set up a tournament course, which we ran on horseback, spearing rings. Tennyson's *Idylls of the King* put me into a world where for months wan lights flickered on plains farther away than Troy. I had heard or read of the music of the spheres and riding alone one night I thought I heard it; after that I would go out at night to listen to it until I discovered that the sound was made by a variety of katydid. Nevertheless a certain pulsation of night has continued to seem to come down from the stars rather than to go up from the earth.

Our ranch house, the main part of which stands, is in an extensive grove of big oaks on a kind of plateau overlooking the valley of Long Hollow. For most of its distance this hollow used to be a mere drainage way, its bottom grassed over in places, carrying water only after hard rains, though it could get on a boom.

Now it is a deep, wide gulch of waste. Erosion. When I first knew it, the valley was a cornfield. Then it was turned out as a part of what we called the horse pasture, where the milk cows as well as saddle horses were kept. That old field is now a dense thicket of mesquites and huisaches. The huisache came to our land about 1930. It is beautiful in bloom and beautiful, too, in its grace of green, but it usurps soil without paying anything at all to it or to the livers upon it.

Thousands of times I have looked across Long Hollow Valley, and something from those vistas remains deep inside me. In the early morning wild turkeys now and then gobbled from the woods on the far side, and the cheerio call of the bobwhite came from every direction. On the slope coming down the valley, about half a mile away, stood a hollow, whitened live oak in which buzzards raised their young every year. "Puke like a buzzard" was a common expression of the country, and I used to ride my horse up close to the tree to observe the young white birds, frightened and unable to fly, verify the saying. Every day nearly I watched buzzards sail. Nothing in the sky is more serenely graceful. Whenever I see a buzzard sailing now, the sight takes me back to the sky over our ranch. One spring the bluebonnets on Long Hollow were up to my stirrups. They bloom that high inside me every spring. In my study hangs a little painting of Mexican primroses. It speaks to me of the Mexican primroses I knew as a child.

In spring and early summer I often awoke hearing the quick, bright cry made by diving scissortails. They nested in mesquites in the calf pasture just north of the house, Long Hollow being to the south. Countless times in these later years a glimpse of the salmon-hued underpart of a flying scissortail has brought back to me those morning awakenings.

The house had a paling fence around it, and in the yard were more flowers—roses, chrysanthemums, cannas, violets especially— than any other ranch in that part of Texas had. The garden, very prolific, was where vegetables grew. They and the flowers were irrigated from a cypress cistern and a supplementary dirt tank into which a windmill, just back of the kitchen, pumped water. The yard was bare of grass, in the pioneer tradition that guarded against snakes. Rattlesnakes were frequently killed near the house. At the corner of a wide L-shaped gallery—"porch" being a literary word that I never heard spoken—grew a cape jasmine. It happened that at the close of school one year I received as a prize a copy of Owen Meredith's *Lucile,* with *Il Trovatore* appended.

> And I swear as I thought of her thus in that hour
> And how, after all, old things are best,
> I smelt the smell of that jasmine flower
> Which she used to wear in her breast.

When I read those line in *Il Trovatore,* the jasmine by our gallery became affixed to them. Its aroma has never left me.

My mother had some sort of help a good part of the time but often none. With or without help, she was too busy cooking, sewing, raising children, and keeping house to garden. Men might come at any hour of the day or night. All had to be fed and bedded. My father tended the flowers as well as the vegetables. He set out orange trees, which never bore. He laid out a croquet ground in the shade of oaks. He could do anything from repairing a windmill to making a coffin for a Mexican child that died on the ranch. He was *patron* for some Mexicans who did not live on the ranch. He liked cutting up meat, and the meat he butchered was all we had. Like many other ranchmen he never hunted. He hoped his eldest son would choose a career better than ranching —that of a clean-collared banker perhaps. He paid 8 and 10 per cent to his banker and liked him.

Back of the house was a rock smokehouse, long ago crumbled down, for the rock was *caliche,* not true stone. Every winter my father, aided by Mexicans, killed hogs and cut them up for curing. The only balloons we children knew were the blown-up bladders of hogs and cattle. No child could ask for better. The way to make a bladder expand is to warm it slowly by a fire, gradually blowing air into it through the quill of a turkey feather.

The Mexicans cut the long, strong-fibered leaves of bear grass (a yucca), heated them lightly over a fire to make them more pliable and then used them to tie the hams, shoulders, and side bacon to poles across the smokehouse. They were cured by smoke from a fire of corncobs kept smoldering for days on the dirt floor. We had no hickory, needed none. Bear grass will always for me mean homemade hemp, also thatches for Mexican huts.

Back of the smokehouse was a big stable combined with corn-crib, hayloft and rooms for tools, saddles and buggies. Along the near end of it grew a row of pomegranates, so hardy that after fifty years, and through a recent drought that killed many oaks, one still exists. Their fruit was a treat. Near them a stout mustang grapevine twined up into the coon tree, an oak in which a coon had been seen. High up across its branches we children had a platform—the "house in the coon tree," we called it—to which we ascended by the grapevine and on which we often sat reading books or playing and in season drinking (without ice, of course) pomegranateade.

Near the coon tree and adjacent to the barn were a shed and three pens. The smallest was for the milk calves, which we boys rode; the largest for driving the saddle horses into and for the milk cows. Except in winter, when two or three were fed, there were twelve or fifteen cows, all of range breeding, more various in color than productive of milk. Two or three of the mildest-natured cows were willing to adopt dogie calves, and as the dogies were given to us children, we took a special interest in these foster cows.

The third pen held hayricks and fronted the horse stalls, but only the buggy horses and work teams were fed. Before daylight somebody—and in time that job was mine—caught the night horse out of the little pasture in front of the house and rode to bring in the *remuda* from the horse pasture. Many a morning I walked stooping over to the ground every few steps trying to sky-light a night horse taking his sleep standing up. He always had a dragrope around his neck, and I would try to get hold of it before waking him. One dewy morning while I was hunting the saddle horses, the cobwebs were so thick between all the mesquite bushes that I had to keep brushing them away in order to see. Cobweb was our remedy for stanching the flow of blood from a cut or a jab in boy or horse.

The sandy ground in front of the stalls for buggy, hack, tools, harness and saddles had been paved with *caliche*. Red ants bored through the *caliche* and colonized below. They are very plentiful in that country, and during warm weather work night and day. They have a vicious sting, the pain of which is alleviated by application of wet soda.

We saddled our horses on the *caliche* or close to it. My father was an early riser, always having coffee boiling long before dawn. When we were running cattle, as the phrase for working cattle went, he had his men away from the house before there was enough light to see by. While we were saddling, the horses would stamp the *caliche* in order to knock off the red ants crawling above their hoofs.

For several years after I went off to college, I half-awakened before daylight every morning to the sound of those horses stamping their feet on the *caliche*. I could hear the low voices of Mexicans saying indistinguishable words, the plopping down of saddles on horsebacks and the metallic clicking of cinch rings and spurs. I never hear those sounds before daylight any more, but the memory of both the actuality and the half-dream is a part of me.

The cattle pens were on down the hill from the ranch house, about two hundred yards away. The well there was one of the oldest in the country, hand-dug and rock-curbed about fifty feet deep, amid magnificent oaks. When the wind did not blow during the dog days of August and the big cypress cistern ran empty, water for stock had to be hauled up by pulley. One end of the rope was tied to a large wooden bucket, the other end to the horn of a saddle. Then a boy or a Mexican rode Old Baldy back and forth, back and forth, hour after hour, over a fifty-foot stretch, drawing water. I can see my father standing on a wide plank over the well curb and hear his hearty "Whoa" as the bucket came up and he reached to pour the water into a trough. In time the well was sunk deeper by a driller and cased with iron up even with the rock curbing.

No cattle ever died on our ranch for want of water, but they died on Tol McNeill's bigger ranch west of us and on the Chapa ranch up about the head of Ramirenia Creek, where my father frequently bought steers. They died on other ranches. I have heard them bawling all night long and all day long for water. No more distressing sound can be made. Men driving herds through the country frequently held them overnight in our pens. If a thirsty herd came when there was no water, it made too much noise for peaceful sleep. My mother saw no romance in ranching. The women of her day had no part in riding, scant time to "stand and stare" like cows and watch buzzards sail into infinity. After she moved to Beeville, I heard her express thankfulness that she would never again have to listen to the bawl of thirsty cattle. Remembering thunder as the voice of hope, I understand how the Hopi Indians worship rain and have little affinity for a religion which uses water merely as a symbol for a theological rite in a medicine-man ceremony.

It was thirst in summer and hunger in winter for drought-starved cattle. The main reserve of the land is prickly pear. It is composed of about 10 per cent fiber and 90 per cent water and defends itself by an armor of thorns. Before the portable pear-burner—a flame thrower fed by gasoline, and air pump—enabled one man to singe the thorns off enough pears to feed one hundred cows, or two hundred, men fed a few of the poorest by chopping the pear down, dragging it to a fire in the open, holding it on the end of a green pole over the flames and then pitching it to the slobbering animals. In January of 1899 Mexicans feeding our poor cows reported that the frozen prickly pear pads were shattering like glass.

About this time my father and Uncle Jim Dobie, the big speculator and operator of the family, went into partnership and bought several thousand cows. They leased a ranch for them on the San Antonio River. During the winter that followed the cows died like sheep. The next summer I rode with a chuckwagon and a "crowd"—as an outfit was called—of Mexican *vaqueros,* led by my father, to gather up the remnant of cows. My chief memory of the excursion is the deliciousness of washing myself and my saddle blanket in the San Antonio River, at which, under the shade of pecan trees, we camped a half-day.

This cow venture so nearly broke my father that he decided to farm. About six lumber cabins were built for Mexican families along Ramirenia Creek, and the men plowed up several hundred acres of open sand hills that never should have been disturbed and that within a few years were turned back to the field mice and the ground squirrels and the hunting hawks. The Mexicans grew enough corn and beans to live on, shooting rabbits and trapping quail to supplement the fare, but the landlord made no money out of four-cent cotton. When we were running cattle, the men quit the fields to work for four bits a day and found. They were better *vaqueros* than they were farmers. It was a torture to me that I could not quit school and ride with them for nothing a day.

One of them entered my life. He is still living, old and nearly blind, on a little piece of land in San Patricio County that my mother deeded to him for a small sum. As long as she lived he brought her a turkey every Christmas and received his "Christmas." From the time the family moved to town, he looked after the ranch. He is little, wiry, quick, with a reddish complexion betokening more Spanish blood than most Mexicans have. He has a Spanish irony. His name is Genaro del Bosque, and his people once had land in Texas. His wife Emelia learned to read English in the school my mother taught at Lagarto before she married. Genaro was the best trailer I have ever known. His intelligence, energy, cow sense and sense of responsibility would have made him a first-class manager of a big outfit.

I and my brother Elrich felt freer with him than we felt with our father and delighted in staying on the ranch with him. He ruined an eye running in brush after a Rio Grande steer of enormous horns and lankiness that had jumped out of our corral while Stonewall Jackson Wright was receiving a herd there. After his men tried on two or three works to catch the steer and couldn't, I bought him range delivery. Genaro roped him, but we never did drive him away. He would jump fences and leave the country when he heard brush popping, and I finally sold him range delivery to a ranchman who reported him in his pasture fifteen miles away.

Genaro del Bosque "had a *mano*," a hand. When a horse threw me on my back across a ridge, injuring a vertebrae that still gets sore sometimes, he rubbed the pain down sufficiently for me to ride to town in a buggy. After the ranch was leased he did not remain on it long under the new employer, but he did not want to leave. *"Yo tengo raices aqui* (I have roots here)," he said. Following the fancies of tradition, I have often fancied that if I were doomed to the everlasting fires of a traditional hell, could be redeemed by a substitute and were such a churl as to call on another man to take my place, Genaro, of all men I know, would without a quiver of hesitation plunge into the furnace. In him and in what he represents, as well as in the land to which we both belong, *yo tengo raices.*

The day before Christmas all the Mexican men on the ranch would come to the house for gifts. My father would have made a trip to Beeville not long before and would have brought back a wagonload of supplies and "Christmas"—sugar and flour by the barrel, molasses and lard by the keg, canned tomatoes, salmon and peaches by the case, bushel sacks of coffee, potatoes, onions and beans. Christmas meant apples, oranges, nuts, raisins, lots of stick and mixed candy, along with special presents. Each Mexican family received a new blanket and a bag of apples and candy for the children. To this day, as common as they are now, I associate oranges with Christmas and its inevitable—and inevitably delicious—ambrosia.

A Plot of Earth

My mother, an eager reader herself, taught me to read and tried to teach me to play the piano. One year after my sister Fannie and I were old enough to be in school, we had a governess. The next year my father, with Mr. Tol McNeill, who was "a sinner," and Cousin Dick Dobie, who improved his mind by reading law and arguing on religion and politics and who begot a child annually, built a schoolhouse. It was about a mile from us on our land. The teacher always boarded with us; only two Mexican children attended the school and they were ostracized. The progress of Mexicans in the Southwest and the progress of English-speaking whites in decent attitudes toward them are among the improvements in life I have seen.

In time the schoolhouse was moved to another site on the ranch, a little farther away for us but located so that three more families to the northwest could attend it. My father organized a Sunday School that met in the schoolhouse. About a mile from it, on our ranch also, were the camp-meeting grounds where, at the time watermelons ripened, two preachers and a dozen or more families camped for ten days annually and were "revived."

So far as religion is concerned, I derived more from my father's nightly reading of the Bible and praying aloud than from the sermons at camp meetings and, every third Sunday in the month, at the Ramirenia church house, eight miles away. Everybody had dinner on the grounds. This church, a store that was also the post office and a stark frame house occupied by the English store-keeper and his common-law Mexican wife, composed the place on the map named Ramirenia. Everybody called it La Posta, for it had been a stage stand where horses were changed. The people who got their mail there were, with a few exceptions, more fron-tierish and backwoodsy and less worldly-minded than those of the Lagarto community, where we got our mail twice a week.

I usually went after it on Saturdays. The coming of the *Youth's Companion* was a red-letter day. I might gallop all the way home in order to read at once "Trail's End" or some other continued story. During the Spanish–American War I read the semiweekly

89

newspaper from the saddle while riding slowly. The newspaper account of Queen Victoria's death could not have been so beautifully written as Lytton Strachey's, but without historical background other than Dickens' *A Child's History of England,* I sensed the end of a great drama. Also, we had a kind of family connection with Queen Victoria. My youngest brother, still in curls at the time, was named Gladstone—Henry Gladstone—not because Gladstone was a great prime minister but because in his great office he was a "militant" Christian of great goodness. The name of Disraeli, his worldly and witty opponent, was unknown to me.

Before my time a railroad, built ten miles away, killed Lagarto. It had had a "college"—a public school of several rooms—in which my mother taught, and the village had three good stores. In my boyhood several families with back yards opening into small pastures still lived on the perimeter of the town. Perimeter, besides a store, a schoolhouse and a church, was about all left to the town.

The house in which my father's mother lived had the coolest hallway for a summer nap after dinner that I knew. Two of her sons would let nothing interfere with their naps, but my father and Uncle Jim napped only when they had nothing pressing to do. Uncle Jim had a ranch not far off. Uncle Frank Byler, my mother's brother, lived on the perimeter and operated a ranch beyond.

The Lagarto people had dances, for which my father had played the fiddle before he married and before he became adamant against dances. The Ramirenia crowd had *bailes,* the Mexican name for dances, and my parents hoped that their sons would never debase themselves by living with Mexican women as some of the young men of the Ramirenia country did. My father went so far as to disapprove of his sons' acquiring much Spanish. I didn't, but Elrich, the brother next to me, dreamed in Spanish and can still outsing any Mexican whose voice has been influenced by coyote howling.

So far as book education is concerned, the only specific pieces of learning I can recall from ranch schooling are how to spell the word *irksome,* on which I was turned down in a spelling match, and knowledge that a branch of science called physical geography existed. I remember the green binding of a textbook on the subject but don't remember a single detail of the contents. I remember a buck deer jumping over a barbed-wire fence in front of the first schoolhouse and the ballad of *Marco Bozaris* in a reader, also the thrilling recitation of *Lasca* by a young lady older than our teacher who had studied elocution somewhere.

Literary associations with the second schoolhouse are limited to a paperbacked novel, *With Leavenworth Down on the Rio Grande.* A boy named Irving Watson brought it to school, and I read it clandestinely behind my desk. It was one of those "blood and thunder" novels that my mother positively forbade. We had a big book about Stanley in Africa, but no book pertaining to the Wild West ever entered our home, not even *The Log of a Cowboy,* by Andy Adams. Andy Adams had been with Uncle Frank Byler at Caldwell, Kansas, after each had gone up the trail with a herd of horses, and he came back to Texas years later to take notes on Uncle Frank's border-country language. We had the best of books at home, but I will not here go into the deep debts I owe to home reading and the direction of it by my parents, especially my mother.

The jackdaws that nested in the oaks about our house and lost young ones that we children rescued and made nests for in fence-staple kegs; the calves sucking their mothers and playing about them out in the pasture; the cows chewing their cuds in the milk pen; the sand-hill cranes fluting their long, long cries on a winter evening; the coyotes serenading from every side right after dark; my horse Buck pointing his ears when I walked into the pen to rope out a mount and seeming to ask if I were going to ride him or Brownie; the green on the mesquites in early spring so tender that it emanated into the sky; the mustang grapevines, the fruit too acid to eat raw but superb for preserves and catsup, draping the trees along Ramirenia Creek; the stillness of day and night broken by windmills lifting rods that lifted water; the south wind galloping in the treetops; the locusts in the mulberry tree and the panting of overridden and overdriven horses accentuating the heat of summer; the rhythm of woodcutting in cold weather; the rhythm of a saddle's squeak in the night: these the land gave me. Its natural rhythms and the eternal silence entered into me.

I never recollect the ranch as being what is called romantic. I was not a good roper or a good rider and never shot a six-shooter until I got into the army of World War I, but from the *vaqueros* and my father I learned to soothe wild or restless cattle with my voice. Sometimes in a way I seemed to become one of them. I became more at one with the sailing buzzard than I have ever become with a human murderer of silence who puts a nickel into a slot to bring forth raucous sounds.

The romantic feature of the ranch was what we called Fort Ramirez. It never was a fort, but it was a fortified ranch house built by a Mexican named Ramirez before Texas became a republic. He had been granted several leagues of land by the Mexican government and was run out by Indians. Not within the memory of the oldest inhabitant of the country had the fort been inhabited. Some of the rock walls were still standing, and a person standing on top of them had a grand view of the S-winding Ramirenia Creek. Granjeno bushes grown from seeds planted by birds that lit along the old picket corrals still outlined them. A patriarch named Gorgonio, who lived about half a mile away and with several *parientes* (kinsmen) farmed a considerable field, used to tell of lights seen about the ruins at night, also of chains making a terrifying noise. People said that a fortune in Mexican gold or silver was buried there. Every year strangers asked permission to dig on the premises. Many holes were dug without permission, some in the night. Digging under the walls contributed to their downfall. Some of the holes in and out from the structure were big enough to bury a wagon and team in.

Uncle Ed Dubose, my mother's half-brother, had a hope for digging up treasure and a faith in divining rods and fortune-tellers not shared in the least by either of my parents. But one time he came with such a plausible legend, together with a map derived from some Mexican down on the Rio Grande—he could talk Spanish better than most Mexicans—and such specific directions from a Negro fortuneteller in Victoria as to where to dig that my father agreed to help. For him it was an adventure without illusion. He and Uncle Ed and several Mexicans spent three days sinking a big hole. They found a fill of earth not like the ground around it, but that was all.

The first thing the recent purchasers of the ranch did after taking possession was to tear down the corrals and burn up the pickets. They were the oldest old-timey corrals in that part of the country. Now they are where Fort Ramirez has gone. In my boyhood there were fifteen or so ranch families around us owning maybe seventy thousand acres of land, all deriving all of their living from the land. At the same time there were probably more than thirty Mexican families living on these ranches. Only three ranch owners now live where fifteen once lived, and the decrease in Mexican families has been greater. Most of the land is owned by absentees; some of it is looked after by men who drive to it from town by automobile.

No matter what is discontinued, evolution continues. A thousand years, ten thousand years, hence, the Dobie ranch will be where it was before the Ramirez grant took in a portion of its pristine acreage. It will have other names, be divided and then be absorbed. The land will always be grazing land, for neither soil nor climate will permit it to be anything else. It is possible that an oil field will temporarily mutilate it. Off and on for nearly half a century, oil companies and oil promoters have paid out more lease money on it than the grazing rights have brought. The time may come when people passing over it will speak a tongue that no one now living down in the brush country will understand.

The thought of times in which I shall not participate disturbs me no more than thought of times in which I did not participate.

93

Nevertheless when I consider the break now made with that plot of land on Long Hollow and Ramirenia Creek—a measure of ground to which I am more closely akin than to any other on earth, not excluding the lovely creekside that has been home to me for a quarter-century—I feel that the end of something has come.

A rural life gives way to urban life and as mobility overcomes stability, human attachments to certain patches of the earth's surface becomes less common. Yet the potentiality of such attachment remains universal. It is very different from attachment to a country, a party, a church, a cause, a person or any group of persons. It is behind much of patriotism. With some people it goes deeper than principles and embodies the profundity of life.

Revenge at Wagon Box Corral

by Bill Judge

"How many Indians were in the attack?" asked the General.

"Wal, Gin'rill, I can't say fer sartin, but I think thar wur nigh onto three thousand uv 'em."

"How many were killed and wounded?"

"I can't say fer sartin, but I think thar wur nigh onto a thousand."

"How many did you kill?"

"Gi'me a dead rest, I kin hit a dollar at fifty yards every time, and I fired with a dead rest at more'n fifty of thum varmints inside of fifty yards."

"For heaven's sake, how many times did you fire?" exclaimed the astonished General.

"Wal, I can't say, but I kept eight guns pretty well het up for more'n three hours."

Such were the questions and answers during the interrogation of a grizzled mountain veteran by the commanding general of the Department of Platte, concerning the Wagon Box Corral fight near Fort Phil Kearny, August 2, 1867.

The night following the Fetterman disaster, Portugee Phillips began a ride of better than 236 miles, in subzero weather, to appeal for help at Fort Laramie. When asked later if he stayed close to the trail, Phillips replied, "Hell no! More'n once I was more'n ten miles off it." Phillips made most of the ride at night, hiding out during the daylight hours. He arrived at Fort Laramie about eleven o'clock Christmas night.

Two days later, on December 27, Colonel H. W. Wessels left Fort Laramie with four companies of infantry and two companies of cavalry for the relief of Fort Phil Kearny. During this march the mercury was continuously ranging between twenty-five and forty degrees below zero. Hampered by blizzards, high winds and drifting snow, often waist high, the relief column practically had to shovel their own route north.

It was necessary to leave a number of their expedition at Fort Reno for the amputation of frozen limbs. Pressing on to Fort Phil Kearny, they arrived on January 17, relieved to find that no further attacks had been made on the fort.

The harsh weather had held Red Cloud's forces immobile in winter camp on the Tongue River.

Shortly after Colonel Wessels' arrival, he relieved Colonel Carrington of the command of the three forts, and the Second Battalion, Eighteenth Infantry, became the Twenty-seventh U.S. Infantry.

Food for both men and horses at Fort Phil Kearny became increasingly scant. The horses were in a starving condition, due to the halting of hay operations by Red Cloud the past summer. With snow two feet deep on the level, foraging was out of the question.

The horses had to be placed on picket lines of chain, rather than of rope. They also had to be tethered apart so they could not eat each other's manes and tails. Raw hides, flesh side out, were placed on posts so that the animals would not eat the wood. Parties were sent out to cut the tenderest branches of trees and bushes to feed them. It required six mules or horses to haul a load that would not have bothered a team of two in normal strength.

The men were reduced to meals of hardtack and condemned sow belly. The latter had so deteriorated that the fat had separated from the lean meat. Bean soup was a luxury served infrequently.

Scurvy broke out and many required hospitalization, further reducing the force available for defense.

After the defeat of Fetterman, Red Cloud's star was in the ascendancy. He now decided that the time was ripe for the greatest of his ambitions—to attack the forts and destroy them. To that end he sent out calls for all warriors to be on hand for the coming campaign.

Delayed by the hard winter, early spring snows and run-offs that filled the streams to overflowing, he cunningly waited the proper time to attack.

His plan was to take Fort Phil Kearny on or about August 1, 1867. The force he had assembled numbered close to six thousand warriors.

Dissension had sprung up among the Indians. Some wanted to fight their way down to the forts, destroying them in turn, starting with Fort Smith.

The argument was settled when the Indians decided they were strong enough to attack both forts at the same time. The largest force, under Red Cloud, numbering three thousand, left for the vicinity of Fort Phil Kearny, arriving there and assuming positions during the night of August 1.

The troops at Fort Phil Kearny had been waiting impatiently for the spring supply trains that were delayed by swollen streams.

So it was not until the latter part of June that the bull train of Gilmore and Porter arrived at Fort Phil Kearny with crowded freight wagons of provisions and other badly needed supplies.

Among the supplies was a most welcome surprise for the garrison. Included in the wagons was a shipment of seven hundred of the new fifty-caliber, breech-loading rifles known as the Allin Springfields. Included with the rifles were one hundred thousand rounds of matching ammunition. These were the first guns of this type to be issued to troops in the Indian Territory.

The guns used by the infantry until the arrival of the new issue were muzzle-loaders. Having been fired, this ancient arm required some time to reload and the use of a ramrod to thrust the new charge home. The Indians, accustomed to this type of gun, would maneuver to draw the fire of this first shot. When they saw the arm raised with the ramrod to reload, they would press in to close quarters. This muzzle-loader was the weapon used by the infantry with Fetterman.

The new guns had metallic cartridges, requiring only a moment to open the breech block and reload. In addition to this improvement in rapid fire, they were more accurate and powerful than the older type of weapon.

The supply train of Gilmore and Porter, rather than make a return trip empty, secured a contract to furnish logs to the sawmill and firewood to the fort. One of the stipulations of the contract was that the fort furnish guards to protect their camp and wagons while transporting the wood. While the cost is not mentioned in published records of Fort Phil Kearny, the price for wood delivered to Fort Smith was $27.50 per cord. The price at Fort Phil Kearny must have approached that closely.

Early in July camps were established by the contractors beyond Sullivant Hill. First was the headquarters camp in the meadows between the two woodcutting camps. The largest woodcutting camp was located on the North Piney, about a mile to the north of the headquarters camp. The smaller camp was on the South Piney, a little over a half mile to the west of headquarters.

The reason for coming so far from the fort for wood is easily explained. The trees near the fort were mostly cottonwood or small pines. Up where the creeks emerged from the hills were pine trees superior to any others. They were described as eighteen inches through at the butt, straight as an arrow and ninety feet to the first branches.

The North Piney "pinery," as it was called, was within plain view of headquarters camp. The South Piney pinery was around a dogleg of the stream bed and out of sight. Both camps were across the streams, away from the headquarters camp.

In addition to these camps the working stock of the wood trains would be grazed in the meadow when not working. The stock was under the care and protection of civilian herders.

Company A of the Twenty-seventh Infantry, Fetterman's old company, was the first to go on guard and escort duty. The companies were almost at full strength due to the replacements which had been added during the spring.

The duties of the men were roughly divided as follows: twelve to fourteen men under a noncommissioned officer were assigned to escort duty for the big woodcutting camp. Seven or eight were assigned similar duties at the smaller camp. Two or three of these men would remain at the picket post on the bend of the dogleg, to keep headquarters in touch with the wood camp.

Empty wagons would go to each of the camps in the morning and return loaded to headquarters in the afternoon. The next morning both wagon trains would be combined in a larger train, leaving headquarters with an escort of a commissioned officer and twenty to thirty men. Combined with teamsters and helpers this would provide a fighting force of approximately fifty men on the six-mile haul to the fort. In the afternoon the empty wagons would return, to be redistributed to the woodcutting camps the following morning, a much different procedure than had been used the previous year.

There were around thirty men remaining at headquarters camp during the day after the wagon trains had departed. All men were rotated at the various posts at regular intervals. Those remaining at headquarters were regarded as off duty.

Headquarters camp was of a singular arrangement that has since become famous. Only the under or running gears of the wagons were used in hauling logs. So the wagon boxes were surplus. Fourteen of these were retained at the headquarters camp and formed in an oval, with the gates facing the fort. Extra side boards were placed on the inner sides, to both protect the stock and to present a higher corral wall. The stock was driven inside each night to prevent stealing by Indians.

Provisions for the men were stored in two wagons, one for the civilians and one for the army personnel. These wagons were still on their wheels and canvas covered, to prevent molestation by wild creatures and to give protection from the weather.

Tents as sleeping quarters were provided for the enlisted men that were off duty at headquarters.

Many army historians and others say that the wagons were lined with boiler plate, as many of the quartermaster wagons on the frontier were said to be. This is the only way that they can explain the small loss among the defenders of the corral during the battle. Those who took part in the fight later insisted that there were no iron linings of any type whatsoever.

During July, Company A was bothered by continuous alarms but had only minor skirmishes to fight.

On July 31, Captain James Powell and Company C of the Twenty-seventh relieved Company A of its guard duties with the contractors' camps. The men were not yet settled in the routine of their duties when Red Cloud struck at Fort Phil Kearny.

The day they arrived at headquarters camp, the men sensed that there were Indians about. They reported this to the sergeant by saying that they could smell them.

The night of August 1 a dog belonging to one of the enlisted men repeatedly ran to the brink of the meadows overlooking Piney Valley to bark furiously at something the men could not see.

August 2 started the same as any other day. The big train left for Fort Phil Kearny with an escort of twenty men under Lieutenant McCarthy.

Thirteen men were left with the smaller train for the wood

camp on the North Piney. One man relieved the noncom at the picket post on the South Piney.

The attack started at approximately seven o'clock. The first Indians were sighted by Captain Powell, who was bathing in the South Piney. The Indians were coming down the slope of the hills south of the creek to attack the herd then grazing in the meadows. He ran back to headquarters, shouting the alarm.

The first Indians, on foot and about two hundred strong, attacked the herders and tried to stampede the stock. While the herders' attention was diverted, sixty additional warriors dashed in on horseback and made away with the herd. The herders managed to escape up the South Piney, one joining the enlisted men at the picket post, the others going on to the smaller wood camp. One infantryman was sent to check on the wood camp. He found that all of the woodcutters, herders and guards had escaped to the wooded hills.

The men at the big camp on the North Piney followed the same tactics. It had often been remarked by the personnel at the fort that if one saw Indians and took to the woods, the Sioux and Cheyenne would not follow. The Blackfeet did and killed several soldiers and civilians, at different times, but not the others. The reason was not known unless it was because they were Plains Indians and distrusted the woods.

The three soldiers and the civilian at the South Piney picket post decided to try for the headquarters camp. Using leapfrog tactics familiar to any infantryman advancing under fire, they alternately fired and ran, each providing cover for the others in motion. The men were more afraid of being captured or wounded than they were of being killed. They remembered Fetterman's men and didn't care for the same treatment.

The Indians rode around them and tried to cut them off from the corral. The Sioux at this time had not formed around the corral, so Sergeant Littman ran out a hundred yards, knelt on one knee and coolly picked off the Indians between the men and the corral, keeping the escape lane open for them. All four arrived safely at headquarters, making a total force of thirty-two men at the corral.

The Sioux and their allies could not be seen coming down the ridge just north of North Piney Creek into the valley below the corral. To the south they were coming up from behind the banks of the South Piney.

Red Cloud took his position on the little knoll northwest of Sullivan Hill. He directed the remainder of the fight from a distance of about half a mile, using field glasses to observe the action and issuing commands with flags, mirror signals and by couriers.

For a short time there was a lull, as the Indians took their positions for the coming battle. This gave the men time to choose and prepare their defensive positions. Each man had one of the new Springfield rifles, a revolver, and forty rounds of ammunition. There were seven thousand rounds of extra ammunition at the corral and extra ammunition was issued each man before the fight started. The men carried the cartridges back to their defensive positions in their caps and hats. One man mentions going back twice for ammunition during lulls in the battle, making three capfuls of ammunition besides the forty rounds in his belt that he used. The four civilians at headquarters fought from the wagon boxes containing civilian supplies. Here were extra rifles left behind by woodcutters and teamsters.

The gate was filled with barrels of salt and beans rolled into place with ox yokes across the top. Spaces between the wagons were filled with whatever was available around the camp. Some of the men fought from the wagon boxes, some from behind the barricades.

Still remembering Fetterman's men, many removed their shoes, unlaced the strings, tied them together and formed a loop in each end. One loop was to go over their big toe, the other over the trigger of their rifle. If they were overwhelmed by Indians, they could place the muzzle of the rifle in their mouths or under their chins and pull the trigger with their toe. None of the men expected to come out of the fight alive, and all were determined not to fall into the hands of the Indians.

The Sioux were now ready to attack, and a force of several hundred detached themselves from the main body south of the corral. Mounted on their best war ponies, brandishing all kinds of weapons, they started slowly, and as they approached their pace quickened until they were going at a dead run.

Within firing distance some of them rode in circles around the corral, others crisscrossed between the corral and the main body of warriors. Still others made sudden dashes and retreats, threatening the defenders.

The main body of warriors approached to a distance of 150 yards, where they sat on their horses watching the first attack. Accustomed to the single shot muzzle-loaders, the first party was to draw the opening round and thereby create an opening in the defense for the main force. The larger group waited for the signal of the uplifted ramrod, showing that the defenders were reloading. In former battles these were the tactics that had been so successful. However, the new rifles were breech-loaders, and the signal never came.

The first group continued their demonstration without realizing what was happening to them. With the ground before the corral becoming suddenly covered with a blanket of dead and wounded warriors and horses, they suddenly found they were up against something new and deadly. The men within the corral did not let up for an instant and caused almost as much damage in the Indians' retreat as they had in the attack. Furthermore, they did not stop here; when the retreating targets became difficult, they opened fire on the main body of warriors, who were within easy rifle range. The volume of fire and the effective range of the new rifles was to Red Cloud's warriors unbelievable.

This was the only attack made on horseback. In fact only one other large-scale attack began from the south. All others were made from the north or the valley side of the defensive position.

Wagon Box Corral was located on a large and fairly level

meadow. Seventy-five yards north of the corral, the meadow sloped sharply to the valley of the North Piney.

Red Cloud's next move was to send a large body of skirmishers to take cover on the valley side of this meadow edge. From this point they were to lay down a heavy barrage of rifle and arrow fire. It was from this direction that the shots came to kill Lieutenant Jenness and two enlisted men and wound two others.

Pitch-fired arrows were shot into the corral. Some of these ignited the hay scraps and dried manure, creating such a dense cloud of smoke and overpowering stench that the men said they could see for only a short distance and could hardly breathe.

The day was hot, with very little air stirring. The smoke, created by black powder ammunition, also hovered over the corral. This continual smoke screen very materially reduced the numbers of casualties among the defenders, because they could find targets among the brightly colored warriors before the Indians could spot them.

The next charge numbered more than two thousand warriors, led by the nephew of Red Cloud. Anxious for honor and recognition of his valor, that he might someday win the right to succeed his uncle as war chief, he led the warriors forward in a semicircle intended to surround the corral. When they reached the area of the first volley on the mounted charge, marked by swaths of downed horses and men, they were again greeted by a sheet of lethal rifle fire. Picture, if you can, twenty-five hundred warriors, all bearing down on an area only seven wagon boxes wide! So densely packed or crowded were they that the men afterward spoke of it as common for two Indians to go down with each shot.

Ignoring their terrible losses, the Indians kept on until they could almost touch the wagon boxes, before giving way. On this and on the following charge, some of the men said they thought it was all over. Quite a number of Indians were killed only five and six feet from the boxes.

During every lull in the battle, pairs of mounted Indians would dash forward to rescue their dead and wounded. Leaning from their pony backs in perfect teamwork and horsemanship, they would grasp a warrior on the ground and carry him off.

They made excellent targets, and the men had no mercy on them. Reference is frequently made by the white men to the torturing of Fetterman's wounded. In this instance they believed the Indian wounded weren't suffering as much as the wounded of Fetterman's party. They also knew that due to the overwhelming number of warriors they had to kill every one they could if they intended to survive. Eventually the Indians rescued almost all of their dead and wounded.

While these last rescue attempts were being made, the men noticed large numbers of Indians riding down into the North Piney Valley from the eastern end of the meadow edge. They, of course, could not see what was developing there, but within a short time they heard a weird humming sound, utterly unlike anything any of them had ever heard.

At this moment, on signals from Red Cloud's group, the remaining warriors on horseback to the south repeated the tactics used in the first mounted charge. The skirmishers or sharpshooters at the plateau edges gave increased cover fire, and up over the edges, in the form of a flying wedge or "V," came another charge by hundreds of warriors on foot. The men fired into the center of the "V" with the same deadly effect, yet the Indians still came on, bounding over their dead and wounded, until they were only a few feet from the corral before giving way.

Afterward Captain Powell said that one more charge would have won the battle. When told of this later the Indians replied that they could not make that charge. They had made six separate and distinct charges between 9 A.M. and 3 P.M. before admitting defeat.

The Indians now had only the desire to rescue the last of their dead and wounded. Creeping forward under the protection of the smoke and camouflaged with clumps of grass, they would attach one end of a rope to an ankle or wrist of a dead or wounded warrior, and other Indians over the meadow edge would drag the men off the field to safety. These ropes were formed by tying several lariats together. Not all casualties could be withdrawn, as some were too near the wagon boxes.

Throughout the battle Red Cloud, with other chiefs, had remained on top of the hill to the southeast of the corral. After the last charge some of the boys elevated their sights and concentrated their fire on this hill top. It may have been their shots or it may have been that Red Cloud had received information that reinforcements were at last nearing the battlefield, for the group moved down the hill into the valley.

Soon the defenders heard a howitzer shell burst over the remaining Indians. Looking in the direction of the fort, they saw an extended blue line of skirmishers approaching. Major Smith had been dispatched to the relief of the corral with one hundred men and a howitzer. Upon their arrival, they saw a most astonishing sight. The plains and valley were filled with rapidly retreating Indians. The corral was still defiantly spitting fire. Many travois heavily loaded with dead and wounded were retreating up the valley of the North Piney.

Realizing the precariousness of his position, Major Smith immediately got all the men under way to the fort. They were joined by the woodcutters, teamsters, herders and guards.

It was known that a terrible punishment had been inflicted on the Indians but not how badly in actual numbers until years later. Some of the chiefs who were present would never talk of the battle. However, others admitted to losses of eleven hundred to fifteen hundred killed or wounded. This against a loss of one officer and two enlisted men killed, two men wounded, among the personnel of the corral.

Red Cloud later stated the loss in a very practical and succinct way, when he told an inquirer that at the outset he had three thousand warriors and that fifteen hundred were lost to him. When questioned again if he meant killed, he repeated that they were lost, that they never fought for him again.

Captain Powell, for his stout defense at the corral, was brevetted the third time for heroism and distinguished conduct on the field.

Murder on the Trail

by Nell Murbarger

On a rocky hill overlooking Tonalea, Arizona, stands a square stone monument, plain and aloof, and seemingly a little defiant. Not many travelers see it, because not many travelers go to Tonalea. Situated in a lonely vastness ninety miles from the nearest railroad, Tonalea is only an Indian trading post—and not an important post at that. Around a murky pond of water stand a few gaunt Navajo ponies, heads hanging listlessly and thin tails switching. Killdeers yammer and run on the sterile flat, and dilapidated Indian wagons occasionally creak past on the sandy road.

Since there isn't a whole lot to see at Tonalea, it is quite probable that you will never go there. But if you *should* go there, and if you *should* leave the road and climb a narrow foot trail that toils upward through the rocks, you'll find the monument at the farther end of that trail, where it seems to be keeping eternal watch over all this great emptiness of bleached land and blue sky. When you have read the bronze plaque on its face, you'll know that this is a memorial to George Albert Smith, Jr. But chances are you still won't know that this is also a memorial to blood and guts, and determination and dreams. . . .

It is a story that had its beginning about one hundred ten years ago, when George Smith was only a little shaver and his parents were trekking overland to Salt Lake Valley with Brigham Young's first contingent of Mormon settlers. One of his father's wagon drivers on that occasion was William Hamblin. As the slow-moving wagons inched their way across the endless plains, it seems likely that Bill Hamblin helped to amuse his employer's little son by telling him wonderful stories of Bill's elder brother, Jacob. This, at least, would explain why this child should have become an ardent hero-worshiper of Jacob Hamblin, a man he had never seen.

As years went by and Jacob became famous for his missionary work among Indian tribes of the Southwest, young George Smith never failed to glory in the older man's exploits, and one of the greatest thrills of his life was his first meeting with the noted "Buckskin Apostle." With his eyes mirroring that special awe and devotion that men reserve for their gods—and boys for their heroes —the lad told Jacob Hamblin that the most cherished dream of his life was to some day be fit to accompany him into the wild Moqui country beyond the Colorado.

Another thrilling time in young George's life was in July, 1860, when at Jacob Hamblin's invitation he and his father journeyed south from Salt Lake to visit at the Hamblin ranch in Washington County, Utah. With the Hamblin boys, Duane and Lyman, and their Indian foster brother, Albert, the Salt Lake youth first experienced the delights of living in the open, exploring the desert on horseback, working with cattle and climbing mountains.

One day as the four youths galloped their horses into the yard after some juvenile expedition, George's father remembered the dream which had lain so long in the lad's heart. Turning to Jacob he asked if it would be possible for George to accompany him on his next trip across the Colorado.

The great Mormon missionary pondered the question gravely.

"It's a long, hard trip to the Moqui villages," he said at last, "but George is strong and self-reliant. I see no reason why he should not go. . . ."

So it was arranged; and when the Hamblin party rode out of Washington County in October of that year, eighteen-year-old George Smith was possibly the happiest person in all the world!

In addition to the boy and Jacob, men comprising this expedition were Thales Haskell, Ira Hatch, Isaac Riddle, James Pearce, Jehiel McConnell, Amos Thornton, Francis—Jacob's younger brother—and a Paiute interpreter, Enos. For the first time, the southbound party also included two women—Ira Hatch's wife Sarah and the Hamblin's adopted Indian daughter, Eliza.

Even before the start of the trip, its leader had been hounded by a mysterious foreboding, and with every mile put behind, that feeling grew stronger. What inspired it, he was unable to say. The men were in good spirits; the animals healthy and strong. The women were taking to camp life like veterans, and the weather was perfect. But still the foreboding persisted. Other members of the party eventually sensed their leader's apprehensiveness and were discussing the matter with him one day when young George joined the group.

After listening to the conversation for a few moments, the lad turned to Jacob. "If it's me you're worried about, you'll find I'll stick to the end!" he declared earnestly. "That's what I came for!"

Jacob smiled. "I'm sure you will, George," he said, giving the boy a good-natured cuff on the shoulder. "I'm sure you will!"

After crossing the turbulent Colorado River without mishap, the party's leader might have felt some surge of relief, except that now they were traveling in Navajo territory. The Navajos were unpredictable. Their nation, large and loosely knit, was governed by many subchiefs, some friendly toward the Mormons, others not. Their main grievance, possibly, stemmed from the fact that the

Mormons had opened negotiations with the Navajos' traditional enemies, the Hopis, or "Moquis," who occupied a few near-inaccessible mesa tops in the heart of the Navajo nation.

As the little Mormon expedition crawled across the plateau toward the Hopi village of Oraibi, any concern its members originally had felt for hostile Indians was dissipated in the face of a new development—lack of water. Two days had elapsed since their crossing of the Colorado, and in all that distance the band had encountered no source of supply. Springs which had met Jacob's needs on all previous expeditions had ceased to flow. And now the mules and cattle were fretting restlessly in their thirst, and lines of worry were creeping into the faces of the men as they plodded across the wasteland, each clothed in his own silence.

Such was the situation when the four Navajo horsemen appeared out of nowhere and boldly joined the party.

Haughty and aloof, sitting their mounts like desert centaurs, they were a fearsome-looking quartet, and not a man but breathed easier when he learned they were from one of the friendly clans.

There was nothing friendly, however, about the tidings they bore. Waiting at the next water hole, a few miles ahead, they declared, was a huge war party of hostile Navajos from Chinle. Unless the Mormons turned back at once, all would be slain.

After lengthy discussion it was decided that neither man nor beast could survive that long, dry journey back to the river, and it was voted to go on to the water hole and gamble on making peace talk. If peace were not to be had, their guns would give them at least a fighting chance for life, whereas they possessed no defense against the hostile and waterless desert.

As the friendly Navajos had warned, the water hole was bristling with Chinle warriors.

Their original ultimatum was that the entire party must die, but after extended palavering through the Paiute interpreter Enos, the warriors offered to spare the Mormon men, provided they turned back immediately and left behind the two women. The offer, needless to say, was rejected.

Because of his wide reputation for truth and honest dealing, Jacob Hamblin had been able to talk himself out of perilous situations on several previous occasions; and now once again the force of his logic was put to the supreme test.

After arguing the matter at length, the warriors agreed that the entire party might go free if the materials they were carrying to the Hopis were surrendered to the Navajos instead. It also was stipulated that the Utah party must turn back immediately without further attempt to reach the Hopi mesas.

With the Hopi stronghold of Oraibi already looming on the southern horizon, this was a bitter pill, and only with great reluctance and in desperation did Jacob agree to the terms.

With time for departure nearing, several of the men were delegated to fetch the saddle stock from the small mesa where it had been feeding. When one of the animals bolted and headed down a side trail, young George Smith left the group to go in pursuit—his companions, meanwhile, continuing to camp.

Learning of the incident, Jacob Hamblin was greatly disturbed and immediately dispatched two men to see to the boy's safety.

They found him lying beside the trail, about a mile from camp. With three bullet wounds riddling the lower part of the boy's body and four arrow wounds piercing his back, the sand beneath him already was saturated with blood, but the boy was still breathing.

When the enraged Jacob demanded an explanation of the treachery, the warriors declared that three Navajo men had been slain by whites in the recent past and that three white men must die as retribution. Not until two others had been surrendered as blood forfeit, they said, would the white party be permitted to leave. Indignantly refusing this demand, Hamblin instructed his men to proceed with preparations for departure. The Navajo braves, meanwhile, continued to mill fiercely about the white men's camp.

111

Protesting that his presence would only delay the others in their attempt to escape, young George begged to be left behind; but although he realized that the lad was in great pain and that there was no hope for his survival, Hamblin refused to abandon him to indignities and possible torture at the hands of the savages. Instead, the wounded boy was lifted to the back of a mule, and, with Jehiel McConnell riding behind to hold him in the saddle, the harried group set forth.

In order to lighten their loads, the Hamblin party had abandoned at the water hole many articles of equipment and food, and with the Chinle warriors remaining behind to loot the camp, the fleeing saints were able to gain a slight lead. Too soon, however, a growing dust cloud on the southern skyline warned that the Navajos again were on the trail and riding hard, and a desperate flight for life was begun. Trail-weary and weakened by hunger and thirst during the several days immediately preceding, the mounts of the Mormons were no match for the fresh horses and lithe, young riders comprising the pursuit, and the dust cloud to the rear grew steadily in stature as the distance narrowed.

When it became evident that there was no possible chance of outrunning their attackers, the Hamblin party whirled with readied guns. Confronted by this sudden turn of events, the plunging horses of the warriors veered down a side ravine, and the Mormons resumed flight, pushing their jaded animals to the limit of endurance.

With the saddle and mule beneath him drenched red with his blood, young George Smith clung tenaciously all that day to his slender thread of life. Not until shortly after sundown, as the beleaguered missionaries reached the present site of Tonalea, did death release the boy from his agony.

With the enemy riding hard on their trail and only minutes behind, Hamblin and his men knew too well that the time it would take for them to dig a grave might mean the loss of their entire party. In this knowledge they sorrowfully wrapped the dead youth in a blanket and left him unburied beside the way.

Murder on the Trail

After pushing on until late that night, the Mormon party was halted by exhaustion. Far to the south the flickering light of a huge campfire told that their pursuers had discovered the boy's body and were holding a war dance over his scalp; and like an icy hand passing through the camp, came recollections of stories that the Navajos ate the flesh of slain enemies. . . .

Traveling with heavy hearts, the little party of missionary-explorers completed the long journey to southwestern Utah. There it became Jacob Hamblin's painful duty to tell a devoted father that his son, entrusted to another's care, would not come back.

Upon learning of the tragedy, Brigham Young directed Hamblin to raise a strong party of twenty men to go immediately into the Indian country and recover, if possible, the body of the murdered boy. It was now midwinter. Ice was running deep in the Colorado and walls of the gorge were frozen and slick. Despite these difficulties the trip was made without loss of man or mount, but little success attended their efforts.

All that remained of the boy's body was the head and a few of the larger bones, which were carried back to the City of the Saints for burial.

And that's why a square stone monument stands defiantly on a hill above Tonalea, Arizona, where a hero-worshiping lad breathed his last on November 2, 1860.

Town of Beer & Sorrow

by Fred Gipson

I still remember Ojinaga as I knew it in the late thirties, a little adobe-walled town sprawling over a low hill on the south bank of the Rio Grande.

It was no place to attract the regular tourist. It could lay no valid claim to singular beauty or historical fame. Yet it always appealed to me; I know of no other place on earth quite so fitting for solitary beer drinking.

Even when others were along, there was a serenity about the town that seemed to quell boisterousness and imbue the drinker with a quiet sense of detachment and melancholy aloneness.

Town of Beer & Sorrow

Many evenings I have sat with a cool beer in one of the open plazas and watched the little umbrellas of smoke rising from the supper fires of the river people living down in the great valley, while overhead the black bats swooped and dived, feeding upon the myriads of mosquitos that rose from the river to hum and swirl in the afterglow of the setting sun. I like to sit there and drink and ponder the mysteries of the bold, ragged peaks of the Chinati Mountains standing in their eternal blue-hazed silence about the surrounding desert.

For how many millions of years have those peaks stood, bleak, barren and silent? What great events have transpired here, back in the long forgotten days before white man came with his methods of "progress," so directly opposed to his Christian religion?

Answers to such questions a man does not find, even in a beer bottle. But it was over bottles of beer that I became acquainted with one Juan Hernandez Jesus Enrique Morales, who explained to me why this is now all desert country.

Juan was one of the river people, a direct descendant of the old ones, who for century upon century have lived in the Rio Grande Valley, cultivating their little island patches among the willows and tall weeds. Today they are sometimes citizens of Mexico and then again citizens of the United States. This is because the main stream of the Rio Grande, considered the international boundary, is of a restless nature and has a habit of shifting ground with each spring flood.

To many this constant change in citizenship might prove disturbing and make for a confusion of loyalties. But to the river people it is of no consequence whatever. After all they were there long before there was either a Mexico or a United States. They have little to do with either country and are in reality only citizens of the river. Nothing more.

Juan, citizen of the river, was a scrawny, dark-skinned little man in tattered clothes who sported a fierce and black mustache and a pair of new *guaraches* made from an old automobile tire. He came to my table with a bottle of beer, his brown eyes eloquent with sadness. Just why he sought me out, an Americano and a stranger, I'll never know, unless it is that there are times when one's need for sympathy and understanding is so great that even the age-old barriers of race and skin coloring cannot stand before it.

And Juan's need for sympathy and understanding were great indeed, I learned, as the empty bottles slowly accumulated on the table before us.

Juan had just suffered the tragic loss of a gamecock, a small stringy bird with a great fighting heart. In the various pits about town, Juan's rooster had won him "many monies," easily keeping him in beer and often winning enough to buy beans and tortillas for his wife and young ones.

But there had come into town from deep within Chihuahua a group of *rancheros* with cattle to be delivered to Texas cowmen on the north bank of the river. The *rancheros* had sold the cattle under agreement to pay the U.S. import duty, rated at so much per pound. Being the shrewd ones, the *rancheros* had penned their cattle at Ojinaga, without feed or water, for three days before making delivery to the Texas side. In this manner they planned to shrink them, thus saving money on duties.

And while the hungry, thisty cattle milled in the pens, bawling out their misery, and while the *rancheros* drank and gambled in the *cantinas,* the Rio Grande played a trick on them. It rose suddenly to flood height and washed out one end of the international bridge, so that when the drunken *rancheros* started the herd across on the day of delivery, the cattle went out to the end of the wrecked bridge and plunged off into the water. The river was shallow here but still deep enough for thirsty cattle to get a drink. Which these cattle did.

The *rancheros* swore vile oaths. They lashed the cattle with whips. They spurred their backs with huge Chihuahua spurs. Nevertheless the starved cattle stood and drank, swelling their sides with Rio Grande flood water, each pound of which eventually cost the *rancheros* so many cents, American, in import duties.

It was a great blow to the well-laid plans of the Mexican

116

rancheros, and they returned to Ojinaga in the evening filled with the wrath of frustration. They drank heavily in the *cantinas* and became unruly.

Then Juan's gamecock, who had the run of the streets and of every bar in town, had the misfortune to hop inside the *cantina,* where he often picked up roasted pumpkin seeds that drinkers had dropped upon the floor. He became excited at the carousing *rancheros* and uttered startled cackling sounds.

That is what started the trouble. One drunken *ranchero* was offended that a rooster would cackle at him. He flung a beer bottle at the bird, knocking him through the open door.

The gamecock came to his feet with a squawk. Someone flung a second bottle. The rooster started down the street at a fast run. And behind him the *rancheros* poured out of the *cantina* and gave chase. The rooster ran faster but so did the drunken ones. Whooping and yelling they chased the magnificent gamecock through the streets, hurling at him empty bottles that made terrible moaning sounds before shattering against the rocky earth.

Juan heard the commotion and left a nearly full bottle of beer sitting on a bar to go chase after the carousing ones who chased after his rooster. Juan shouted great obscenities at them. He called them drunken dogs of dogs, lizards' bellies and goats with the stench of the Evil One upon them.

But Juan could not stop them. They chased his rooster out to the end of the street where the ground cut sharply away toward the river. And there the poor bird took wing and sailed out over the Rio Grande, squawking his fright.

And while he was still in the air, the devil, disguised as a great gray hawk, swooped down upon him, sinking cruel talons into the back of the rooster and carrying him to the ground in a cloud of feathers.

Broken, bitter to the core, Juan retraced his steps to the bar to drown his despair. Only to find that in his absence someone without honor had stolen his beer.

Thus it has been with his people for centuries, Juan explained.

117

Always the devil, in one guise or another, has been ready to pounce upon the weak and unwary. It is a curse that the old ones brought upon themselves back in times so remote that not even the great-grandfathers of his grandfathers could remember when it happened.

But it was in the days when there was still peace upon the land, when all this great tumbling country, from north of the Chinati Mountains in Texas to far below the Santa Cruz range below the river, was a fertile land of green hillsides and flowering meadows and brooks that gushed cold, clear water from under the ledges. It was a beautiful, bountiful land then, and in it the river people lived lives of the blessed.

But then the devil came to live in a hole, there on the western shoulder of the Santa Cruz. And he made himself a great rope, one end of which he tied to the point of the mountain, the other to the great boulder that stands there in the middle of Ojinaga's main street. And nightly, hand over hand, the devil came down the rope into the village, where he waylaid young maidens, started bitter fights among friends and spread disease and pestilence among the people.

Alarmed. at these things the old ones prepared to trap and destroy the devil. With great labor they carried rocks and mortar to the top of the peak and built a slabstone hut over the mouth of the devil's hole, meaning to trap him inside.

But the devil was a smart Indian. While the old ones were struggling to slide into place the last great stone that would seal up the hole forever, the devil changed himself into a buzzard and slipped between their legs.

And in his anger at the people, the devil spread his wings and sailed out over the Rio Grande Valley in ever-widening circles. And wherever the black shadow of his wings passed over the earth, it was as if fire had touched it. Flowers, trees and grasses all died. The springs ceased to flow. And great floods came and washed the soil away, so that the bare rocks stuck out like the bones of a carcass gnawed clean by the coyotes. And ugly plants sprouted from the rocks, to grow sharp spines that reach out and stab one, leaving wounds that become sore and festered.

So today there is desolation in a once fertile land. And still the devil lurks in his hole in the mountain or in the mesquites and tall weeds beside the river, coming nightly to haunt the village.

Juan could prove that the devil is still there. He waved a beer bottle dramatically and said: "Look at the floods, the droughts, the famines, the disease and sorrow."

I looked. I looked at the huge boulder in the middle of the village and up at the high shoulder of the mountain where the light of the sinking sun touched the side of a tiny slabstone hut. I looked at the barren land, spreading for miles away from the river on either side. And at the maze of sun-blistered peaks, the slopes of raw unwatered soil, the foul greasewood, the weird ocotilla with its groping, octopus-like arms. I looked and thought of Juan and his tragic loss of a rooster. Then, sorrowfully, I turned and ordered more beer.

Farewell Peacemaker

by Hart Stilwell

Two things happened not long ago in the Texas Ranger Service that marked the end of the trail for the most romantic firearm ever devised by man—the Colt Frontier Model Forty-five, or Peacemaker.

Captain Roy W. Aldrich, after thirty years of continuous service with the rangers, hung his Peacemaker on a peg beside his bed and retired.

And way out in west Texas, sixty-nine-year-old Bob Coffee, still on active duty, reluctantly retired his beloved Peacemaker and buckled on a .357 magnum. It wasn't exactly orders from headquarters. In the ranger service they don't like to give flat orders—against the tradition of the service. But headquarters in Austin let it be known that they'd like for the last of the Peacemakers to be retired, along with Captain Roy Aldrich. As long as he was on active duty, the men at the head of the service were reluctant to take steps to retire the Peacemakers. They had too much respect for Captain Aldrich. They knew he would never abandon the great old gun that had served him in time of need.

But when he retired . . .

Farewell Peacemaker

Well, the Peacemaker is through. Movie and radio and television and Wild West stories to the contrary, it has been retired to its peg on the wall. If you doubt this, go to Texas, where the Peacemaker and its forebears climbed to fame and where it lived on in active service long after it had been replaced in most other parts of the nation.

Cross the state from the panhandle to the Rio Grande and from the Gulf of Mexico to El Paso and count the Peacemakers carried by officers in line of duty. You'll find a few of them. Down in the south Texas brush country Ranger Captain Alfred Allee sometimes buckles on his forty-five if he's riding out on horseback. It's still about as good a gun as any in the world for fighting from a horse. And remember—there is no flat order against its use by a ranger. Just a preference, which is generally observed, even by Captain Allee. When there's real work to be done, he carries something else.

In the same part of Texas, Rangers Joe Bridge and Dudley White have a strong hankering for the old single-actions they toted for years. But they carry something else.

In the piney woods of east Texas Dick Odhom made the switch only recently. And last of the lot to change was the real old-timer of the service, Bob Coffee.

There you have them, five men out of fifty-one who still like to carry the grand old side arm. But on active duty about forty-five of the rangers carry the .45 caliber Colt auto-loader, the others carry double-action Smith and Wesson or Colts, in .38 or .357. When Captain Aldrich retired, the Peacemaker retired with him. He was the last unreconstructed Peacemaker man—the last of those rangers of a different era who flatly refused to carry any other gun.

You'll find about the same situation in other fields of law enforcement. In the Texas Highway Patrol the Peacemaker isn't on the approved list, which includes the .45 auto-loader and the .38 double-action in Smith and Wesson or Colt. Among the sheriffs of Texas you must hunt to find a Peacemaker man. There are a few, such as Jim Scarbrough of Kingsville and H. R. Rarsdorff of Refugio.

Here and there a deputy sheriff or constable still lugs the old gun. And, of course, many ranchmen and cowhands carry it, mainly to shoot at rattlesnakes or kill sick cattle.

But all this isn't generally known throughout the nation, and, strangely, there is a reason. The American people flatly *insist* that the Peacemaker lives on. And the Texas Rangers are perfectly willing to keep the tradition alive. Here is the way it goes:

Fred Olson, captain of headquarters company, in Austin, buckled on his six-shooter, an ivory-handled, single-action Frontier Model Colt .45—a Peacemaker. The ranger captain climbed aboard a spirited paint horse and did a little fancy riding, fast drawings and accurate shooting.

All this was for the benefit of the cameras, grinding away, recording on film the Texas Ranger in action as millions of people visualize him—as the American people insist that he be.

The camera shooting was interrupted by a different kind of shooting—the genuine article. O'Neal Massey, escape artist, had broken out of prison again. Within two minutes Captain Olson was on his way. He drove off in a fast automobile. Hanging from the belt he buckled on before leaving was a .45 auto-loader. Beside him in the car was the rest of his shooting gear—a Winchester .30-30 carbine and a Remington 12-gauge auto-loading shotgun full of buckshot and slugs, loaded alternately.

Captain Olson trailed the escape artist to a little cabin in the woods. The ranger stepped through the doorway and saw Massey lying on a blanket on the floor, asleep. When Massey's eyes opened he was looking at a shotgun pointing at his belly.

"Come up with hands high," Captain Olson ordered.

Massey obeyed. Captain Olson kicked the blanket aside and revealed Massey's pistol, only inches from the spot where the convict's right hand had been.

"Why didn't you come up shooting?" the ranger asked.

"I would have, Captain," Massey replied, "if you'd had a one-ball gun. I can't do any good against that thing."

While all that was happening, the spirited paint horse was in his stall, munching hay, and the Peacemaker hung on a peg in Captain Olson's office—at peace.

The Peacemaker is the most famous shooting iron ever made. So great is its fame that such terms as six-shooter, thumb-buster, forty-five, hog-leg, plow-handle, and six-gun all identify it in the minds of most people. Coming into being in 1873, it blazed a bloody path to glory that kept it in active service long after better guns were being made—right on down to the present.

The end was in sight for the Peacemaker soon after the Bandit Days along the Rio Grande in 1917. Probably the real turning point came in 1934, when ex-Ranger Captain Frank Hamer, Ranger Manny Gault, and several Louisiana peace officers cut short the bloody careers of Clyde Barrow, the modern Billy the Kid, and his gun moll Bonnie Parker.

Frank Hamer grew up as a Peacemaker man, and a remarkably able one—fast on the draw with either hand and deadly accurate. But when he and his fellow officers blotted out Clyde Barrow and Bonnie Parker, Hamer had an auto-loading shotgun in his hands, and the other officers used submachine guns and rifles. All carried handguns, none Peacemakers; none used in the shooting.

You have to match the criminal with firepower. When the criminal switched to submachine gun and sawed-off shotgun and auto-loading handgun during the gangster days of prohibition, officers had to do the same. When crime moved from the country to the city, from the brush to the highways, from horseback to automobile, the auto-loader, the double-action and the automatic took over. The Peacemaker was eased out.

As Captain Olson, himself a Peacemaker man at one time, said, it just doesn't measure up. He discovered that back in the early thirties, when he set out in an automobile hot after some high-jackers. When he shot his thumb-buster dry he . . . "well, you try to reload one of those things while you're going as fast as the car will go," Captain Olson said.

Many people have puzzled about the tremendous fame of the Colt Frontier Model Forty-five, and some have sought to make a mystery of that fame. They cite the fact that both Remington and Smith and Wesson were making almost equally good revolvers in the earliest days of the Peacemaker, and they cite the further fact that Remington and Smith and Wesson brought out fairly good double-action revolvers in the early days of the Colt single-action weapon.

Then, they ask, why did the Colt almost completely hog the picture?

There are a number of reasons. Some have to do with such things as simplicity of design and operation, reliability, ruggedness, durability.

But there is this important fact, often overlooked: the Peacemaker was a famous gun the day it was born. It simply carried on, and in noble fashion, a tradition. The Colt revolver became famous almost forty years before the Peacemaker showed up on the scene in 1873. The Peacemaker simply carried on.

One reason for the pre-eminence of the Colt both before and after the birth of the Peacemaker was the sensational record of the weapon in the hands of the Texas Rangers. The manner in which the career of that band of men and the career of the Colt single-action are interwoven is remarkable. They have supplemented each other, complemented each other. It is quite possible that neither would have achieved its high place in history without the other.

They came into being the same year, 1835, and for a hundred years their courses ran parallel. Colt secured his first patents in England and France in 1835. Texas organized its ranger service that year. Some historians claim that a few early-day Colt revolvers were used by the rangers in capturing the Mexican "navy" in 1836. They're probably wrong.

It definitely is true, however, that the earliest serviceable Colt, the Patterson, did its first deadly work and started up the glory path in the hands of the Texas Rangers under Captain John C. Hays. Colt even called the gun the Texas Arm, and much of his output was shipped to Texas. Captain Hays was the first to arm his rangers with this repeating handgun, and in the Battle of Plum Creek in 1841 he and twenty-five rangers completely routed one hundred Apache Indians.

It was one of the important battles of history. It was the first time the white man had fought from horseback—the first time he *could* fight from horseback. Prior to that he had dismounted to handle his musket, and the Plains Indians gave him a hell of a going-over while he was on foot, for the Indians fought from horseback.

The Battle of Plum Creek marked the beginning of modern cavalry as it was known until the machine gun whittled it out of existence. It made the white man the equal of the Comanche and pointed to the doom of that noble race, also at the hands of the Texas Rangers, a few years later.

With the Colt revolver the white man could pursue the Indians, chase him and keep on shooting—and exterminate him.

The stirring deeds of Captain Hays and his men came too late to save the Patterson Colt factory, which closed in 1842. But four years later the rangers were to step into the picture once more and bring Colt back into business to stay.

In the war of 1846 with Mexico, General Taylor took the Texas Rangers into his army. Captain Samuel H. Walker, a young ranger who had fought under Captain Hays, was sent to find Colt and induce him to turn out some of his guns for the rangers. Thus came into being the Walker Colt, a far better arm than the Patterson Colt. Captain Walker helped the gunmaker iron out a lot of flaws in the earlier model, flaws revealed in actual fighting. Captain Walker had two of these famed six-guns in his hands when he was killed in the battle of Huamantla while routing Santa Anna's troops. But his men were using Patterson Colts. The Walker Colt got to Mexico in time for action, but in the hands

125

of the rangers headed by Captain Hays, who had arrived at Vera Cruz only a short time before Walker's death.

Throughout the entire war the Texas Rangers were in the thick of fighting, both at Monterrey and between Vera Cruz and Mexico City. And they struck terror into the hearts of the enemy when they showed up with their Colts. So great was the havoc that the London *Times* a bit later raised the question whether this ". . . most terrible weapon of destruction ever placed in the hands of man" should be loosed on the world.

Those guns, and the Colt Dragoon, which came soon afterward, were the granddaddies of the Peacemaker. And their work wasn't finished in Mexico. In 1858 they wrote in lead and blood the obituary of the Comanche Indians as a free people. Captain Rip Ford at the head of 102 rangers, all armed with Colt revolvers, and accompanied by 113 friendly Indians, followed the Comanches into Indian Territory, engaged 300 of them in battle, and routed them completely, leaving 76 dead on the field.

It broke the Comanche power and stopped forever their raids into Texas.

There was more work. The Colt and the rangers did it. Rip Ford took his rangers to the Rio Grande, met and vanquished a much larger force under Juan N. Cortina, the raider who had captured the city of Brownsville, Texas.

During the Civil War all cavalry men who could beg, steal or buy a revolver got one. Cavalry troops armed with them could ride almost at will through foot troops. The Confederacy even manufactured an imitation Colt. It is quite possible that had either side in that war armed all its soldiers with revolvers, that side might have won in a hurry.

But just as officers of the law sometimes lag behind criminals in using the newest and best weapons, so the military often lags behind both. The Civil War was fought with muskets.

But the Colt continued adding to its glory in that war and immediately afterward, with the result that the Peacemaker was already a famous weapon when it showed up in 1873.

126

Farewell Peacemaker

To almost all people who can read and see and hear, the Peacemaker achieved its lasting glory in the hands of the gunmen, both outlaw and marshal, in the roaring cowtowns and mining towns of the Old West—Dodge City, Abilene, Tombstone, Wichita and others.

As a matter of history, the gun was blazing a path to glory in the hands of the Texas Rangers before those cowtowns were generally known in the nation. When Captain L. H. McNelly and his rangers startled the nation with what has been called "McNelly's Bloody Ride to the Rio Grande," he and his men were using Peacemakers. That was in 1875.

When McNelly and sixteen men met a force of sixteen cattle rustlers and killed every one of them in a running fight while losing only one ranger, history for the Peacemaker was being made. When McNelly rode on across the Rio Grande, and at the head of thirty-five rangers stood off a force of three hundred men in a pitched battle, it was the Peacemaker that turned the tide. Its fame was established before Wyatt Earp and Bat Masterson and Wild Bill Hickok and other gunmen were heard of.

It just happened that there were no Ned Buntlines or other dime-novel writers on hand to record in detail the deeds of the rangers. It also happened that the rangers worked in companies —and a lone gunfighter makes a more striking story.

Yet there were other good revolvers, notably the Smith and Wesson and Remington, available at the time. How did the Peacemaker manage to hog the show?

There was, of course, that prior fame. The Colt was already standard, due largely to the work of the rangers. There were other reasons. The Colt had the simplest, strongest action—fewer parts, something quite important to men far away from gunsmiths. The old gun would even work with some minor part broken. And its toughness was proved for all time when it was chambered in recent years for the .357, the most powerful of all pistol cartridges, developing a muzzle velocity of more than 1500 second feet.

Army tests made soon after the Peacemaker was produced demonstrated its superiority over other pistols of that day.

As for the early double-actions, they were poor guns—not reliable. Some had a trigger pull so hard a man had to use both hands to get off a shot. And if a weaker spring was used, the gun sometimes misfired, a painful development when lead was flying.

Then there was the looks of the Colt and the feel of it—its famed grip. Even though its symmetry is marred a trifle by the attached shell ejector, the Peacemaker has the most striking lines of any handgun ever made. In this it follows closely the lines of earlier Colts—it is a tribute to the artistic talent of Samuel Colt.

The grip of the gun fits more naturally into the human hand than that of any other handgun, including the best of today. A man with a small hand, such as Billy the Kid, could hold high on the grip. It fit. A man with a big hand, such as Ranger Captain Ben McCulloch or Big Foot Wallace, could hold all of the grip. It fit.

There was one more reason, having to do with human nature.

The Peacemaker early in the day became standard. So it followed that any man showing up with something else saddled on him, a .38 or .41 or any double-action, was inviting a gunfight. He was certain to hear slurring remarks about his "dude" gun, inviting him to prove its worth.

So the gunmen of the Old West, with the lone exception of Billy the Kid, who sometimes carried a .41 double-action, clung to the single-action .44 or .45 caliber, and almost every one of those who achieved fame or notoriety used a Colt. Some, such as Wild Bill Hickok and Jesse James, balanced off their Colt with a Smith and Wesson.

In the hands of those gunmen—Curly Bill, Sam Bass, Hickok, Ben Thompson, John Wesley Hardin, Bill Tilghman, Wyatt Earp, Doc Holliday, Bat Masterson, Frank and Jesse James, the Daltons, the Youngers and a host of others—the Peacemaker did things, according to writers about the Old West, that were astonishing to behold.

Farewell Peacemaker

Millions of words have been written, telling of almost miraculous feats of quick drawing and quick, accurate shooting by those men. And almost as many words have been written trying to prove it couldn't be done.

Did they fan a six-shooter? If so, could they hit anybody in the process? Did they shoot from the hip? How about slip-shooting? Did they shoot with two guns at once? Were they as fast and as accurate as some claim?

Nobody will ever know. But of one thing there is no longer any doubt. They *could* have done all those things and more. It has been proved, and the results checked by flawless timing devices and witnessed targets. It has been done by a short, stout pistol genius of Montana named Ed McGivern.

Here are some of the things McGivern has done with the Peacemaker:

Draw and put one shot in a standard bull at eighteen feet in from one-quarter to two-fifths of a second.

Fire all five shots (no Peacemaker is loaded to the gills unless the man loading it has an empty head—if the hammer, in down position, is rapped smartly it may fire any live shell under it) without drawing by fanning in from one to one and one-fifth seconds and put all shots in a group the size of a man's hand—this at a distance of eighteen feet.

Draw and fire five shots by fanning in around one and three-fifths seconds—and fire them accurately.

Draw and do the same by slip-shooting in a fraction of a second more. And hit a man-size target near the center with every shot.

McGivern did still more. He plunked them into the target at lightning speed using a Peacemaker in each hand, firing them alternately.

He proved that cocking the single-action while it is being hoisted from the holster into shooting position comes natural to a man who has had practice—he proved the first shot with the Peacemaker can be turned loose just about as fast as the first shot with a double-action. Most revolver men claim that the auto-loader

129

is a shade slower in delivering the first shot—they claim getting off the safety catch is not as natural an action as cocking the Peacemaker's hammer. Auto-loading devotees don't agree.

But on one score there is little doubt. The Peacemaker is plenty fast in getting off that first shot. As to the other shots—well, McGivern drew and got off all five shots with a double-action in the time it took him to draw and fire twice with the Peacemaker. And his fastest time for firing five shots with a double-action, without drawing, and firing accurately, was two-fifths of a second as against a shade over a second in fanning the single-action.

He proved that the gunmen of the Old West could have done those things they are said to have done. But did they?

Chances are they didn't. And one reason is that strange things happen to the human animal when lead is flying both ways. When John Wesley Hardin, traveling in Florida in a railway coach, looked up and saw the long barrel of a Peacemaker coming through the door, he shouted, "Texas, by God!" and grabbed for the gun in his fancy vest—the vest he invented. The gun stuck, and Hardin almost pulled his britches over his head while Texas Ranger Captain John B. Armstrong polished off Hardin's companions and nabbed Hardin.

Most people agree that Wyatt Earp and Doc Holliday were two of the best gunmen of the Old West—fast on the draw and accurate. Yet in the O. K. Corral battle at Tombstone, Wyatt and his brothers and Doc Holliday on the one side, and their enemies, the Clantons and McLowerys, on the other, fired more than thirty shots at close range before three men finally were killed, one by a shotgun blast.

Those old-timers did a surprising amount of missing at short range. In one of the famed duels of the Old West, Charlie Harrison, one of the finest shots of them all, blazed away five times at Jim Levy, a careful, cool customer. Levy was only nicked. But the three shots he fired did the job.

Earp tells of seeing only one gunfight in which there was any fanning of a forty-five. Levi Richardson, a good man with a gun, got fancy and let go all five shots at Frank Loving, a youngster who had never shot at a man before. Richardson was fanning the gun—and fanning the air. When Loving was able to see through the thick cloud of black powder smoke, he shot Richardson in the heart.

Probably the all-time record for wasting ammunition was set by Hank Vaughn—a tough Oregon gunman—and a cowhand whose name has not come down in history. They clasped left hands, drew on signal and emptied their six-guns at each other, doing some hitting, some missing. Both lived.

Undoubtedly one reason some men could absorb so much lead in those days and survive—Cole Younger carried seventeen slugs in his body, and Emmett Dalton had more, counting the "blue whistlers" from a shotgun—was the low velocity developed by the black powder charge.

The men who lived to tell the story said there was very little Fancy Dan shooting when the chips were down. Earp and Emmett Dalton spoke with scorn of hip-shooting, fanning, two-handed shooting.

Yet McGivern's feats in hip-shooting and two-handed shooting show it could be done, and accurately. Undoubtedly the question of distance was a determining factor—and still is. Firing at very close range, the man who undertakes to aim by sighting is likely to have his aim marred by death. But at fairly long range, aiming should be the poison.

When Wild Bill Hickok killed Dave Tutt at what was said to be seventy-five yards, he waited until Tutt fired (so they say), then took careful aim and killed his man. Here again McGivern's tests tell the story. Although he can draw and hit a target at close range in a quarter second, shooting from the hip, he found that it requires about two seconds for a good man with a gun to draw, aim and hit a man-size target at fifty yards. Somewhere in between, the system favored by Earp, holding the gun a little above the waist and pointing, not aiming, should be best.

How would the gun-handlers of today stand up against those

old-timers? It's like that other oft heard question, how would Jack Dempsey in his prime stand up against John L. Sullivan in his prime. Nobody will know.

But this much is pretty certain—men such as McGivern are undoubtedly more accurate and probably faster than any men of the Old West, and for a very good reason. They've done more shooting. The chances are Ed McGivern has fired more shells through revolvers than all the well-known gunmen of the Old West put together.

But when it comes down to drawing and firing at a man who is doing the same thing—trying to kill you—the men of the Old West had a kind of practice that made up for the limited target practice. They were used to the genuine article. They would probably come off with at least some honors today.

The Old West and the Peacemaker blazed in their hour of bloody glory. When the Old West faded, the Peacemaker didn't. In the hands of such men as Ranger Captains George W. Bailey and John B. Armstrong and Lee Hall and John Hughes and Bill McDonald, it saw service on two frontiers and in Texas cowtowns.

It's quite possible one reason Texas cowhands raised so much hell in Kansas was because the rangers kept them in line in the Texas towns. The rangers moved out into far west Texas, took on the Apaches raiding out of Mexico and stopped the raids. They moved down on the Rio Grande and battled bandits and cattle rustlers. They moved in on the bloody feuds in Texas—the Taylor-Sutton feud, the Kimball County War, the Mason County War, and stopped them—usually without firing a shot. They disbanded so-called Minute Men and Vigilantes. *They* were the law.

But the show for the Peacemaker was nearing an end just the same.

In 1892 the U.S. Army switched to the .38 double-action. The rangers were hamstrung by a loophole in the law depriving them of most of their power, and their glory faded. The frontiers were quieting down.

The Peacemaker came into the limelight again at the turn of

the century. American soldiers in the Philippines began setting up a tremendous howl, demanding some side arm that would stop the wild charges of the Moros. The .38 wouldn't. So the army rushed a shipment of Peacemakers to the scene. They did the job.

Then came real trouble along the Mexican border, the so-called Bandit Days from 1913 to 1917, and once more the Peacemaker in the hands of Texas Rangers blazed away. The old gun came back in grand style and upheld its reputation. Unfortunately, some of the men handling it didn't uphold the tradition of the Texas Rangers.

Two politically-minded governors had saddled a host of incompetent, hare-brained and sometimes downright murderous political appointees on the service. The manner in which some of those men killed innocent Mexicans came near spelling the end of the ranger service.

Still many of the old guard of the service were on hand, and with Peacemakers in hand, they fought some bloody battles with bandits, and won. The gun and the man still could do the job.

The real fadeout of the Peacemaker and the old-style ranger started then. A few of the old-timers still are around, but not in service. There's Captain W. M. Molesworth, who at eighty-six is the oldest of them all. He was in the thick of the border fighting in the Bandit Days. His old thumb-buster hangs on a peg beside his bed.

He won't discuss any other gun. To him there is no other. "You hit a man with it," he says, "and he goes down and stays down. And there's no jamming. If you want to buffalo a man, you bend that barrel over his head and he's real quiet for a spell."

And there's Captain Aldrich, and there are a few others—all retired.

The change had to come. Men of the Old West fought by a code —at least they were supposed to fight that way. Officer and outlaw alike were obliged to face the enemy with gun in holster, then draw at will. Sometimes the code was carried to fantastic extremes. Clay Allison, "Wolf of the Washita," and Chunk Colbert fiddled around for hours, buying each other food and drinks, stirring their coffee with their six-shooters, carrying on like madmen as each waited for the other to make his break. Chunk made it—and lost.

The code was blotted out by blasts of machine-gun fire and shots fired from guns concealed in coat pockets—often fired into the victim's back—when gangsterism came into being. Officers had to match the gangster.

"Other guns are faster and more accurate and have more fire-power," Captain Don Lawrence, gun instructor for the Texas Department of Public Safety, explains. He doesn't even like the grip of the Peacemaker. The gun slams back in the hand when fired, he says. The barrel is too high above the grip, making for poor accuracy and an upward swing on the recoil. The hammer is too long and too heavy—a gunner can get off his target while it's falling, or it can jar him off when it hits.

There are some other reasons for the fadeout of the Peacemaker.

It was never intended to be concealed. It is a proud gun, thriving on display. That fine-looking and fine-feeling grip doesn't slide easily into an inside pocket. When guns ceased to be a part of man's wearing apparel, those who began carrying concealed weapons turned to something trimmer.

And there's the matter of weight. The thumb-buster weighs around 37 ounces, depending on length of barrel. The newest Colt auto-loader weighs 26½ ounces. The .38 double-action weighs around 32 ounces, depending on model and barrel length.

Then there's the business of display. An officer wearing a Peacemaker today, even in Texas, gives the impression that he is actually trying to make a show. His fellow Texans look at him, then look at each other and grin.

The old gun is through. Yet it barely missed another brief moment of glory in 1940. Although few people know it, if the Germans had landed on English soil, 108 of the Britishers facing them would have banged away with Peacemakers. England, in her desperate effort to rearm, took what guns she could get. Included in the lot were 108 Peacemakers. They are still there, souvenirs of a great past for gun and country.

In 1941 the Colt Arms Manufacturing Company stopped making Peacemakers because of the war. After the war, manufacture was not resumed. It won't be. Parts are not easy to get. Shells are becoming scarce.

The Texas Ranger carries on, in a somewhat different manner. The frontier fighter is gone. The ranger of today is a crimebuster, modern style.

The Peacemaker carries on—but only in the imagination of man. It will live there forever.

The Vengeance of Joe Meek

by Norman B. Wiltsey

Joe Meek was running his winter trapline far back in the Blue Mountains of Oregon when Jimmy Rabbit, a half-breed Nez Percé, brought him word of the Cayuse uprising and the pitiless massacre of the kindly missionary-doctor, Marcus Whitman, and his lovely wife, Narcissa.

Jimmy reported that fourteen persons had died through violence or exposure in the Cayuse raid on the mission at Waiilatpu; among them, eleven-year-old Mary Jane Bridger and ten-year-old Helen Meek.

Both little girls were born of Indian mothers. Helen's mother, a pert and pretty Shoshone girl named Moon-on-the-Water, had been killed in a ruckus with the Blackfeet when Helen was three years old. A great worry had lifted from Joe Meek's troubled mind, and the pain in his bereaved heart lessened a mite when he'd placed his small daughter under Narcissa Whitman's gentle, expert care at peaceful Waiilatpu. Having lost their only child in a tragic drowning accident, Marcus and Narcissa Whitman had lavished affection upon all children brought to sanctuary at the mission.

Joe was stretching beaver skins in his cabin when Jimmy Rabbit arrived to deliver his terrible news. The lean trapper listened in grim silence, gripping a stretching board in his powerful hands until the brown knuckles strained white. Finally he spoke: "Tell me one thing more, Jimmy. Did those Cayuse devils torture Helen before they killed her?"

Jimmy shook his head. "No torture little girls. Both die of fever —outside house on ground."

The stretching board snapped in Joe's fingers. "Why did they do it, Jimmy? Doc Whitman and his missus wuz mighty good to the Cayuses; fed 'em in the hard winters an' took care of 'em when they wuz sick. Jimmy, this turrible thing don't make *sense!*"

The half-breed shrugged, and replied in Nez Percé, "I do not know for sure. It was said in council that sick children died after taking the white doctor's medicines. Tiloukaikt and Tomahas— he who is called The Murderer—told the people that the white doctor had poisoned the children. You know the tribal law that says a medicine man must die if his medicines kill the sick instead of curing them?"

Joe nodded. "I know the law. It is a bad and foolish law—but then, so are many of the white man's laws. . . . Who took the sick little ones from their beds and put them on the cold ground to die?"

Jimmy Rabbit evaded the mountain man's piercing gaze. "I am not sure; I was not at Waiilatpu on the twenty-ninth day of November, when the raiders came. My uncle, Singing Hawk, told me that Tomahas killed the white doctor and that Tiloukaikt, Kiamasumpkin, Isaiachalakis and Klokomis led the attack on the others. I know not who carried your small one and the daughter of Big Throat (Jim Bridger) outside the mission house. I came to you quickly because I thought you would like to hear what I knew."

Joe Meek dropped the broken stretching board and took the half-breed's right hand in both of his. "I understand, Jimmy," he declared huskily. "My friend, I thank you. . . ."

January of 1848 was half spent before Joe Meek reached the burned ruins of the Whitman Mission at Waiilatpu. A bleak wind mourned through the circling spruces as Joe worked furiously at digging deep, permanent graves for the fourteen victims. All had been buried in hastily dug, shallow graves by compassionate Catholic missionaries arriving at Waiilatpu soon after the massacre. Hungry wolves had found the burial spot and dug out the frozen bodies, and the scene wasn't a pretty one to contemplate.

Joe was sick to his stomach when he finished his grisly, self-appointed task. Among the hideously fang-torn corpses, he'd recognized the bodies of his daughter and the daughter of his friend Jim Bridger by the bright ribbons in the girls' hair. He knew those ribbons; he'd given them to Helen and Mary Jane months before. They'd been such eager, earnest young'uns; trying so hard to learn the white man's difficult way of life in a changed and confusing world. Seemed like God must've been napping to let their brave struggle end like *this!*

The mountain man dropped the final shovelful of earth on the last grave and turned blindly away. Unaccustomed tears wet his bearded cheeks as he mounted his cold-hunched horse and rode back down the trail away from those ugly mounds of raw earth. The grimly solemn words of the Shoshone blood oath gritted between Joe's clenched teeth as he put distance behind him:

"Hear me, Mighty One Above! I will have blood for blood, though twice ten snows whiten the ground before I find the ones who have wronged me and made desolate my heart. Hear me, Mighty One!"

Two winters passed before Joe Meek's vow was fulfilled, and Tomahas, The Murderer, and four of his comrades in the Cayuse uprising were arrested and brought to trial at Oregon City, seat of the territorial government. No written record survives today of Joe Meek's relentless hounding of the killers through the misty mountains of the Northwest until the five leaders in the Whitman massacre wearily decided to surrender to "save our people from further persecution by the white men." Trial of Tomahas, Tiloukaikt, Klokomis, Isaiachalakis and Kiamasumpkin began on the morning of May 22, 1850. Joe Meek—now a United States Marshal—guarded the five prisoners during the progress of the trial.

This "white man's council" was a deep mystery to the five Cayuse prisoners. Frankly they admitted killing the white medicine man Whitman, his squaw, and twelve other whites and half-breeds at Waiilatpu. Why then all this silly fuss, with one bull-voiced white man bellowing that they were murderers and yet another bull-voiced white man roaring back that they were not? They had deliberately "thrown themselves away" to help their oppressed people: why not kill them at once and get it over with? Stand them up against a wall and shoot them, split their skulls with a hatchet or cut their throats with a knife—but kill them quickly and honorably. All they asked was a warrior's death, that they might join their brother braves unashamed in the Spirit Land.

Sixteen-year-old Cathy Sager, one of the survivors of the Waiilatpu massacre, proved to be the star witness for the prosecution. Calmly, almost as if she were reciting a "book story" learned in school, Cathy related how she had seen Tomahas strike down Dr. Whitman with his tomahawk. She told of her two brothers slaughtered before her eyes and of little Helen Meek and Mary Ann Bridger—both children wretchedly ill with the measles—brutally yanked from their beds and hustled outside the mission house to die on the frozen ground. Quietly yet vividly she told how Mrs. Whitman had tried to shield the screaming victims as the maddened Indians beat them with war clubs and lashed them with rawhide quirts. Tears came to the eyes of the audience when Cathy described the pitiful scene when mortally wounded "Mother Whitman" collapsed beside the mutilated body of her husband. The girl finished her testimony by telling of the death of her baby sister from exposure the second day following the Cayuse raid and how she had cuddled the tiny lifeless form in her arms for hours in the wild hope that the tot was not dead.

Cathy's clear, unfaltering testimony made a verdict of guilty virtually certain. In vain, defense attorneys Clairborne and Pritchett thundered that the court had no jurisdiction—that Oregon was not a territory at the time of the massacre. Pritchett boldly declared that the massacre was not really a massacre at all but simply an act of war as war was realistically waged by the Cayuses. Clairborne, in the course of arguing that the raid was actually a reprisal, pointed out that war meant total extermination to the Cayuses. The able lawyer eloquently reminded the jury that white men, times innumerable, had murdered Indian women and children with impunity. The Cayuse uprising, "in defense of their invaded hunting grounds," was long since crushed and the once powerful Cayuse nation defeated, humbled and stripped of all its richest lands. Now let the one-sided white man's laws be magnanimous for once and permit these persecuted warriors to go free to support their impoverished families!

The five killers listened to Joe Meek's running translation of all this impassioned oratory with undisguised amazement and contempt. Here they sat on the prisoners' bench, utterly in the white man's power, and the white man made much windy noise with his mouth and delayed putting his enemies to death. There could be but one answer to such sickly nonsense: the white man was both timid and a fool! Tomahas and his mates began to glower and mutter on the bench, and their gratified primitive egos were not deflated until the third and final day of the trial when the jury brought in a verdict of guilty as charged. Judge Pratt gravely pronounced sentence of death by hanging, the execution to be carried out nine days hence on June 2.

The Cayuses took the death sentence with impassive stolidity, but again back in their cells at the jail they complained bitterly to Marshal Meek.

The Vengeance of Joe Meek

"Why is this, Joe Meek?" demanded Tiloukaikt. "We are warriors; what have we done to deserve a coward's death?"

"You have killed treacherously a man who had done nothing but good to your tribe; you have murdered sick children and weak and helpless women. Were those the acts of warriors?"

Tomahas, the Murderer, laughed scornfully. "War is war—whether it be killing men, women or children. The white medicine man was evil, so we killed him and all those around him. We Cayuses are not soft, like the white man!"

"You will find that *some* white men are not so soft as you think!" Joe told him grimly.

"You know our religion, Joe Meek," hopefully persisted Tiloukaikt. "We cannot face our brothers in the Spirit Land without wounds to show them. You are a warrior; not a wind-mouth like those other white men at the council. Surely you will see that we die by bullet or knife or hatchet instead of the rope?"

Joe shook his head. "You must die by the rope, Tiloukaikt. I—Joe Meek—will be your hangman!"

The morning of June 2, 1850, broke calm and beautiful across the rolling Oregon hills. In Oregon City a crowd gathered about the place of execution a full hour before the time set for the hangings. Settlers had brought their families in wagons to see the Cayuse murderers die at last for their horrible crime of nearly three years before. Fellow tribesmen of the doomed braves waited sullenly to view the multiple execution. Stalwart Nez Percé warriors, handsome of countenance and haughty of bearing, stood aloof at the rear of the throng to witness this shameful spectacle of five braves hung by their necks until they were dead.

Two hours dragged by and the crowd began stirring and murmuring impatiently. Suddenly the prisoners emerged from the rear door of the jail, walking stiffly erect between armed guards led by Marshal Meek. In the front rank of the motley assembly, a grizzled old Cayuse medicine man whooped shrilly. The whoop was a signal for every Cayuse in the crowd to sound off in a weird

141

death chant. The five murderers walked to the scaffold to a barbaric dirge provided by their swaying, wailing tribesmen.

On the lofty platform Tiloukaikt appealed once more to the
executioner. "For the last time, Joe Meek, we call upon you as
a brother warrior. You—who have lived and hunted with Indians
and twice taken an Indian woman to wife—*know* the importance
of the thing we ask. Shoot us, cut our throats with your knife!
Do not send us to the Spirit Land unwounded with rope marks
on our necks. It is little to ask of you, Joe Meek."

"It is too much to ask of me," snapped Joe. "You must hang,
according to the white man's law." The mountain man hesitated,
remembering something else from his years of wilderness living
"Injun style." "Yet you also die according to another law—the
vengeance law of your people. Have not the ancients written that
there is no shame when a man is killed *in any manner* by a close
relative of one he has slain? 'Blood for blood until the dead is
avenged!' Is this not true?"

"It is true," somberly agreed Tiloukaikt. "But we have shed
no blood of yours, Joe Meek. . . ."

"Ah, but you *have*, Tiloukaikt! Do you remember the little
Shoshone girl at Waiilatpu—one of the two sick little ones you
put out on the frozen ground to die? She was my daughter,
Tiloukaikt! I swore the blood oath against you when I found her
body. You die by that oath!"

Surprised, the five killers talked briefly together. Below, the
restless settlers roared angrily at this added delay and demanded
that the hangings proceed. Klokomis stalked to the edge of the
platform and spat disdainfully at the upraised white faces. The
menacing roar increased in volume. A lanky farmer snatched a
rifle from his wagon box and bawled hoarsely: "Quit the pow-
wowin', Meek! Hang them red devils *quick,* or we'll shoot the lot
of you like crows on a rock!"

Tiloukaikt turned again to the hangman. "It is well, Joe Meek.
You know and respect our ancient laws and customs; we also
believe that you speak with a straight tongue. Our brothers in the

Spirit Land will accept the strange manner of our death and welcome us to their lodges. We die as warriors. We thank you."

Joe nodded, stony-faced. Swiftly he adjusted the hempen ropes, careful to place the sinister knot in each noose in exactly the right position to mercifully break the neck of each murderer as he reached the end of his drop after falling through the trap. Deftly the hangman completed his gruesome task, stepped back to receive the hatchet from his assistant.

Not a sign of fear or panic appeared on the expressionless bronze faces before him; only Tiloukaikt smiled slightly in gratitude and farewell.

The hatchet swished down, severing the trip rope cleanly with the single stroke. The greased trap sprung smoothly; the five killers dropped together into eternity.

Joe Meek turned away from the yawning trap hole and descended the ladder. He strode through the suddenly silent, fascinated crowd without once glancing back at the grotesquely dangling bodies behind him. His lips moved rapidly, framing words in Shoshone:

"Hear me, Mighty One Above . . . ! With my own hands I have killed the murderers of my child. . . . My heart is cleansed of hate and anger—it is lifted from the ground. . . . Hear me, Mighty One. . . !"

When Booger Red Rode
the Man-Killer Gray

by J. Frank Dobie

I have heard that somebody is writing a book about Booger Red. Few people in his lifetime knew his baptismal name and fewer know it now, but the name Booger Red lives on. He may not be worth a whole book, but any man whose tradition stays green for fifty years is worth at least a biographical sketch. It has been almost that long since I saw him ride a bad pitching horse. This was before rodeos were organized as they are now, and Booger Red was going about the country with a wagon, two or three helpers and several horses giving exhibitions of bronc pitching. The fee for spectators might have been as high as four bits. I forget.

This story about a ride he made and the horse he rode is not mine. The by-line belongs to Joseph J. Good, who used to be a Texas cowboy and who is now writing his reminiscences. He has given me permission to publish this episode. He was at the Fort

Worth Stock Show about 1898 when he saw the horse and the man. At that time the arena was a patch of prairie land on which some corrals had been built. The spectators were in buggies, on horses, on foot. There were no stands of seats. When a horse came out of the corral, he had the whole country to pitch in.

Suddenly a dappled gray horse about fifteen and one-half hands high, weighing around one thousand pounds, that had been roped inside the corral broke through or over the plank fence and was out where everybody could see him. But the roper held on to the rope and with help soon choked the struggling horse down. Then a saddle was put on him while he was held down, men rolling and pulling him around so that it could be girted up. A very young man, just a boy, got into the saddle, taking the reins, as the horse was allowed to rise. In a flash the gray was upright. In another flash he had "bogged his head" and was pitching as hard as a cornered tiger fights for life. His motion was one jump forward and the next jump a zigzag in which he writhed all the muscles of his body. That close-coupled body was beautiful, the short back, rounded hips, beautifully proportioned neck and legs all magnificently muscled. The sun brought out the dapples in his sleek gray. His mane and tail flowed with his powerful movements. His head, broad between the eyes, bore little resemblance to the jugheads of some demented outlaws. He looked like a top cutting horse—except for the whites of his eyes.

As he pitched there on the Fort Worth prairie he seemed to put increasing power into his fierce zigzags, but the boy on his back kept a perfect seat, pulling hard on the reins for maybe forty feet. Then, as suddenly as if he had been shot by a bullet, he dropped down over the gray's left shoulder. By the time he reached the ground the gray had plunged forward far enough to kick him a full blow in the chest. The horse seemed to step on him, bearing down with full weight, and to kick him with one movement.

Among the explanations that followed, one was that the left stirrup leather broke, another that the string lacing the stirrup leather broke. The way the rider fell indicated that something

145

beyond the action of the horse had detached him suddenly and completely from his firm, balanced position in the saddle. It was about ten o'clock in the morning when he fell. A horse-drawn ambulance took him to the hospital. The horse was caught and taken back to the corrals. The show went on. By eleven o'clock the rider was dead.

During the morning the reputation of the gray horse spread—and grew—among the spectators milling around the arena. It was said that no man had been able to ride him to a standstill, that he had thrown them all, that this was the twenty-third man he had killed. Perhaps no man had yet ridden him to a finish. Even if this was only the first man he had killed, he was a terrible horse.

Among the riders present was Booger Red. He was approaching the peak of his riding career, through he was to be much more widely known in years to follow. Certain men now approached him and asked him if he would ride the gray that afternoon. He said he would if they would make a purse for him. A little before twelve o'clock four men on gentle horses started riding among the people with big Stetson hats held out for contributions. Dimes, quarters, half-dollars, and silver dollars—for dollar bills were then unknown—were pitched into the hats from all sides until between two and three gallons of silver had been collected.

Whatever the amount was, Booger Red earned it that afternoon. He mounted the gray near the corral. As soon as he was turned loose, the "man-killer," as he was now being called, started out in the one-jump-forward and then zigzag lunging style that had brought him victory a few hours before. After he had gone forward about a hundred yards in this way, he changed his style and went to fence-rowing. After the one-jump-forward, he would make a twisting turn first to the left and then to the right, bringing the side of his body within the turn so close to the ground that had Booger Red loosened his leg grip his foot could have almost touched the earth. Booger Red did not loosen anything.

When the gray started fence-rowing, he was headed east. After a jump in that direction, he would pitch crossways, headed north,

146

and then twist back to the east and the next time pitch crossways to the south. He kept this up until he had pitched around and over maybe ten acres of land, covering half of it twice.

The crowd, people afoot as well as in buggies and on horses, followed the pitching horse, keeping back far enough not to interfere. He did not seem to notice them. All his attention was on the man cemented to his back and quirting him at every jump so as to keep in rhythm with his motions.

After pitching all over those acres of ground and halfway over them again, the gray made one last lunge and then set out on a beeline run for the corral. "I was standing near the gate," Joseph J. Good says, "when the horse, of his own accord, stopped right at it. Two men seized his ears, bridle and headstall and held him while Booger Red dismounted. He was so exhausted that he had to lean against the fence in order to stand up.

"The horse was totally blind. He had pitched himself blind. He was led away, and I never heard what became of him. The worst pitching horse I ever saw and the best rider I ever saw were together that afternoon at the Fort Worth Stock Show. I doubt if Booger Red ever rode a worse horse than the dappled gray man-killer."

Flowers for
Charley McDaniels

by Fred A. Stone

I remember the day that Charley McDaniels rode into town. I saw him coming down San Antonio Street. I didn't know who he was at the time, so I didn't pay him any special mind. To me, just a little old knot-head kid piddling along the dusty, 'dobe-walled street when I should have been home an hour before, the sight of another tough-looking gun-hung rider meant nothing. Along in the 1890's his kind rode in and out of El Paso every day.

But few of his kind, or any other kind, had the sort of horse he rode. That's what caught my eye. I loved fine horses, and this

148

was one of the finest I'd ever seen—a big lanky, stocking-legged sorrel with a white star in his forehead. He was hardly more than a colt, by the looks of him, yet he stepped along under the saddle with all the pride and assurance of a much older horse.

I stood and stared at the beauty of the sorrel and dreamed of the far-off time when I'd be big enough to own such a horse.

It wasn't till Dad arrived home later in the day that I learned the name of the man who rode the sorrel.

Dad (Lewis W. Stone) came into the house with his customary long, quick stride, calling to Mother: "Get dinner on the table as quick as you can, Reb. Got some business downtown that can't wait."

Dad always called Mother "Reb" because her maiden name had been Lee and she was the granddaughter of a general in the Confederate Army.

The extra cheerfulness in Dad's voice didn't fool Mother. She waited awhile, then asked quietly: "Who is it this time, Rocky?"

Dad's face sobered. "Charley McDaniels," he said, just as quietly, then added, as if to divert her thoughts: "Riding one of the finest sorrel horses I ever saw."

Mother turned to her cooking, and they said no more. But for me they'd already said enough.

I knew who Charley McDaniels was. I'd never seen him till he'd ridden past that morning on the star-faced sorrel, but I knew all about him. Kids learn things a lot faster than most grownups realize, and Dad had been United States Deputy Marshal for the southwestern district of Texas too long for me not to know the names and general histories of most of the badmen in our part of the country.

And Charley McDaniels was bad. There was no doubt about that. He was as bad as they came. He was on the wanted list of every law-enforcement officer within the radius of a thousand miles. He was half Irish and half Mexican.

His main specialties were horse-stealing, cattle-rustling, hiring out as a gunman in local range wars and plain murder, for whatever price he could command. He was one of the few real badmen who never drank; his weaknesses ran to gambling and women. He loved the game of monte. He had a reputation for never cheating but a still better one for gunning down any man who tried to cheat him. He preferred Mexican women to white ones, and generally any time he wasn't to be found around a monte table, he'd be down in the red-light district, throwing his money around among the Mexican whores.

I felt a quick surge of excitement as I thought of Charley McDaniels' reputation as a gunman and killer, then recollected the choice Dad always issued to every badman who rode into El Paso: "Get out of town, go to jail or go to Boot Hill."

Dad had made that order stick so far. In one instance I'd been on hand to watch him do it. That was the time he put me behind a telegraph pole with orders to stay there, then walked up to confront a drunken hoodlum who had a reputation for being mighty careless with his guns. Nothing had happened that time. Dad had merely talked for awhile, and finally the man had unbuckled his belt and handed over his guns. But I was betting it wouldn't be that way this time. Not with Charley McDaniels.

Just why the possibility of a gunfight between my father and Charley McDaniels should have stirred me with a sort of exhilaration instead of fear and dread, I'm not sure right now. I was young, but not too young to understand the danger to my father. The only explanation that I can give is the fact that in those days I was so inordinately proud of my father, so sure of his courage and ability to handle any situation, that I may have felt him invincible.

And looking back now I still have the feeling that he was as nearly invincible as any man ever was.

I remember following him that day from the kitchen to the back porch, where he went to wash up for dinner. I remember how he looked bent over the washbasin—the whole six-feet-two-inches-one-hundred-ninety-six-pounds of him. He was straight as an arrow, with broad, thick shoulders and trim, gun-hung waist.

Flowers for Charley McDaniels

He was of Scotch-Irish and Indian origin—two kinds of Indian, Cherokee and Comanche. He looked more Indian than white with his coppery skin, dark eyes and jet-black hair. Yet that hair must have been a throwback to some Scotch-Gaelic ancestor, for I never knew of a curly-headed Indian among either the Cherokee or the Comanches.

I remember how Dad always wound up his face-washings by trying to slick back that unruly hair with his wet hands and never having any luck. And I remember how he failed this time and gave me a solemn wink as he carried the washpan to the edge of the porch and splashed its contents into my mother's flower bed.

We ate. And while Dad did a lot of talking, there was nothing more said about Charley McDaniels. When he rose Dad said, "I won't be gone long, Reb," and left the house, walking as casually as if he'd been going out to shoe a horse.

What happened downtown right after that, I didn't learn about in detail until years later, so many years later in fact, that no doubt some of those details were minimized or exaggerated. Yet with all its many tellings, the main story has never varied much, so that what I tell here can't be far off track.

Dad searched first among the whorehouses, but if the gunman had visited there, the Mexican girls wouldn't admit it. Which didn't surprise Dad. After all McDaniels was young, not hard for a woman to look at and was a free spender. Why should the girls give him away to a peace officer who made a habit of killing or jailing or running out of town some of their very best customers?

It wasn't till Dad entered the Gem Saloon on El Paso Street that he got wind of his man. McDaniels, according to one talkative elbow-bender, had just left, headed for the Ranch Saloon a block or so down the street.

Dad left the Gem through the back door. He hurried down an alley and entered the Ranch Saloon through one of the little wine rooms that were reserved for family drinking, women not being allowed to drink in the main saloons in those days. He walked quietly into the narrow hall that led to the main barroom.

He nudged open a door and took a close look at the customers ringing the gaming tables. His man wasn't there either.

He entered the room then and spoke quietly for a moment to Jake Sullivan, the barkeep, then left by the main front door, walking out as unobtrusively as he could.

He hadn't fooled anybody, however. Behind him every customer in Jake's place pushed through the swinging doors and stood in the street, watching him. Some followed for a ways, then finally lost interest as Dad turned a corner and went around to Utah Street.

Again he searched the red-light district, combing it as carefully as a squaw hunting lice in a buck's hair, and again he had no luck. Then just as he was coming out of a big red brick building known as Tillie Howard's place, his deputy Elmer Wagner came across the street to meet him.

"Been a shooting at the Wigwam Saloon on San Antonio," Elmer reported.

Dad asked quickly: "Who was in it?"

"A gambler and a deputy city marshal," Elmer said.

"Anybody else?"

"Yeah. The fellow what done the shootin'. Didn't get his name. The deputy was Tom Glover. The gambler was that big, black Mex monte dealer at the Wigwam."

Together they hurried toward the Wigwam. Turning west on San Antonio, they saw a crowd making a rush for the far side of the street, taking cover wherever it was to be found. Across the street on the south side stood a lone man. The man stood hesitant, as if not quite sure where to go next.

"That's our man!" Dad exclaimed to Elmer, then added: "Get to the other side of the street and keep out of this fracas till I'm down or till I invite you to take a hand."

Charley McDaniels caught sight of Elmer crossing the street and burst into sudden loud laughter. Then he stepped out into the middle of the street, turned his back on Elmer and faced toward Dad, who also had stepped out into the clear.

152

"Marshal," he called to Dad, "I'm coming after my horse. I'm fixing to leave town."

Dad called back to him. "It's too late for that now, Charley. I'm arresting you for murder, and where you're going you won't need a horse."

"That gambler was cheatin', Marshal," McDaniels argued. "And I warned that law feller to stay out of the deal, but he went ahead and drawed on me. First!"

"Can you prove that, Charley?"

"I sure can."

"All right then," Dad said. "You got nothing to fear. Just drop your guns, and we'll go talk to the judge. I'll see that you get a fair trial."

Dad didn't any more expect Charley McDaniels to drop his gun than did the hiding onlookers who peeked from every doorway and window along both sides of the street. But he stood waiting, giving McDaniels a chance. And while he waited he could hear the old-timers calling bets to each other up and down and across the street. He took what comfort he could from the fact that the odds offered seem to make him a favorite to win.

Dad called again. "Drop those irons and lift your hands, Charley. Like I said, I'll see that you get a fair trial."

But the killer grinned and shook his head. "Sorry, Marshal," he said. "I can't hear you. Not when you talk like that."

"You better hear me," Dad said. "If you don't, I'm going to have to come and get you, Charley, and you're not going to like that."

McDaniels, as if stalling for time, studied on that for a moment, then tried to make a deal. "Tell you what, Marshal. Let's save us both a lot of trouble. You let me get to my horse, and I'll leave town—and promise not to come back as long as you're the King Pin of the butcher shop here!"

Dad shook his head. "You've got me wrong, Charley. I don't make deals with outlaws. You're not getting out of this town till you've settled your bill."

153

"Well, then," McDaniels said reluctantly. "I reckon you better start walking. I'll be coming to meet you."

There was a span of ninety-six feet between them when they started. I know this because Old Chipmunk, a deputy city marshal, stepped it off the next morning—"Just to keep the books straight." There wasn't a soul in sight between them, but from a hundred different points of cover, there were eyes squinted against the hot glare of the afternoon sun. There was no sound either except their slow, deliberate footsteps, muffled by the powdery dust of the street.

Moving slowly, speaking no word, they closed the gap to sixty feet, to forty, then to thirty.

From that point on, the only thing either man watched was his opponent's eyes. Each knew that the other walked with his hands held level with the gun butts at his belt, but it wasn't hands they watched. It was the eyes that would give the telltale signal.

A listless breeze trailed along the street, picking up a tiny wisp of dust, then dropping it almost before it cleared the ground. The leaves on a big cottonwood overhanging the street trembled slightly and grew still.

Then it came and was over with such shocking suddenness that it was almost a disappointment to the onlookers. There was just that one brief instant when the hands of both men were filled, and the guns were bucking and crashing. Then the guns were still again and, through a haze of light, bluish smoke that hung in the dead air, the onlookers saw one of the men lower his guns as if he no longer had the strength to hold them. Then as one gun slipped from his hand, he pitched forward, plowing into the dust with his head and shoulder.

He lay there still and quiet, while the second man, bare-headed now, advanced cautiously toward him, still holding a smoking gun in each hand.

Elmer Wagner and Chipmunk were the first to rush out.

"You hurt, Marshal?" Elmer queried, excitedly. "You hit anywhere?"

Dad looked behind him to where his black hat lay in the dust. "No," he said. "But I think he ruined a damned good hat for me!"

Chipmunk brought Dad his hat, and Dad poked a finger through one of the jagged holes in the crown and seemed to study his finger for a good long while. Finally, clapping the hat on his head, he said to Elmer: "You and Chipmunk take care of things. I've got business at home that can't wait."

I was there at the house when he came through the yard gate. His steps seemed faster and wider apart than ever and there was a wider-than-usual grin on his face. And I remember how Mother was sitting there in the old granny rocking chair, watching him come up the steps, like she was seeing a dream come true.

Dad caught her up out of the chair and kissed her and said, "Hi, Reb; is supper ready?" and winked at me to show that he knew it was way too early for supper yet. Then he headed for the water cooler, where he got himself a big long drink of water.

When he finished Mother asked quietly: "When will the funeral be, Rocky?"

"At ten o'clock in the morning."

Mother nodded. "I'll hunt up my hymnbook," she said, "and cut some fresh flowers at daybreak."

Dad said: "Make them something special, Reb. He was a game one; I liked him."

"Then why did you kill him?" she asked. Her tone wasn't accusing; she just wanted to know.

"Why, for a couple of reasons, Reb. First he was too old a dog to teach new tricks. Second you're too young and pretty yet to be left a widow."

Dad grinned at her, pitched his hat onto the couch, hunted up another and left the house, headed back for town. Mother picked up the hat, stuck a finger through one of the holes in the crown, then finally went to hang the hat in a closet.

"Now," she said to me, "if he can just get a shirt and a pair of pants, we'll have a whole outfit."

She was smiling at me as she said that, but when I happened

to wander into the next room a few minutes later, I found her stretched out, face down across the bed, weeping silently, like Dad always said a woman had to do now and then.

The next morning I helped carry the flowers that Mother and Dad took to put on Charley McDaniels' grave, after they'd buried and sung over him. But the sorrel horse wasn't anywhere in sight.

I never did learn what happened to him.

Nineteen Months with
the Comanches

by Jack Derden

On May 19, 1836, a huge war party of Comanches and Kiowas swooped down on Fort Parker, on the headwaters of the Navasota River in Limestone County, Texas. Employing a flag of truce to effect entrance to the stockade, the Indians massacred most of the forty or so whites inside the fort, but carried off Rachel Plummer and her two-year-old son and little Cynthia Ann Parker and her brother John. The story of Cynthia Ann is well known, the dramatic tale of Rachel Plummer comparatively unknown. Yet the story of Rachel Plummer's nineteen months with the Comanches forms one of the most stirring accounts of pioneer courage and fortitude ever known on the American frontier.

Knocked senseless at the start of the Indian attack, Rachel remained in a dazed condition until she found herself being hustled north by her captors at daybreak next morning. For five straight days the Commanches hurried her on, allowing her no food and very little water. On the fifth day the Indians brought her son to her because he had been crying since his capture. When they discovered that little Jimmy had been weaned, they tore him loose from her arms. She never learned what became of him, for she never saw him again.

From the fort Rachel moved northeast with the Comanches until she reached the Red River. Crossing the Red River, the band hurried on northwest until the Rockies were reached. Although it was now July, snow had appeared on the higher slopes, and it was bitterly cold at night. Rachel suffered greatly, as she had no shoes and few clothes. Her feet became badly frostbitten, but the Indians ignored her sufferings.

All this time she was forced by her captors to dress buffalo skins by day and wrangle horses at night. Usually she had so many buffalo hides to dress she had to do them at night while attending the horses.

An old Indian with a wife and only one daughter adopted her. The dreary months passed, and by October she had learned to speak the Comanche language. The other two women of her household were hard but thorough teachers. She had to refer to them as mistresses and to address the old man as "Master."

In October she gave birth to her second son and had to be up and moving the same day. A birth did not delay the Comanches if they wanted to travel. In fact the lives of both mother and child were in jeopardy if they hindered the band in any manner. Knowing this, Rachel began to fear for her newborn child.

Her fears were soon realized. Seeing that the infant was hindering Rachel's work, the old man ordered it killed. Three Indians entered the lodge, grabbed the six-weeks-old baby from her arms and started to tear it apart. The mother screamed in horror and rushed at them, but the burly braves pushed her aside and tossed the child through the lodge opening to land on the frozen ground.

They gave it back to her then—but when they saw signs of life in the tiny body, they tore it again from her arms, tied a rawhide rope around its neck and dragged it through prickly pears until it died.

Rachel Plummer never forgave her captors for this horrible act. Her feeling was not softened by the realization that her child had been "executed" according to tribal law. The Comanche edict was inflexible—death was meted out mercilessly to anyone, no matter how helpless, who could not contribute to the tribal welfare. Rachel saw more than one aged Indian man or woman left to die alone on the cold mountains because they were too old and weak to travel. Death was a daily occurrence in the Comanche camp. Rachel herself often prayed for death to release her from her bondage.

From the mountains she traveled with the Comanches to the prairie, to the Salt Plains (or sand dunes) and then on to the Great Salt Lake. On these journeys she acquainted herself with the wild animals, for her captors taught her that her new religion was handed down to them through the lesser deities—the animals. The otter, the mink, the bear and the eagle had received the story of the origin of Creation direct from the Great Spirit, and these lower animals had imparted this information to the Comanches. Her immediate clan worshiped the eagle, so Rachel was given an eagle's wing to wear as the symbol of her tutelary god.

Dancing became a part of her new religion. Torturing prisoners was also a part of her new faith. She offered sacrifices to the gods through the shaman. Of course Rachel did not believe in the Comanches' religion, but it was expedient that she pretend that she did. Savage and terrible as the Comanches were, they were devout in their religious beliefs. During her stay with them Rachel saw several braves expelled from the tribe because they expressed disbelief in a supreme power.

She listened to her old mistress tell about the preposterous Man Tiger—a nine-foot-tall animal with features of a man, yet with paws and claws like a tiger. The Man Tiger was the protector of

159

the cave men, the pygmies of the mountains. The old squaw cautioned Rachel never to go into the mountains alone or to molest the three-foot pygmies for fear of frightful retaliation by the Man Tiger.

Rachel was always on the go. At one time or another she passed through the country of the Pawnees, the Navajos, the Chemuhuevi, the Apaches and other tribes. Once in the Rockies she picked up so many gold nuggets she had to get her young mistress to help carry them, but was forced to give them up to the old squaw who ruled her lodge. (This was twelve years before the California Gold Rush of 1849.)

At another time in the foothills of the Rockies, Rachel discovered a cave with rocks guarding its mouth. She made candles of buffalo tallow and explored the famous Carlsbad Caverns of New Mexico for two days and a night. Her description of the underground stream and her portrayal of the large rooms are proof that Rachel Plummer should long ago have been recognized as the true discoverer of this wonderland of North America.

She wrote, in part:

> . . . I felt a great anxiety to find out the cause of this strange scene, which upon close examination, was more splendid than the mind can conceive. Reader, you may fancy yourself viewing . . . an entirely new planetary system, a thousand times more sublime and more beautiful than our own, and you will fall far short of the reality I here witnessed. I soon discovered that these lights proceeded from the reflections of the light of the candle by the most innumerable crystallized formations in the rocks above, and on either side. The room I was in was large—say 100 feet wide—and its length was beyond my sight.

Bravely, Rachel Plummer pursued her journey to the bowels of the earth.

> For a distance of three or four miles [she goes on] the cave differed in appearance and width, but nothing worthy of notice was observed. The cave forked, the ceiling or roof of

the right hand fork being ten feet high and six feet wide. I went on and entered one of the most spacious and splendid rooms my eyes ever beheld.

On one side of this room was a clear, beautiful stream of water. She followed the stream until she heard the ominous roaring of the water as it fell down a precipice, before turning back.

When she came out of the cave, the Indians were astounded. They thought she had been lost in the bowels of the earth.

Life continued to be hard for Rachel. Rebelling against harsh treatment by her young mistress, she fought with the woman and knocked her down with a buffalo bone. The squaw begged for mercy, so Mrs. Plummer spared her life.

The Indians who had witnessed the brief fight surrounded Rachel, shouting and gesticulating wildly. She resigned herself to being killed, but the warriors patted her on the shoulder, crying *"Bueno! Bueno!"* The Comanches applauded her because they admired anyone who showed strength and courage, and they also approved her trait of showing mercy to a fallen foe. They named her "The Fighting Squaw."

But the fight with the younger woman led to a second and more serious encounter with the old mistress of the lodge. First ordering Rachel to bring in some hay, the spiteful old crone tried to tie her hands. Fearing treachery, Rachel resisted. The squaw then set fire to the hay and threw the blazing bundle on her. Painfully burned, Rachel grabbed her tormentor and held her close to the flaming grass. The wiry old woman fought furiously, and before the fight was over the old mistress was beaten almost into unconsciousness and the lodge was a shambles.

This was the second mistress that Rachel had subdued, and each had lost much face with the tribe. Again Rachel administered to the bruises of her defeated opponent.

But now Rachel was forced to stand trial in the Council House. The chief and twelve of the tribe's head men presided. After Rachel had been seated the chief rose, raised his right hand and beckoned her two mistresses to rise.

"Is it true that each of you has fought The Fighting Squaw?" he asked.

"It is true," they answered.

"Are all the facts true that we have discussed here?" went on the chief.

"Yes," they replied.

"Do either of you have anything further to say?"

"No," they answered.

"Then you are dismissed," concluded the chief.

Then came Rachel's turn to take the stand. The same preliminary questions were asked of her. She answered them, waiting tensely for the final question.

"Do you have anything to say before the Council passes sentence?" asked the chief.

"Yes, I have plenty to say!" she cried.

"Then speak!" the chief sternly bade her.

Rachel Plummer, in a cool, dignified manner, made her speech.

"I am going to tell you honorable men the truth if you kill me for it. My people had done nothing to the Comanches. We were living a quiet, peaceful life disturbing no one. We were close to your hunting grounds; perhaps that is why you attacked us.

"You took me dishonorably. You used the white flag of truce to trick me and my friends into death or slavery. You have killed my children.

"I have been with you many months, doing everything you asked of me. I have done slave labor because I was afraid you would kill me if I refused. But now—from this very minute—I will show you that I am not afraid of death. I await your sentence, but I warn you that the Great Spirit will punish you for the great harm you have done to me and my people."

Rachel sat down, hardly caring what the judges' decision would be. The head men powwowed briefly with the chief, and then the chief rose to speak.

"You—who show mercy on fallen foes—are part of the Great Spirit. We admire you, for no Indian shows mercy like you do.

You are now one of us, for anyone with courage and mercy can be Comanche."

The chief paused, then said solemnly, "I sentence you to go out and cut another tent pole to replace the one you tore down."

Almost fainting with relief, Rachel accepted her punishment provided that the mistresses helped her with the job. The judges agreed to The Fighting Squaw's request. From that time on, The Fighting Squaw was a respected personage in the tribe.

Though she had established herself with the Comanches, Rachel Plummer could never be reconciled to their ruthless, nomadic way of life. She had been on the move with them for nearly nineteen months. All that time she had worked like a slave, for the women were obliged to do all the heavy work of the camp. No woman could sit in the tribal councils, nor could she ask anything about the proceedings of the council. She was never told when or where the tribe was going to move.

A woman was bound with innumerable taboos. She could not broil and boil meat on the same fire. She could lose nothing or waste nothing in the preparation of the buffalo for food. She was forbidden to walk close enough to the fire to cast her shadow, as that would produce a dread spell of evil for the whole camp.

When one member of her lodge became sick, the shaman, or medicine man, appeared on the scene. In an opening between two lodges, the shaman started his weird incantations. He dug a hole under each tepee. In one hole he built a fire, while in the other he placed an exact mud replica of the patient's head. He then stuck willow twigs all about the two holes.

At sunrise the strange healing rites began. With solemn ceremony, the shaman led the patient into his makeshift hospital. Musicians accompanied the procession with weird music. The drums beat all day. No one was allowed to walk close enough to the fire to cast a shadow, for if this happened the sick man was doomed. If the patient died, the shaman conveniently laid the blame on unseen forces that had ruined his magical incantations. If he recovered, the shaman could collect a fee from the grateful relatives. Either way he couldn't lose.

Always curious, Rachel Plummer made many inquiries about the shamans. She learned that some of them pledged their life's work to becoming medicine men. They would go through one of the medicine lodges, which granted three or four degrees. Each degree cost the student a large amount in barter, and the farther he advanced in these secret meetings, the more each successive degree cost. At times a shaman had to pledge his life's savings in order to achieve the highest degree.

War chiefs and some other leaders usually inherited their positions within the tribe, but there were cases where some outstanding personal achievement helped to win a brave some coveted position. This was a way of rewarding those who possessed special skills, abilities or knowledge. Thus Rachel Plummer became "The Fighting Squaw" because of the prowess she displayed in the fights with her two mistresses.

When a comrade fell in battle, the Comanches shed no tears over him. If a slain warrior was scalped, however, his whole village swore vengeance.

One day a war party of Osage warriors attacked Rachel's camp. A few of the fallen Comanches were scalped. After the enemy had been driven off, the Comanches scalped the dead Osages, cut their bodies up and held a cannibalistic feast. Rachel's young mistress offered her a roasted human foot, but the captive politely declined the choice tidbit.

Some time later at a camping point somewhere west of the Rockies, a party of Mexican traders came into the Comanche village. They spotted the white woman at once and began negotiations with her master for her release. After much bickering, Rachel heard the old man agree to release her for a stipulated sum.

Rachel and the Mexican traders spent seventeen days on the trail before they reached Santa Fe, New Mexico. At the post there she was turned over to a Mr. Donaho, who had been working for her release ever since her capture. The people about the post collected $150 to send her back to her people in Texas, but for some unknown reason the pastor of the village church refused to give her the money. She then decided to accompany Mr. Donaho on his return trip to his home in Independence.

Mrs. Plummer was met at Independence by her brother-in-law, Mr. Nixon, who told her about the ones lost and the ones saved on that memorable day of the attack on Fort Parker. In return Rachel told of her own harsh experiences and the fate of her children. She could tell Mr. Nixon nothing of the whereabouts of Cynthia Ann and John Parker.

Rachel rode horseback from Independence, Missouri, to Texas. She found that her people had moved farther south in Texas to Montgomery County. They welcomed her joyfully and listened with rapt attention to her story of the nineteen hard months she had endured with the Comanches. Dry-eyed, she told of the tragic death of her second son and the disappearance of her little Jimmy. Her relatives were weeping when she finished speaking.

The experiences of Rachel's cousin Cynthia Ann Parker were quite different. Captured at the same time as Rachel, when she was only nine years old, Cynthia Ann lived with the Comanches for twenty-eight years and married Chief Pete Nocona. The last fourteen years of her life were spent with her uncle and brother-in-law, Mr. O'Quinn. Her small daughter, Prairie Flower, was buried near Edom, Texas, but her son Quanah became a chief of the Comanches. Cynthia Ann was buried in 1874 a few miles south of Poynor, Texas, in the Foster cemetery. Quanah removed her bones in the early 1900's to the Indian burial ground in Oklahoma.

Cynthia Ann's brother John Parker was released before he was grown, to become a substantial citizen in west Texas.

James Pratt Plummer was never seen again by his mother after his disappearance in the Comanche camp, but the Indians released him when he was thirteen years old. He became a good citizen and lived with white people for the rest of his life.

Rachel Plummer, health impaired by her long ordeal, did not live long after her liberation from the Comanches. She died on the nineteenth of February, 1839, one year after she reached home. She lies buried in Montgomery County.

Haze Over Chilkoot

by Charles McKenzie with Mac Hecht

In 1897 I had never heard of the snow-covered mountain of Chilkoot, nor of the old Injun warning concerning her. But I *did* have the uneasy feeling that I'd reached my last frontier— reached it the year before, in the wind-swept sheep country of Malheur and Harney counties of eastern Oregon.

The solitude of sheepherding that had seemed so satisfying two years ago had gone sour on me. Even the rattle of a wild-lily pod, shaken by the wind (that dry rattle that was identical with that of a coiled snake) didn't send me on a wild jump, my heart pounding, as it once had.

166

Haze Over Chilkoot

I wanted new scenes, new experiences, but I didn't know where to find them. My feet were always itching to move on, and so in my twenty-eight years of life I'd pushed westward halfway across the continent.

Born in Buchanan County in 1870, I'd moved with my parents to Gallatin County, Montana, in 1880. We'd farmed and raised cattle there until 1888. Then we took another hitch westward. We landed in Lane County of western Oregon, near Eugene. I worked with my father on the farm there until 1896.

Restless, I looked westward once more. But now, only eighty miles away across the fir-clad coast range, lay the rugged Pacific. But I *had* to keep moving. So I back-tracked to Eastern Oregon and settled down to sheepherding. I didn't stay settled long.

Just about the time I heard the blat of the first spring lamb, a fellow found gold on the Klondike River in the Yukon Territory. While I listened to the endless bleats and "baa-a-aas" of ranging sheep, others across the nation were hearing another sound. The sound of the big stampede.

The big stampede of 1897!

Men and women, fired by dreams of untold wealth, rushed by crowded boatloads towards the Klondike and the treasure hidden there. Hardly had the thunder of their passing died, before tales concerning them came flooding back. Tales of fabulous strikes, of nests of nuggets big as hen's eggs, of paupers becoming rich overnight.

Other tales drifted back too. Tales of disaster and privation. Tales of the penalties the untamed North exacted from those who would rob her of her treasure. These stories were discounted or cast aside. Only the golden tales counted. Those—and getting North as fast as one could.

I was like the rest of them. The gold fever flamed in me, and I knew I'd have to go.

So I came back to Eugene in the fall of '97 and made preparations for departure. By late February of '98 I was ready. I had a little under $1,000 in my pocket and was crazy to be off.

167

I went to Portland but had to wait there until I could get a boat to Juneau. At last I booked passage on the *George W. Elder,* paying $35 for my ticket.

Then the *George W. Elder* was on her way, and I was headed towards the land of gold. But Nature stepped in right away. We only got as far as Astoria, Oregon, a distance of 105 miles, then found out that it was too stormy to cross the bar. We laid overnight in Astoria.

It was rough next morning, too; but we sailed anyway. Right away the *George W. Elder* got a new name. We called her the *George W. Roller.*

We had a rough voyage, but it didn't scare us much. The boat was loaded to capacity and we were potential millionaires—every one. None of us were too uneasy about a group of soldiers on the boat. These soldiers were being sent to Dawson as a relief expedition by the government. Rumors of famine had drifted back to the States; and the soldiers were being sent to relieve it.

We made Juneau in about a week's time. I stopped over for a week or so and laid in my supplies. I bought flour, bacon, beans, evaporated potatoes, rice, coffee, sugar, dried fruit, lots of tobacco, salt, soda, and a few simple medicines. Then I bought a tent, a Yukon stove, blankets and an endless variety of needed tools and clothes. Last of all I bought my Yukon sled. It was seven feet long and sixteen inches wide. The gee pole was seven feet long. It was fastened to the side of the sled and functioned as both brake and steering apparatus. When I had finished my buying, I had an outfit of around sixteen hundred pounds.

The next step was to decide where I was to land in Alaska. There were two places possible—two trails to take that would eventually lead to the chain of rivers and lakes that was the route to Dawson. Dawson was where the Klondike and Yukon rivers met.

These two settlements each lay on a fork at the head of the Lynn Canal. The mountain bordering Lynn Canal extended north of Juneau. Dyea lay on the left fork, Skagway on the right. A few came into the Klondike by way of Edmonton, capital of Alberta, but I never did find out the exact route they took.

Dyea was an Injun village before the gold rush. The Dyea Trail started here and ran up the towering mountain of Chilkoot, through the pass, on her summit and on to Lake Linderman.

Skagway settlement was an Injun village before the gold rush too. The Skagway Trail was a high trail and could be traveled by horse. It bypassed Lake Linderman and ended up at Lake Bennet. But the Skagway Trail was longer. So I decided to take the Chilkoot Trail, even if it did lead up to the clouds.

My mind made up as to my destination, I caught a small Alaskan steamer for Dyea. This little boat was overloaded with men and supplies, but we got along all right until we reached the Lynn Canal. As nearly as I can judge, the canal is about eighty miles inland.

We'd just entered her when a wild storm roared down on us. The *George W. Roller* was a rocking chair compared to our little boat then. The rain lashed and froze on everything it touched. We wallowed an entire day in the canal. When we finally sighted the lights of Dyea that night, our boat was covered with ice with the exception of her smokestack.

Dyea sat on a long, sloping beach, just above tidewater. The beach was fully a mile long. Our boat took us in as far as she could. Then we scrambled ashore and staggered groggily up that long beach towards those twinkling lights. Our goods would be floated in during the night. Lighters, or small boats, from Dyea met each steamer and floated the goods in on high tide. This service was sold to us by the steamship company along with our tickets.

My legs felt like rubber, and my stomach kept doing somersaults as I plodded through the night. I found a bed in a hotel and rolled into it.

The next thing I knew the sun was shining in my face. It took me a while to realize where I was. Strange sounds beat against my eardrums. Even as I lay there I sensed the urgency of those sounds.

169

Then I remembered my outfit, waiting to be claimed, and I lost no time in getting dressed.

As I hurried towards the beach, the strangeness of this new land jarred the cobwebs from my brain. My home, in the rain-swept Williamette Valley, 1,300 miles away, seemed to belong to another world.

It was the last of March now, and there was a sting to the snow-chilled air. The sun was blazing down, though, and the temperature hung just above the freezing mark.

Dyea was only a huddle of raw shacks, saloons, gambling houses, a hotel, boardinghouses and tents. Snow-clad mountains reared in every direction. A river flowed through the town. This was the Dyea River. Willows, cottonwoods, elders and some spruce grew along the river. In the distance loomed the white-topped coast range. That mountain range I would have to cross to get into Canadian Territory on my way to the Klondike.

Thousands milled around Dyea. They crowded the saloons and restaurants. They overflowed the street and beach. Injuns were everywhere. They lugged packs up from the beach and worked for the white man in any way they could. Their guttural voices mingled with those of men shouting at their teams, the barking of dogs, the crunch of footsteps on snow and the shushing of sled runners. The smell of spruce intermingled with the wood smoke of a thousand campfires. Over all hung the sweat-tainted smell of man.

Excitement flooded through me. This was my world now. It was what I'd been seeking so long. This—and what lay ahead. But I was only one of the raw *cheechakos*. That's Chinook for "newcomers." Chinook is a jargon gotten up by the Hudson's Bay Company. "One is never a sourdough until he has seen the ice come and go on the Yukon," I'd been told on the boat.

I'll outstay them all! Charles Edwin McKenzie, an old sourdough.

I grinned as I headed towards the beach.

The lighters had floated our stuff up the beach to within one half-mile of Dyea. A great mountain of stuff was piled on the beach. A fellow read out our names and checked us off as we claimed our goods. My goods were all marked C. E. McK. I answered for three fellows from the boat who hadn't shown up yet.

I moved my outfit up the beach a way, then went to find a driver and a team to sled me up to Sheep Camp, the next step in my journey.

I couldn't find a team at first. Workers and horses were few; the gold seekers many. Finally I put my name in with a driver and, wild as I was to be off, had to wait my turn. The price for sledding an outfit up to Sheep Camp, twelve miles away, was ten dollars. It didn't seem too high to me.

I had to wait three days in Dyea. The time wasn't wasted, though. I studied maps and learned all I could about the treacherous chain of lakes and rivers that I would have to travel. Long Lake, Lake Linderman, Miles Canyon, with its deadly twin whirlpools, Squaw Rapids, White Horse Rapids, Five Finger Rapids and Windy Arm took their places on the maps and in my mind. The more I heard about what lay ahead, the more anxious I was to get started.

I saw our soldiers again during my wait in Dyea. I was glad to learn that the famine rumors were unfounded. They were still in Dyea when I left.

A fellow told me something while I was in Dyea that made me realize how far gold hunger can drive a man. He said a man had an old gray mare. He hauled outfits and supplies from Skagway to Lake Bennet with her. The mare brought a fat sum into her master's pockets, and he loaded her heavily. On one trip to Lake Bennet the mare plodded along slower and slower. Just as she reached her destination, she collapsed and died.

Man talked with man while we waited, and I heard again and again of a strange party of three who were going into Dawson with us—a woman and two men. The woman, her husband and—her ex-husband. All traveling together, cozy as you please.

There was another strange party of three in the Dawson-headed crowd. There were two men and a woman in this party too. The outstanding thing about them was that they were all Negroes and that one of the men had flaming red hair. He weighed around 160 pounds and was light-colored. Among the thousands of faces his was unforgettable. His companions were much darker and of average size.

Seeing the mountains of goods piled around, lots of times with nothing but markings to protect them, worried me at first. "What about all these outfits stacked in the open?" I asked a big fellow with friendly dark eyes and an easy grin. "They'd be a big temptation to anyone with itching fingers, wouldn't they?"

The grin left the man's face and his eyes grew rock hard.

"I don't think anyone will be anxious to steal from the other fellow. *Not* when they hear what we did to a thief last week."

"Treated him pretty rough?" I asked.

"We just gave him the beginning of what Nature will probably finish." He spit a stream of tobacco juice and started after it as it stained the snow. Then he turned to me. "We caught him at Sheep Camp," he went on. "We stripped him of every supply he had. Even his pocketknife. Then we sent him kiting off down the trail. We passed along the word of what he'd done, and you may be sure no one is going to take pity on him. Even the Injuns hate a thief.

"Up here, we figure a thief is the same as a murderer. A man's outfit is his life line. Robbed of that, he'll die."

"Wouldn't he have any chance at all to get out?"

The big fellow eyed me queerly. "The only way would be to catch the first boat out. *But—his reputation went ahead of him.*"

I kept a close watch on my team and driver. Boats kept coming in all the time; new arrivals swarmed up the beach. I grew maddened at the delay. It seemed that everyone was moving ahead but me.

Men drifted back down from Dawson too. Some with gold to scatter at the gambling tables, others wild to catch the first boat out.

172

I teamed up with Billy Hardwick from Nebraska, and we asked all the questions we could. Then my turn came with the team.

Sheep Camp lay twelve miles or so up the canyon from Dyea. It was a rough little plateau of three or four acres part way up Chilkoot Mountain. It was said that it got its name from a party of American explorers while Alaska still belonged to Russia.

These men came upon a party of Russians camped there. They tried asking them questions. The Russians talked back as hard as they could, but one of the explorers exclaimed in disgust, "Might as well talk to a bunch of sheep!"

Sheep Camp was a beehive of activity when we arrived. Teams were working up from Dyea. Hundreds of camps were crowded together, and goods were piled sky high. Men, and a scattering of women, bent under heavy loads, staggered up the mountain to the summit three miles above Sheep Camp. Far up on that dizzy summit was Chilkoot Pass, gateway to the Klondike.

"Think we'll ever make it, Charlie?" Billy Hardwick squinted his eyes as he watched pack-burdened men digging their way up its snowy sides.

"We can if they can," I said. "Let's get started."

I built my pack up to two hundred pounds. Then I cut a heavy club to use in climbing. When I rested I could slip the club under my pack and take the weight off of my shoulders. Then I strapped the pack on my back and started out.

There were thousands ahead of me on the trail. It was just above freezing, but the sun was blazing down. I had on a hooded mackinaw but hadn't gone far before I had to throw it back. I was sweating before I'd gone half a mile.

Two miles from Sheep Camp the spruce timber stopped, and I came out above timber line, at Stone House. Everything was white from here on.

Stone House wasn't a house at all. It was a huge, house-shaped rock. It was covered with snow, so I don't know how it really looked. Someone had put a can here and dug a deep, well-like hole in the snow at the base of the rock. This hole was five or six

173

feet deep, with running water at its bottom. No one passed up the chance for a drink of water. My tongue felt like cloth as I waited my turn at the can. Then I stepped down in the hole and scooped up a drink. It tasted wonderful.

Some teams sledded up as far as Stone House, at an extra-high fee; but from there on clear to the summit it was a back-packing job. The trail really got rugged from Stone House on. One could just make it without hewed steps. I divided my pack here and restrapped a hundred-pound sack on my shoulders.

As I went along I noticed outfits stacked along the trail with "For Sale" signs on them. My shoulder straps cut my back, and breathing became more difficult. A half-mile beyond Stone House, a fellow had a tarpaper shack. He had a restaurant here and sold good meals. The shack was about ten by twelve feet. If anyone lugged a good-sized piece of wood up the mountain to him, he got his dinner free.

A little beyond the restaurant was another place of business. It was a snow dugout or cave. A man served water or lemonade here. Both drinks were the same price, fifteen cents each.

A few feet from the snow house were The Scales. A tarpaper shack housed them. Injuns and others carried packs up The Steps to the summit. They charged two cents a pound and weighed in at The Scales before the big climb.

The big climb! I stared upward for 1,000 feet, and there was a stairway of ice-carved steps all the way. These were The Steps. Injuns had carved them in the dim past to get up to the summit of Chilkoot and the pass. A white man had charge of them now. A huge rope hung down the side of the steps from the summit. It was anchored at the bottom with stakes driven into the ground. A great heap of rocks held the stakes down. The rope was fully an inch thick at the bottom and was used exactly as a stair rail. Thousands of hands, pulling on the rope, had worn it as thin as a man's finger at the top. It was anchored here, too, with stakes and rocks. The steps were about one and one-half feet wide.

A money box was at the bottom of the steps. We dropped ten

cents or fifteen cents in for the keeper every time we made a trip to the summit. He kept busy at them all day long, with a shovel and a broom.

I took my place in line. Grabbing the rope with one hand and digging down with my club. I started up those icy stairs. When I finally came to a resting place, I stopped to get my breath. A resting place was a pair of twin side steps, just large enough to hold a man and his pack.

The summit was rough, but I found a high place and started my cache.

The pass was a gap at the summit. Through this pass, on the other side of the mountain, lay Canadian Territory.

A fellow packed his entire outfit to his cache on the summit. He then slid them down the Canadian side, a sled load at a time. About 1,000 feet below the summit he hit frozen Round Lake. This lake was the first of the chain of lakes and rivers on his route to Dawson and the Klondike.

I was watching a fellow riding a canvas down the slide, behind his loaded sled. A mountain of goods was piled at the lake's edge. His sled got away from him, and I saw it plow into that pile of goods. A second later a golden cloud exploded into the air. He had hit someone's cornmeal sack.

I made two trips a day from Sheep Camp to the summit. As I packed I noticed an outfit with a blame good pocketknife stuck carelessly into one of the boxes on its top. Thousands passed and repassed that outfit every day, but when I made my final trip the knife was still there.

I saw things take place at The Steps during that time that were hard to believe. I saw a medium-sized Injun pack a two-hundred-pound barrel of pitch up The Steps. A barrel, or anything round, was the hardest of all loads to carry. They wouldn't fit to a fellow's back. I found that out when I packed my Yukon stove up The Steps. This Injun did it again and again.

Another big fellow from Eugene packed for hire all the time.

I've seen him pack four one-hundred-pound sacks of flour up at one time.

But the most amazing thing of all was "the crazy German." That's what I called him in my mind. Impatient to reach the summit and refusing to take his turn in line on The Steps, he clawed his way up the rough ice beside The Steps. None of us believed he'd make it, but he did.

I learned a quick way to get down the side of Chilkoot without going the long way back by the Peterson Trail. A slide ran parallel with The Steps. After I'd slid down once, I found out that the seat of a man's pants can feel mighty thin. I used a canvas to ride down on after that.

A little over a week's hard packing, and I had my outfit all cached on the summit. I was really relieved when I boosted my Yukon sled to the top of the pile. It was early April now, and the sun blazed down; but a sharp wind was blowing. I felt so good that I made two trips to the summit for hire. The four dollars that I earned on those trips made me feel better than ever. I could hardly wait to go through the pass. But I'd promised Billy that I'd spend a night with him before I shoved off.

The wind was still blowing and a thin haze was forming over the summit as I turned back. It was snowing when I got back to Sheep Camp.

It was still snowing heavily the next morning, so we decided to stay in camp. I kept thinking about my cache up on the summit and wondering how soon I could get back up there. *Delay again! It's what I'd had from the start! Would I never get started?*

About eleven o'clock the snow thinned and the wind died. I'd made up my mind to start right away, when a man came plunging and yelling down the trail.

"Snowslide!" he panted. "A lot are caught in it! Help!"

He collapsed on the snow.

I grabbed up one shovel, Billy another, and we joined the hundreds streaming up the trail. We met several survivors. They told us what had happened. Fifty or more of them had been at the summit when a blizzard started up. Afraid, they had started back for Sheep Camp. They all took hold of one guide rope as they worked their way down the trail. The avalanche roared down upon them as they rounded a slight curve about a mile beyond The Scales.

By the time we had covered the two miles to where the slide blocked the trail, we found hundreds ahead of us, all digging desperately. I saw right away what had happened. This was a straight snowslide, with no rocks or dirt in it. The wet, new snow had piled up on the old crusted snow and had started sliding. It gathered up more snow as it went along, until there was a slide of twelve to fifteen feet deep and two hundred to three hundred feet wide. It gathered weight and depth as it went along.

I couldn't get in where the rest were digging. But someone told me that there was a smaller slide just off the main trail, between Stone House and The Scales. It was in the location of a worker's camp, so I went there.

I didn't see how anyone could have been caught in this slide. It was only about a hundred yards long and not much wider than across the trail. It wasn't more than ten or twelve feet deep in any place, and it petered out at the trail.

I dug my shovel into the wet snow and loosened a chunk the size of a bushel basket. Others joined me and we worked frantically. Lifting that wet snow was back-breaking work, and I was sweating and panting before I'd worked ten minutes. But I kept at it hard as I could. If anyone was under there I wanted him out.

I'd been digging about half an hour when my shovel slipped down suddenly. I brought it up full of snow, and saw a hole underneath. Another shovelful showed me that I'd struck a hollow in the snow. Underneath the vaultlike hollow was a body.

The body of a man lying in a sleeping bag. The hollow was caused by the warmth of his body melting the snow. One look at his face jarred me to a standstill, my shovel rigid in my hands. It was congested. Almost black.

Others were finding victims too. They uncovered two more

bodies. Both were lying in bed. Each body with its vaultlike hollow above it. Each face congested.

Silently, feverishly, we worked.

Then we found *him*. The sole survivor of that tiny workers' camp of four. We uncovered the ox. We found him chewing away at the baled hay that had saved his life. Those piled-up bales had made a little margin of safety. So slight it was that one of the dead men's feet was touching the hind foot of the ox.

I stared at the chewing animal, hardly believing my eyes. In the week or more that I'd been packing up the trail I hadn't even heard of an ox.

Satisfying ourselves that there were no more victims here, we went back to the big slide. Victims were being uncovered here too. The guide rope aided the searchers in their task. They had only to locate it, dig down and uncover a victim.

I had no idea that a doctor was going into Dawson with us until I found him busy at the slide. His name was Dr. Cleveland. He gave first aid to anyone brought up alive. He had the living taken up to the powerhouse. This was a tarpaper shack put up by the tram company at the summit, but neither tramway nor house was finished. All of the survivors were in bad shape. I don't know how many of them died.

The dead were taken down to Sheep Camp. A tent was set up as a morgue and the stiffened bodies were placed in it. At last fifty-three lay there.

Then came the task of trying to identify those congested faces. Dr. Cleveland took charge of the identification. As soon as a man was identified, the doctor made out a report to be sent to his relatives in the States.

One woman was caught in the avalanche. She was buried upright but was still alive when she was taken out. Her condition was bad, and she was rushed up to the powerhouse. She was the woman traveling with two husbands.

Those that escaped, at the end of the rope, told how she was caught in the slide. She was on the very end of the rope when they started down the trail. But she became worried over her husbands, who were farther up, and had started up the rope to catch them. She hadn't caught up with them when I went over the pass. They were both taken out dead.

We dug for three days and were finally satisfied that there was no one else under the snow. Those taken out alive told a curious thing. They said they could hear us running over them, could hear our voices and our shovels, but found it hard to shout for help.

I began sledding my outfit through The Pass and down to Round Lake. We had the trail opened, and everyone was wild to be on his way. The dead had only to wait. The ice waited for no man.

They were holding an auction on the summit the day I went up there for the last time. An auction of the slide victims' goods. Someone told me that the proceeds were to be sent back to the men's families.

I stood there watching the bidding. "Outfit—J. M. B. What am I bid for this one?" The auctioneer's voice singsonged. There was no laughter among the bidders. No joking. Each of us was thinking of the men who had gotten these outfits together. They had struggled up Chilkoot only to be defeated in the end. We thought of their loved ones, waiting back in the States. *Waiting for the men who might have been us!*

"Twenty-five! Who'll make it fifty?"

I turned and stared in the direction of Sheep Camp. I couldn't see the tent of the dead from here, but I knew where it was. Its occupants were still unburied, unmindful of our rushing by. Then I wondered how many of us would reach the Klondike with its golden promise.

Footsteps crunched past me, hurrying through the pass. I glanced up. It was the Negro party. For a moment before they went through the pass, the sun flamed on a Negro's red hair. I had no way of knowing then that Death waited for him at White Horse Rapids or that I was never to know the fate of the other two.

"Going—going—gone!" The auctioneer was hurrying now. I glanced up at the sky. It was clear and blue. Perhaps if we had known about the old Injun warning I wouldn't be hearing his singsong now.

"When the wind blows and haze gathers over Chilkoot, there's danger ahead. Stay away from the summit."

That was their warning, but we'd learned it too late.

I threw myself down on my canvas and clutched the sled runners. Then I shoved off. Five hundred miles away the Klondike beckoned.

Laughing Killer!

by Norman B. Wiltsey

Many of the old-time Western badmen were, by modern psychiatric standards, real gone crackpots. Clay Allison was one of the worst. Clay's weird behavior indicates conclusively that he was of the manic-depressive type of psychopath, alternating between moods of wild elation and blackest despair. On the mad upswing of his emotional curve, Allison was about as fantastic a character as you'd be apt to meet outside a padded cell.

There was the time Clay put on a frontier "Lady Godiva" act for the amazed and amused citizens of Canadian, Texas. Stripped to the skin—except, of course, for gunbelt, boots and sombrero—Allison rode down Main Street at full gallop on Saturday night, standing upright in his stirrups and whooping endearing remarks to the scandalized women on the sidewalk. Proud as a prince and naked as a jaybird, he rode the entire length of Main Street and

181

dismounted in front of a saloon. Posing gracefully in the doorway, Clay doffed his sombrero with a grand flourish and invited his fascinated audience inside for a drink.

Not all of Allison's mad stunts were as harmless. Challenged to a duel to the death by an outraged Texan, Clay promptly chose Bowie knives as weapons and a deep, open grave for a dueling ground. The grave would also double as a last resting place for the loser. Clay's shaken opponent, pale but game, accepted the unique terms. Allison carved him up and left him dead in the grave. Well-sliced himself, Clay climbed out of the gory trench dripping blood and laughing insanely. The tendons of his right leg were injured so badly in this sanguinary affair he walked with a limp the rest of his life. Maybe it made sense to Allison; it failed to impress the sickened spectators.

Uneasy ego drove Allison to challenge any rival six-gun ace to a showdown—which he generally maneuvered to look like a case of "shooting in self-defense."

Wyatt Earp was one gunfighter who turned the tables neatly on Clay. Allison, who displayed twenty-one notches on his gun at the time, boasted that he had killed six lawmen and planned to add Marshal Earp of Dodge City, Kansas, to his "dead list."

Warned of Allison's boast, Wyatt said merely, "Let him come and make his play. I'll be waiting."

Up from Las Animas, New Mexico, rode Clay on his cream-white "war horse," dressed all in black and white, with his jet mustache acurl. Six feet two in height, slim-hipped, wide-shouldered, with flashing blue eyes, Allison could have made any of today's cowboy film stars take a back seat when it came to good looks and dramatic appearance. In addition to being a screwball, he was a terrific ham and as inordinately vain as a chorus girl.

Marshal Earp and gunman Allison met in front of the Long Branch Saloon on a warm summer morning in 1877. Both men were dressed similarly as to color scheme, but where Clay sported a showy white buckskin vest trimmed with silver *conchos*, Wyatt wore a plain white shirt adorned only with his silver star of office.

Earp stopped short at sight of Allison and leaned against the wall of the saloon, thus forcing Clay to approach him from in front. Around the two crack gun-slingers, space was suddenly cleared as if an invisible, giant hand had whisked away the apprehensive bystanders.

Allison advanced mincingly in his fancy high-heeled boots.

"You Earp?" he demanded.

"I'm *Marshal* Earp," corrected Wyatt significantly.

Clay strutted closer, "I've been *lookin'* for you."

"You've found me, then."

Allison lurched suddenly against Earp; the marshal felt Clay's stomach muscles tighten as he went for his gun. He hadn't cleared leather when the muzzle of Earp's "Buntline Special"—a presentation .45 Colt with a twelve-inch barrel—prodded Clay in the belly.

"Drop it, Clay!" snapped Wyatt.

Allison dropped the half-drawn weapon back into its holster as though it were red hot. "Hell, Wyatt, I was only jokin'," he grinned.

Earp failed to smile. "Get out of Dodge and take your jokes with you," he suggested grimly.

Clay wheeled, climbed aboard his cream-white horse and left town on the gallop. His humiliation was complete; he never made trouble in Dodge again.

Basically Allison was always unsure of himself, so his ruthless, neurotic mind was constantly scheming to get a decisive edge on a dangerous opponent. He once sat facing gunman Chunk Colbert across a restaurant table in Clifton, New Mexico, for two solid hours in a marathon test of nerves. Both men acted in the same maniacal manner: laughing, talking, stirring numerous cups of coffee with the barrels of their six-shooters. Colbert's shrieking nerves snapped first, and he made his belated break. Clay—who had his countermove planned precisely in advance—upset the light table with his knees, dumping it in Colbert's lap, coffee and all. Chunk got off one shot that flew wild; Clay threw one slug that drilled Colbert through the forehead. Another case of "shooting in self-defense" for killer Allison.

Once Allison, game leg and all, "danced" his way out of a situation that could easily have wound up for him in a one-way trip to Boot Hill.

Cowpuncher Frank Cattlin accidentally jostled Clay's elbow at a bar one day, spilling the gunman's liquor. Deep in one of his black moods, Allison still retained enough sense to realize that the crowd would not stand for his shooting an unarmed man. Accordingly he jerked his gun and ordered Frank to dance to the tune of bullets chewing up the wooden floor around his feet. Cattlin danced as ordered—but when Clay's gun was empty and the surly killer had turned again to his drinking without bothering to reload, Frank stepped outside and borrowed a Colt from a friend. Returning, the angry cowboy pushed the muzzle of the cocked .45 roughly into Allison's ribs and barked, "Now, damn you, *you* dance!"

Dance Clay did, wincing at the painful sting of powder blast accompanying each shot. His bad leg gave out at the fourth crashing shot, and he tumbled down in the dirty sawdust at Cattlin's feet. Lying in this undignified position, head resting on a filthy spittoon, Allison underwent a lightning change of mood. He grinned up at Frank Cattlin and bawled, "Goddam it, boy, you've taught me a good lesson! Help me up and I'll buy you a drink!"

Professional gamblers in the joint offered odds that Frank Cattlin would be a dead pigeon before sundown and got no takers. Inexplicably Allison never sought to rectify his loss of face by killing Cattlin. He drank steadily for an hour, mumbled something about having a toothache and reeled out the door, seeking a dentist.

The tooth-yanker, understandably nervous at having the famed gunman in his chair, pulled the wrong tooth. Sobered by the pain, Clay discovered his loss immediately. Bellowing like a wounded buffalo, he lashed the terrified dentist to his own torture seat and

184

pulled three of his teeth in retaliation—with his own forceps and *without* benefit of anesthesia.

In Dodge City, Clay had meekly knuckled under to Wyatt Earp —but in New Mexico he was a law unto himself. Hank Lambert's saloon in Cimarron was his unofficial headquarters. Here he ruled as sadistic tyrant or benevolent despot, as the mood hit him. One night he roared out his intention of shooting out all the swinging oil lamps in the place. The worried proprietor summoned the marshal to pacify him. Marshal Pancho tried to talk Clay out of the brainless idea. Allison listened sullenly without saying a word. Finally, in a nervous gesture, Pancho removed his sombrero and dropped hand and hat to the level of his waist. Instantly Clay pulled a gun and shot him dead.

Allison was not even arrested for this shocking, cold-blooded murder. He claimed that the marshal had used his sombrero as a shield to hide his gun hand while he attempted to draw. As Pancho had no warrant for his arrest, Clay maintained he had a legal right to protect himself. Nobody challenged this ridiculous assertion.

In Las Animas Clay and his brother John attended a shindig at a local dance hall. It was western etiquette to check all shooting irons before shaking a merry hoof with the gals, but the Allisons delighted in breaking all rules of genteel conduct. Marshal Charlie Faber politely asked the swaggering brothers to turn over their guns and was told to go to hell. Faber left the hall and returned with a double-barreled shotgun. He ordered John Allison to throw up his hands. John went for his Colt instead and took half a dozen Number-0 buckshot through his gun arm. Firing from a far corner of the room, Clay put a slug through the marshal's heart. Miraculously only one "innocent bystander" was hit by flying lead in this scrap, and he was not seriously wounded.

Again the crafty killer pleaded self-defense. "Faber had another load of buckshot in his gun and was out to get all the Allisons he could," argued Clay in a Las Animas courtroom. The bemused jury agreed with Allison and set him free.

Shortly thereafter Clay bulldozed his way into an appointment as foreman of a grand jury in Las Animas. He proceeded to lead the jurors in a twenty-eight-day-and-night session, during which no court business was transacted but everybody stayed happily drunk on liquor provided by Foreman Allison. When the bills came in it was discovered that Clay had indeed paid for the whiskey—but with county warrants signed by himself.

Allison took a short "vacation" after this escapade, and came whooping back into town to find court in session. He rode his war horse into the courtroom and ordered court adjourned until he left town again. The judge hesitated to obey—and Clay put a bullet through the wall just above the judge's head. Court adjourned.

For all the foregoing indictment it must not be rashly assumed that Clay Allison was a totally bad *hombre*. In his lucid moments he fancied himself as a sort of frontier Robin Hood, fighting gallantly for the weak, helpless and oppressed. For example Clay personally avenged the brutal holdup murder of Cimarron's beloved Methodist preacher, the Reverend F. J. Tolby. Allison helped run down the murderers, "assisted" at the hanging of one and summarily "executed" the other. It is also claimed by some folks that Clay staked the widow and her two small children to train fare back East.

In 1880 Allison sold his ranch and left Cimarron to buy a new and larger "spread" of land on the Blackwater in the lower Pecos Valley. Ranch house built and a responsible foreman hired, he returned to his old home in Tennessee to marry his boyhood sweetheart and bring her back with him to New Mexico.

Marriage put an end to Allison's career as a badman and killer. His somnolent conscience awakened at last, he strove mightily to atone for past crimes. He was kind to the poor Mexican kids who lived in the 'dobe huts of his field workers, bought them clothing and candy and provided medical care when needed. In every way possible he tried to even the long, bloody score against him and—who knows?—perhaps he partially succeeded. He paid in suffering when his first-born child arrived cruelly deformed in body; he paid in bitter remorse throughout the long nights when he couldn't sleep and drove his matched team of trotters to a steaming lather across the dark countryside.

The strange manner of Clay Allison's death has been attributed to grim retribution and to sheer, blind chance, according to varying viewpoints. Contemporary reports reflect this confusion; some state that Clay was drunk at the time of his death, others indignantly deny the harsh allegation.

Driving near his ranch one day, Clay overtook an old teamster trying feebly to restrain his nervous young horses on a steep grade. He stopped his trotters, offering to drive the skittish team to the bottom of the hill.

The old man thankfully accepted, setting his brake and climbing stiffly down from his precarious perch on the big load of saw logs.

Allison, an expert horseman, anticipated little difficulty guiding the wild young team safely down the hill. Maybe he *was* drunk—in any case, he forgot one all-important factor in his own physical condition. Halfway down the rocky grade he shoved his right foot down hard on the brake to slow his plunging descent. The atrophied leg muscles and weakened tendons were not equal to the sudden strain. The leg buckled, and the frightened team lunged forward as the brake slacked off. Clay grabbed for the iron rail of the seat, but the tilting wagon struck a rock at the side of the road and hurled him to the ground.

The right rear wheel crunched over his head, killing him instantly.

Mi Ashe Ton Gaxas

(Stealths of the Dark Moon)

by Shatka Bear-Step

AUTHOR'S NOTE: The following events occurred in the lives of three American Indians—tribal renegades and horse thieves, who established a precedent that saved the lives of many white pioneers of the early West.

"Put fun in your life while you may, young man. The downhill slope is steeper than you think!" Those were the words of one of the great leaders of his profession; Go Don Bear-Step, Sagamore of the *Mi Ashe Ton Gaxas* of the Bear-Step Clan, horse thieves par excellence.

A half-century ago, when it was winter in Oklahoma and Jack Frost painted fantastic pictures upon glass windows, a proud youngster was permitted to keep an open fire burning, the pipes well filled and the coffee ready for three heroes of another era.

The privileged one was looked upon with envy by other young-sters because he was allowed to "sit in," almost within the circle of the "Old Bloods," and to learn their secrets and listen to wild adventure tales of three silver-haired demigods of yesteryear, while they smoked and lived in retrospect the many events that had been crammed into their thrill-packed lives. The voice of the "coffee cooler" was not to be heard—except in laughter at their unique humor—but his ears were well open and his memory retentive enough to reiterate here a few of the pranks played by the three Indian heroes of a bygone era.

There was Heconida (White Horn), the proud Omaha who had served with the Dog Soldiers of the Cheyenne to learn their philosophy and, incidentally, their horse-heisting technique. He was well built and straight as an arrow. His regular features, snow-white hair and unique philosophy branded every inch of him the aristocrat. The many pierces in his ears showed that he had once been a man of great wealth.

There was Otopasco, the Pinal Apache—deep-chested, powerful and silent. His laughing eyes and immobile features made you wonder whether he had the goods on you or was just glad to be alive.

Then there was Go Don Bear-Step the Cherokee-Comanche, recognized as a great leader by Heconida and Otopasco many, many moons before he became the idolized grandfather of this writer.

There was, indeed, an All American Indian combination that puzzled most of the people who knew their Indians. It was similar to the dog, cat and raccoon combination—natural enemies getting along together like bread and gravy. It couldn't happen, but it did. And others would say an Omaha and a Comanche could not trespass so far into the Crow, Shoshone, Ute, Paiute and Hopi

189

countries without being killed. It couldn't happen, but Bear-Step and Heconida did it.

Grandpa Bear-Step was born of an aristocratic mother, "Cherokee the Civilized." He was taught to speak, read and write in English, Spanish and Sequoia, (written Cherokee). He also spoke Comanche. All through his boyhood days the culture of the Cherokee was instilled in his heart, while the muffled wolf song of the Comanche tormented his soul. So, typical of the mix-breed when the wild goose called, he succumbed to the stifled thirst for adventure in faraway places, and the instinct of his Comanche father held sway.

In Montana, where the Big Missouri flows north, he cut an Arapahoe arrow from a young Omaha-Ponca named Heconida, or White Horn, and thus began a lifelong friendship. Food was plentiful, and the stinking hide-and-fur business was no fun. So trading in high-spirited horses led them down the wind from cold winters southward through Ute, Paiute, Navajo, Hopi, and the very dangerous Mormon countries.

While retreating from some hot-headed Mormons, they all but overran a Pinal Apache who had also met with Mormon rebuff for his unsuccessful attempt at horse stealing. Sunrise found the three renegades in hiding together in an ancient ruin of the Verde Valley. Here it was learned that the three of them had much in common; mainly, a great love for good horses, a feeling of appreciation for each other's company, and a limited knowledge of the English language.

So Otopasco, the Pinal Apache strong man, was accepted as third member of the party without ceremony. Here were the waters that had sought and found their own level; here were three exceptional men, each in his own right a skillful pony heister. But what made practical sense, here was a combination of three hellions who among them could converse in Omaha, Ponca, Sioux, Cheyenne, Cherokee, Comanche, Apache, Spanish, English and the universal sign language of all the tribes. Here was condensed the cream of the cunning, skimmed from the aforemen-

190

tioned tribes and now under the shrewd supervision of a Cherokee with a Great Smoky education and the sure instinct of the Comanche. Here were representatives of three of the greatest tribes of horsemen (and horse appraisers) on earth. They were destined to go places together.

"*Mi ashe ton gaxas,* stealths of the darkened moon," Heconida translated his native Omaha into English. "We should do well together."

There were no articles of corporation, pledges or oaths of partnership. Silent mutual nods of approval linked the friendship that never was broken. And it was there on the Verde River, while the three stealths were camped in the cottonwoods near the ancient ruins of Sugarloaf, that the Bear-Step Clan was born.

So the three *Gaxas* plied their crafty trade and improved with practice. Vacationing during light of the moon and working seven nights out of the twenty-eight, they enjoyed life and did well. They were wily and alert at all times, and caution was their watchword.

White Horn was the official daytime scout. While Otopasco tended camp and the stolen horses, Grandpa Bear-Step would sit on a high spot and smoke his pipe and keep an eye on both of them. Sometimes White Horn would be miles away, but his signal mirror blinked the message—"strange riders coming." Then Grandpa relayed it on to Otopasco, who destroyed camp evidence and stood by to herd the string of stolen mounts up or down a stream of water to obliterate tracks. If the riders drew uncomfortably close, White Horn would ride almost within their rifle range while pretending not to see them. He made straight, unsuspicious tracks for them to follow, indicating that he would lead them to his camp and their missing horses—but he never did!

Sometimes the riders were too smart to fall for this old trick and would chase White Horn. But his weapon was the finest of rifles—the Atkinson—and his aim was deadly. And there was no mount in the West to match his broad-chested Nez Percé war horse for speed and endurance. There had been occasions when a vein had been tapped and the life of White Horn saved from death by starvation and thirst by drinking of the royal blood of the horse with the iron heart, his beloved Appaloosa, Sooloocy, heisted from the Sioux.

The three comrades moved southward through the Yavapai and other Apache countries, where Otopasco, as front man, did well among the scattered tribes of his Apache cousins. Smooth diplomats, they presented chiefs with fine horses and made friends everywhere. The southwestern tribesmen began to look upon the renegades as gentlemen soldiers of fortune, to be admired and treated with great respect. Young braves became eager to join the wandering horse hunters, but the three adventurers gently but firmly refused to take on any recruits. Theirs was a tight, profitable partnership and they intended to keep it that way for the present.

For ten years *Mi Ashe Ton Gaxas* of the Bear-Step Clan were free to come and go among many tribes. They who extended them welcome were amply repaid with excellent horses and other loot. Many dogs were killed to provide feasts in their honor. Tribal chieftains asked that some of their finest young braves be permitted to work with the Bear-Step Clan and become masters of the polished skills of the three Stealths of the Darkened Moon. Grandpa Bear-Step became official *Wathon* of the horse hunt, and his name symbolized the fraternity emblem of the graduated *Gaxa* of the *Mi Ashe Ton,* as selected recruits were finally accepted.

Teaching the Apaches how to steal was like carrying coals to Newcastle, as the cavalryman of the 1850–1860 period well knew. But it was the superior Comanche technique that elevated the Apaches from the unimaginative "dry gulch" hijack into the clever Jimmy Valentine category of scientific horse-heisting.

Every American Indian is born with inherent love for the game where skill is combined with chance, and the stiffer the penalty the more pride he takes in beating the game. No other race has ever had as many gambling games as the Indian. There are more than three hundred that can be played in a basket, with penalties ranging from busted knuckles to a form of Russian roulette. Sometimes more lives were lost in tribal games than in tribal wars. Sequoia, for example, was crippled for life in the game of Cherokee Ball, a sort of "lacrosse in the rough." Two-timing squaws were bad medicine then, same as now. The age-old triangle game was risky and rough. Left hands of the two male participants were lashed together, and they slashed it out with knives. To the winner went the spoils—*after* her nose had been amputated by the virtuous wives.

Horse stealing was the Indian's favorite game. Taking chances on getting shot by one who was clever enough to catch him gave him his greatest thrill. Dying on the battlefield was a great honor, and a happy hereafter was his who died in that manner. But when the eyes of the gods were dimmed by darkness, the Great Unknown of the *Gaxa* wasn't so certain. Between the gain and the loss, the gap was great indeed. He gambled with his hereafter. If he were captured by other Indians and tortured, he stood a pretty good chance of getting right with the gods by jeering and tormenting his captors. But getting killed or hanged in the night for horse-heisting was exceedingly bad luck, and tribesmen gave the *Gaxa* credit for great bravery in taking such chances.

Heisting was worth the chance. It paid off in excitement, horseflesh and tribal honors rated according to the distance between the actual win and what the brave stood to lose. The hoof print painted on the rump of his horse was the honor mark for which the *Gaxa* had taked his life, and won. It was second only to the "pat hand," warpainted symbol of an enemy killed in action and scalped.

Great importance was placed upon the method in which the horse was heisted. According to *Mi Ashe Ton* doctrine, it was bad taste to potshot a rider (not an enemy), and ride away on a captured horse. One could easily vex the gods by killing a person (or any living thing) without having just cause and making oath and promise beforehand in due and ancient form. Killing a nonenemy was sinful, and doubly so after sundown or when the eyes of the gods were dimmed with rain, self-defense excepted. Grandpa Bear-Step often boasted of having never killed or scalped a man he wasn't mad at because he was above that sort of thing. His statement was usually followed by one from Uncle White Horn, who would lift eyebrows at Grandpa, sadly shake his head and soliloquize, "Those quick-tempered Comanches!"

Heisting for the thrill of tormenting the enemy became tops in clan honors. Humiliating the army by making off with their mounts without molesting *remuda* guards, making officers appear ridiculous in the eyes of their subordinates, making infantry out of cavalry troops, gave them their greatest satisfaction. The "Walking Soldier With Spurs" was jeered with distant owl hoots and crow calls, but permitted to live and bring disgrace to his camp. If he slept his canteen was filled with sand; but they saw to it that he lived to return in humiliation to his comrades. The officer in "Walking Spurs" was made to feel like a one-man parade through an invisible zoo of every rodent with vocal cords, and the "Bronx Cheer" was used in the same salutation then as now. Apprentice *Gaxas* were allowed to practice their art of stalking him. Then, from behind boulders and bushes, they would spring out and "BOO!" make faces, and "child frighten" him! But they were forbidden to touch the messenger who carried misfortune back into his camp.

The sport of heisting from the whites became rather monotonous, and they found that it was more fun stealing from other tribes. The Indian guarded his mount better, slept lighter and killed the heister just as dead but quicker. If he were good enough to capture a *Gaxa* alive and turn him over to the women for torture, he became a hero, and the *Gaxa* was in for a bad time of it. The high-spirited Indian pony had Indian habits, being broken to hackamore, foot guiding and bareback riding. To the *Gaxa*, he was considered a greater honor and better prize than the lazy, oat-fed, heavy-footed cavalry plug, with saddle sores and the disposition of the milk cow.

In the mid-nineteenth century Indians were pestered by heisters more than the white man, and the unfortunate one usually lost his mount in the same manner in which he had won it. He began to look upon his pony as a prize to be maintained, which he owned to the same extent he would own a branded buffalo. But the honor belonged to the brave who rode the prize mount. He risked his life to gain a trophy, which he guarded with the same enthusiasm a heavyweight champion defends his belt. Uncle White Horn defined the situation with the following quotations: "You may possess, but never own, what the Great Wahkonda has given life. The hide is yours, but the tracks of the living horse, never." This bit of Omaha philosophy may have been first offered in condolence to the brave who lost his prized trophy to a better *Gaxa*.

So the horse was the Indian's most treasured gift from the whites. It was the table stake of his most fascinating game and the cause of most of the tribal wars. Even the scattered Apache cousins were becoming hostile toward each other and feuding amongst themselves over captured horses. The technique of the *Mi Ashe Ton* was backfiring and causing bad blood to flow within one of the strongest and fiercest nations of the Southwest.

A powerful young chief of the Chiricahuas, named Cochise, was regarded as one who could bring all Apache tribes together and put an end to intertribal heisting; but it was whispered that he was fraternizing with soldiers and advocating that his followers adopt the humdrum habits and customs of the sodbusting whites. His subchiefs and small bands were seceding and renegading from the mother tribe.

The older Apache wise men had no doubt that the tall and good-to-look-upon chief of the Chiricahuas was a great genius; but it was known that he was handicapped with high principles and a code of decency that was unfitted for one in his high position. It was foretold by older chiefs that someday he would become the victim of his own misplaced confidence in others.

In the year 1860 the young chief Cochise bought a bill of goods disguised in a fancy and "decent" wrapper. Predictions of the "Old Bloods" came to pass. Cochise was seriously wounded under the white flag of truce violated by a greenhorn cavalry officer whose ambition outweighed good sense. Had not Cochise escaped, the amateur soldier would have become a hero, and the defiled truce flag whitewashed for further use.

But such was not the case. The genius of the infuriated Cochise was finally reckoned with at the expense of fifteen thousand white casualties, abandonment of stage lines, ranches, mines and cities and millions of dollars' worth of livestock and provisions. It took six Civil War generals and five thousand troops twelve years of blood, sweat and tears to clean up the mess made in a few seconds by a boy-soldier who defiled the traditional white flag of truce by attempting to use it as a camouflage for the sneak punch that narrowly missed its mark.

But in 1860 the Great White Father in Washington was having the same trouble experienced by Chief Cochise. His generals and subchiefs were likewise seceding and renegading from the mother tribe, and he too was being whispered about. Soon he was fighting on two fronts. There was intertribal warfare with blood brothers slashing at each other, while royal families of the Old World prepared to move in from Mexico. Soldiers he could spare for his western frontier twisted his orders and executed them in the manner they chose.

In the succeeding fifteen years the *Mi Ashe Ton* Clan of Bear-Step reached its peak, and roving bands of his graduated *Gaxas* captured the finest horses. A small secret society had become a great organization that controlled the horsepower, pride and glory of the western frontier, and the finesse with which Apache Stealths did their heisting well rated the high honor marks painted upon the rumps of their excellent mounts.

So around their open fire during those sacred minutes when it is neither daylight nor dark, three old cronies sat silently and smoked—and remembered. The "coffee cooler" patiently waited for the inevitable, "Do you recollect when . . . ?" The introduction of the bull session to come forth with glowing coals and darkness and more unique stories from an unquestionable source.

There have been told and written many tales about the Arizona ranchman and frontiersman, Pete Kitchen, who survived Apache raids between 1854 and 1880. There is no doubt that Pete was hit by many marauding bands and renegades and was plenty bad medicine. The Apache quickly learned that. But the main reason he remained alive was that the Apache respected him, wanted him to live and stay in business. They had little or no love for him but they understood his code of decency. He would give them no trouble if they left him strictly alone. In short he was a hell of a good neighbor. If they had killed him, his boots would have been filled by one with less common sense than Pete Kitchen possessed. The Apache found early in the game that his plow-pulling nags were too old to eat and too slow to ride, so were useless to the Indian. They looked upon his kingdom of hams and cabbages as a reservoir to be tapped only in case of total depression.

There was no doubt that Pete was a good shot, because he was a Kentuckian and all Kentuckians are good shots. But Pete was hot stuff in his home state before he went west, where he shot a stalking Apache six hundred yards away. That story came from the Apache side of the fence, so it must have been on the level. But for every Apache Pete saw to shoot at, there were ten he didn't. He seldom, if ever, told about the five-hundred-yard shot through the head of another, but the head was made of adobe and didn't count. An important part of *Mi Ashe Ton* technique was to draw attention and fire from one direction, while signal mirrors blinked in the other.

Concealed within the adobe walls of Pete's corrals were boulders and smaller stones, so it could not be cut with a horsehair lariat. His gate was built of massive timbers and held shut with log chains and brass padlocks which made his horses secure at night. A Mexican sentry created havoc by reporting that a band of Apaches was loading Pete's hogtied porkers on their ponies and leisurely riding away with them. His boys buckled on their pistols and raced to the corral with saddles and bridles, to give chase to the impudent pig-heisting Apaches. Pete fumbled with his keys and unlocked two of the padlocks; but there was another for which there was no key, placed there by the Apache *Gaxas.*

The Butterfield Stage Line threatened the Apache stronghold and was a sure sign of trouble. If Texas Confederates and war shortages hadn't defeated them, the Apaches would have done it later. Indians of many tribes went for their excellent horses that were purchased on the "Marshall Plan" of that era. Arapahoe, Kiowa and Comanche heisters were riding the iron-shod Butterfield horses and liking them. The canny New Yorker got the idea of using watchdogs in assisting his drowsy Mexican remount-station guards. But Indians and dogs have had a mutual understanding for more than three thousand years. In Indian camps were female dogs, some of them in heat. By simply borrowing the bitches' bed blanket and unrolling it on the upwind side of the watchdog, his one-track mind was quickly taken off the sentry business while *Gaxas* from the downwind side plundered the corral.

Mr. Butterfield eventually found an Apache weakness. Someone told him Indians do not ride mules. So here was aspirin for his constant headache. Stolen horses from his remount stations were replaced with young, high-spirited mules. The party who told Mr. Butterfield that Indians don't ride mules was absolutely right. But he should have told him Apaches love to eat them. So his corrals were heisted as usual.

A remount-station master was presented with a beautiful hand-woven bridle, a present from the wife of one of his Mexican chore boys. Though she spoke better Spanish than her husband, it was later learned she was Apache, and the bridle was made from the tail hair of the Butterfield mules. It was sent in token for the heisted muleburgers. This was typical of the *Mi Ashe Ton* technique. Frequently a pair of wornout moccasins was left in exchange for a prized horse. The *Gaxa* method of poking fun at the loser.

A prominent horseman whom Grandpa did not like awoke one morning to find inverted hoofprints painted upon his bedroom window. Rushing to the stable, he found moccasin tracks and a dead jackrabbit hanging from the hitchring of his prize stallion. Almost two years later the unshod stallion was returned to the same stall, gray with wisdom and worse for wear. There were two hoofprints painted upon the same window, one up, one down; one coming and one going. A thorough nose count in the corral revealed that the old stallion's spirited young offspring was missing. The hoofprint tracking upward was the Indian's honor mark of the captured horse. It was painted upon the rump of his favorite mount and upon the leg of the brave that turned the trick. The inverted hoofprint was the heckle mark, or what the whites called "the Indian sign." The marauding red man painted this sign on windows, over stable doors and sometimes upon the very horses picked for heisting. This was done to torment the owner and warn him. It was a bad-luck sign and worried him greatly.

The hoofprint sign was adopted by the whites. Horsemen of today nail horseshoes over their stable doors with the open ends upward, so that sickness will be driven away from their stables and their mares will foal beautiful and healthy colts. But the inverted horseshoe remains a symbol of very bad luck.

Through his powerful glass a cavalry officer once sighted what he believed to be two horses heisted from his command. Upon arrival at the distant hilltop where he had spotted the "horses," the angry officer found two crude dummies resembling horses, bearing squeaky military saddles which Grandpa did not like. Moccasin tracks disclosed that Grandpa and another *Gaxa* had spent hours patiently constructing the dummies especially to fool the gullible cavalry. It was a jest he played on them several times.

Humiliating a cavalry officer in the presence of his command was more fun than killing him, according to the *Mi Ashe Ton* doctrine. The methods used in such humiliation were often fiendishly ingenious. In one such incident some cavalry mounts of inferior quality were heisted. Three days later, their saddles painted with "pokie," an invisible sap of the poison oak variety that causes an agonizing itch for about nineteen days, the horses were quietly returned at night. Thus a cavalry unit was reduced to foot soldiering for a period of three weeks.

The finest cavalry horses were ridden by the higher officers, who took great pride in their horsemanship. Since riding a horse lame reflected upon its rider, enlisted men were gazing askance at a certain high-ranking officer who had lamed five horses in five days. The five splendid mounts were put to pasture to recuperate.

Soon white people of peculiar character were rounded up and questioned about the disappearance of the five high-spirited but slightly lame mounts. But they were not recovered. It was known that the Indians regarded an ailing horse as bad medicine. Being possessed with evil spirits, they would not ride, eat or come near it. The convalescing horse at pasture was much safer than those behind rock walls, iron gates and padlocked log chains.

A few months later this happened again. The same officer (whom Grandpa, White Horn and Otopasco did not like) had lamed five more beautiful mounts. Again enlisted men looked upon him with lifted eyebrows, and the injured horses were put to pasture. Again white men of peculiar character were rounded up and questioned about the disappearance of the slightly lame horses.

This hurt Grandpa's feelings very much because retrograde whites were stealing his thunder, getting credit for his work and taking the sting out of his bite. But the *Mi Ashe Ton* technique eventually leaked through the White Curtain. With red faces the officers learned that their prize mounts had been "stippled" by the *Gaxas* in the dark of the moon and were put to pasture for lame.

A small needle threaded with horse hair was run through the leg slightly above the hock. It was scarcely felt by the horse. Protruding ends of the hair were cropped at the surface of the skin. The slight wound was almost impossible to locate. The horse had gone lame somewhere between the hoof and the hip. Where? The question could be answered only by the *Gaxa* who stippled the horse.

All through the years of my childhood, I served as official

"coffee cooler" for the three cronies when they met and smoked together and sat in silence through the twilight. Then with the darkness came coffee and refilled pipes, and the chips were down. The *powmini* started with the customary, "Do you recollect when . . . ?" And invariably one of the three was the villain of the incident. The conversation was carried on between the other two as though the culprit were absent from the group. They lifted eyebrows and shook their heads in shame for having once associated with such a scoundrel. Grandpa would heckle Uncle Heconida with one similar to the following:

" 'Pasco, do you recollect the time that Omaha fellow, Heconida, blinked the antelopes and got Mormons?" Then Grandpa and Otopasco would chuckle and shake their heads at the thought of the shameful event, while custom demanded Uncle Heconida keep quiet and pretend to be embarrassed. Fragments of the story were tossed back and forth by Grandpa and Otopasco until the shameful tale had been unfolded in its entirety.

The hard-riding sons of Nauvoo were bad losers when their horses were heisted. They were good frontiersmen and better trackers. Many an Indian heister was run ragged by them. Grandpa used to say, "They would run six good horses to death to catch a heister with one bad one." The moral to that one was, "When you heist a Mormon, be sure you get his fastest." The brush with them resulted from Heconida's hunger for fresh antelope meat, and he employed the Omaha technique in hunting them. Concealing himself in mesquite on the downwind side, he blinked the antelope in the eye with his mirror. While its curiosity drew it closer to the blinking nuisance, Otopasco, with bow and arrows, had hidden in a crosswind position near the course the curious animal would instinctively take toward the flickering light. But Uncle Heconida's mirror had simultaneously aroused the curiosity of a band of Mormons out searching for heisted horses. It took two days for the *Gaxas* to lead the determined Mormons away off and lose them, then circle back to where some mighty thirsty Mormon mounts were hidden.

With the close of the story the two old men would chuckle, and then pretending to discover that the culprit was among those present, they would point fingers at Heconida and have a good laugh at him. But it was now his turn to carry the ball and another's turn to blush in shame at his retort.

"But don't you recollect, Otopasco, that wasn't the end of the trouble? Remember that Bay Mormon?" The two of them lifted their brows at Grandpa and he would hump his shoulders and hang his head in shame as the private conversation of Heconida and Otopasco revealed the second chapter of the story. "I knew that Bay Mormon of Bear-Step's was bad medicine. Recollect how the young mare got in heat and kicked the stuffings out of the Hopi geldings and seduced that Whipple Stud? Their tracks led, like the crow flies, back to the Mormon settlement where she'd given birth to her first colt."

Every stolen horse was named after the settlement from which it was admitted to membership in the clan, and in many cases before. They appraised the stock and planned their moves in advance. The cream of the corral was carefully selected before the heist. Such names as "Bay Mormon," "Paiute Paint," "Whipple Stud" (souvenir of Fort Whipple) were self-explanatory. The Hopi Indians gelded some of their horses, and the heisters loved them because they gave the least trouble. A mare got mean spells and would bite and kick other horses and then run for home wherever it was. A stallion would whinny and raise the devil at the very time he shouldn't. So when other horses got near, they had to make him sniff tobacco. Then he would get so busy sneezing, he neither heard nor smelled them. But Grandpa said that was not true. With a sniff of that awful Apache tobacco, neither horse nor man would give a damn.

To this very day the Indian doesn't live who isn't a pushover for the Appaloosa, the war horse with the spotted rump. The Nez Percé Indians had spent two hundred years of gelding and scientific breeding to develop the wonder horse with unbelievable stamina. The breed outdid the mounts of General Wright's cavalry so badly he later conceived the idea of defeating the Indians by destroying the magnificent strain and ordered them shot on sight. The horse with the spotted rump was marked for death. Eight hundred of the riderless mounts were destined to be slaughtered and the breed to become almost extinct.

About the year 1855 some of these mounts had been traded and stolen from the Nez Percé tribe and were possessed by the Crow, Blackfoot, Cheyenne and Dakota Sioux tribes, later to become annexed to the clan and identified as "Loosy Crow," "Loosy Foot," "Shy Loosy," "Soo Loosy," etc. The term *Loosy* meant the horse was tops among the blue bloods of horsedom, the Horse A'Palouse,' *pièce de résistance* and *grand prix* of the horse thief. The *Gaxa* would gladly risk his life and his hereafter for a chance to heist the "Loosy."

And so the chain of talk went on and on into the night. Three white-haired cronies drank coffee and smoked, while three young braves rode in retrospect through sawtoothed mountains and blistering deserts; fighting, feasting, flirting with death, thirsting and drinking raw blood from their mounts to keep on living, and "putting fun" into their adventurous lives.

Then suddenly the flash of fresh fuel on dying embers would destroy their delusions. Interim years fell away like shattered glass and shocked them with sudden realization—those events had taken place many, many moons ago. The hideous future was here and was stifling them. Horse stealing had become looked upon with disrespect. Yes, the downhill slope was steep, very steep indeed. Silently each old brave would puff his lifeless pipe, knock the dead tobacco ash into his hand, then stand and drop it into the fire. Rubbing his hands together, he would say, "I go now," and without further adieu he would disappear into the night. Then Grandpa Bear-Step would sit alone and stare at his fire late into the night. Sometimes he would be smiling, and I wondered what he was thinking about.

Jack Frost paints fantastic pictures on bedroom windows when it is November in Oklahoma. One early morning sun revealed phantom forests of palm trees and glistening jungle ferns, and I fancied seeing an inverted hoofprint there.

Then I found Grandpa Bear-Step with his pipe. There were dead tobacco ashes in his cold hand and he was smiling into a fire that had died in the night.

Silently, expressionless and seemingly without emotion, Heconida and Otopasco stood beside me, while a Christian minister dropped a handful of earth onto Grandpa Bear-Step's casket. But in the red soil of the Cimarron country, broken Apache and Omaha hearts were buried with their Cherokee-Comanche *Wathon.*

Otopasco and Heconida came with me to erect a small stone marker; then we opened the grave and put in tobacco and corn, and Otopasco put in a small piece of turquoise. Then the grave was good.

Grandpa Bear-Step was happily hunting.

Nowadays Oklahomans may respectfully tell you, "This is one of the many graves of our Indian dead." But a half-century ago some of those Indians could have told you, "This man was, perhaps, the greatest horse thief the West ever knew; and his method of heisting probably saved more lives of white prisoners than did any other person, because he believed and taught that it was sinful and bad luck to kill a man for his horse."

I continued to build the open fire, cook the coffee and load the pipes. The two remaining braves came back to "sit in" through the sacred minutes of twilight, and on into the darkness of night, to stare at the glowing coals in silence. Another story was never told. With Grandpa Bear-Step, many stories that will never become known were buried.

With the following dark of the moon, Heconida, White Horn the Omaha, was dead because he cared no longer to live.

It was winter, and I kept the open fire burning, coffee hot and filled pipes in readiness, for the lonely Otopasco often came and "sat in" in silence. It was then the stone-faced Apache strong man paid me my greatest compliment, when he asked me to sit beside him. He offered me his pipe and I smoked it and became dizzy with the realization that I was no longer a "coffee cooler." I smoked with the great Apache Brave, Otopasco. I smoked his pipe as his equal and became a man. I was very proud as we men sat side by side during those sacred minutes when it is neither daylight nor dark.

Then when sky and earth no longer met and the gray horizon of the West became lost, it was again dark of the moon and time to make talk with the mouth. I gave him back his lighted pipe, and he smoked. Then peering at familiar faces within the glowing embers, he spoke:

"Heconida the Omaha has saved my life many times. Now he is dead. Cherokee Bear-Step, the Comanche Man, has saved my life many times. Now he is dead. Only I now live and walk alone to their fire to look upon dry cups and feel cold, empty pipes of them and to hurt bad and die inside of me. I go now."

And the grand old Apache strong man, last of the great *Gaxas,* tossed white tobacco ash into the fire and silently disappeared forever into the black shadows of *Mi Ashe Ton.*

Race for Half a Million

by Curtis Bishop

Colonel C. C. Slaughter gave his ten-year-old son a boost into the saddle. Then the cattle baron cleared his throat.

"You'll make it all right, boy," he said in his gruff way. "You know the trails as well as I do."

The Colonel was trying to reassure himself as well as to steel his son against the ordeal ahead. For Bob Slaughter, no more than a tyke, did not present an imposing appeaance atop the Steeldust mare. The boy shivered in his thin shirt, for the night air was crisp and chill. He sat the strange saddle a little awkwardly; he had never ridden on a four-pound English saddle before. He missed the comfortable bulk of the high-horned Spanish-type gear.

But he must ride without warm garments or his usual saddle. Every ounce would count in this race of 366 miles with a half-million dollars as the purse.

Bob Slaughter touched the thoroughbred mare with his spurs

and was off at a gallop. He did not like the horse's gait; he preferred the easy swinging lope of a mustang. But in a distance run —a fabulous distance—blood lines counted . . . in rider as well as horse.

The moon was just coming up; in the next three hours before midnight, Bob Slaughter would have a clear, pale light before him.

And a fresh horse under him. Soon the horse would tire. Gold coins clanked in Bob Slaughter's saddlebags to buy a fresh mount when the mare faltered. But for the ten-year-old horseman, there would be no relief.

From Dallas—a frontier village in 1881—into the plains country, to a line camp twenty miles north of Big Spring . . . every one of the grim 366 miles was Bob Slaughter's to ride at breakneck speed.

There could be no rest, no delay. The ten-year-old was racing to overtake, and to pass, a coach and team which had left Dallas three days before. He had spotted his adversaries a full seventy-two hours in this race for a cattle empire.

Back in Dallas, in the lobby of a two-story frame hotel, Colonel C. C. Slaughter gnawed at his shaggy mustaches and cursed in a soft monotone. Representatives of the English syndicate had approached him five days before; after forty-eight hours of wrangling over a price, the Colonel had signed an order to his foreman for the immediate transfer of all his range holdings.

The price—an even $500,000—seemed fair enough for the cattle, the gear and all the other physical properties bearing the Lazy S brand. At one time C. C. Slaughter had owned nothing more than the mustang under him and his *reata*. But he had dragged many a protesting *ladino* out of the South Texas brush country. He had traded for wild cattle in San Antonio until he had a herd he could drive into the open West Texas country and turn loose upon free grass.

For a time his "headquarters" was no more than a sod-covered dugout. But he sold herds in Kansas and put his profits into more cattle.

After fifteen years the Lazy S was some outfit. Line riders made a human drift fence from the banks of the Colorado River to the Cap Rock, 55 miles away. Lazy S cattle stormed into Dodge City and onto the Indian reservations of New Mexico.

A half-million was a fair price, but not an exorbitant one.

It did not shock the Colonel when men posing as British noblemen offered to buy him out lock, stock and barrel. English and Scottish investors were buying outfits all over the west. The Rocking Chair, bought by Baron Tweedmouth and the Earl of Aberdeen; the Matador, the LX, the RO, the Prairie Cattle Company—Englishmen had bought these ranches in just such a transaction. Britons believed that yearlings could be bought at four dollars per head, fattened at the cost of an additional dollar per head and sold at sixty to seventy dollars each.

The Colonel knew the cattle business wasn't that easy. He was afraid of a falling market (and justly so). When the Englishmen met his price of $500,000, he agreed to sell.

When the Colonel made up his mind, he went "whole hog." He stood for the whiskey until the last Briton was asleep. Then he rented a coach and team from the Dallas livery stable and sent the Englishmen on to their new properties at his own expense.

With the imposters went the Colonel's orders to his foreman to deliver, on sight, eveything that was the Lazy S, even to ropes and saddles.

Then things happened. The Texas Land and Mortgage Company, an English loan corporation with a branch office in Dallas, refused to cash the draft without investigation. The loan company smelled the rat before the Colonel did.

A cablegram to England confirmed these suspicions. Colonel Slaughter had turned over his ranch to three bogus noblemen whose draft wasn't worth the paper it was written on.

Or had he? Not yet, not if word could reach his foreman to refuse delivery of the ranch despite this order. Possession was still nine points of the law; in range country it was perhaps more.

There was still a hope, a faint one. There was ten-year-old Bob

Slaughter racing across a rugged, unsettled domain. But there still remained over three hundred miles ahead of him when he galloped into the sleepy town of Fort Worth and watered his horse at the village trough.

And why not have hope in the boy? Bob could ride as well as any grown man. His weight would tell far less on a horse than the weight of an adult. And he knew every trail between Dallas and the Slaughter range.

Through the night Bob kept the saddle. The Steeldust mare was a staunch animal; she could still run when Bob reached Weatherford though she was near white in color from sweaty foam.

A friendly doctor sold the boy another mount and agreed to take care of the thoroughbred. Bob wolfed down breakfast and rode on.

The sun came up; no longer did his slight body shiver with cold. Over the Palo Pinto Mountains galloped the young courier, on to the Clear Fork near Phantom Hill. He drank when his horse did and did not stop to eat.

In midafternoon his horse developed a limp. At first Bob tried to push on, then was forced to stop. The ten-year-old was already wise in animal lore. He found a sharp, jagged pebble lodged in the frog of one hoof. The horse could hobble along with no danger of maiming.

It was ten miles to a ranch headquarters at the Cottonwood's mouth; the horse had to make it. Bob used the spurs relentlessly. The animal bore up until a half-mile from Seth Barnes' corral, then collapsed.

Bob left the horse and ran on afoot, carrying his light saddle on his shoulders. One of Barnes' Mexican *vaqueros* went to care for the tired animal.

Barnes and his crew of riders were gone. Worse still there was only one horse in the corral—a stallion which had been ridden only once.

The Mexicans called the ten-year-old "loco" when he asked to borrow the unbroken animal. But they helped strap the light saddle on the outlaw and lifted the boy astride.

The outlaw "sunfished" twice, then seized the bit in his teeth and bolted. Bob could hold the horse to the trail, that was all.

His hopes sank, though their direction was right, westward. At this rate the stallion would run himself out and collapse.

Gradually the horse slowed up. Finally to a walk. Finally to a trembling wall-eyed stop.

Luck was with the ten-year-old rider. A creek was close at hand; he let the stallion drink and blow. Then he vaulted into the saddle.

The outlaw yielded. The horse picked a pace it could hold, and darkness found the young horseman in the Taylor County foothills.

Bob Slaughter dozed off in the saddle again and again, until finally the night cold made him crouch in low discomfort over the horse's neck.

The first tint of dawn found them nearing the Colorado River. Bob veered his direction so as to make for a spring near the river bed.

Then suddenly he reined up. He smelled smoke.

He went on more carefully. Breasting a sharp ridge, he looked down upon the spring-fed valley.

There was the coach his father had rented, and there, eating breakfast at a campfire, were the three bogus noblemen who had given a worthless draft for the Lazy S empire.

The aroma of frying bacon and boiling coffee drifted up to the youngster. It was almost too much to withstand. But Bob unhesitantly skirted the camp and took to the road again.

He was ahead of the Englishmen, but the race was not over yet. Soon they would be on the trail again with rested horses and a rested driver.

Another mount purchased; a fresh horse. But the same ten-year-old. The sun came up, came high. Now he did not stop even for water. Now he was in Lazy S country and that spurred him on.

Noon, high noon. The first dead hours of afternoon. The last gray, dreary miles.

One of the Lazy S hands saw the horse plodding along with a spent boy hanging to its neck. The ten-year-old was a light, unconscious weight which the Slaughter waddy speedily bore to the ranch headquarters at German Springs.

He was asleep, dead asleep. They could not rouse him. But they found in his pockets the order from his father not to surrender the ranch despite what papers the Englishmen could show.

It was two o'clock then. Ten-year-old Bob Slaughter had ridden 366 miles in forty-one hours. He had made it in time, for the Englishmen did not reach the headquarters until late afternoon.

They received a rude welcome. They were told to "git back" in that "ther coach" and "git." They were not ordered to any particular destination, nor given much of an explanation, but they got the general idea. The Lazy S hands were sometimes very outspoken and sometimes emphasized their words with appropriate gestures.

The Colonel, coming on at a less exacting pace, found the Lazy S realm still intact and his ten-year-old son fully recovered from the ordeal. In fact young Bob Slaughter was very happy over the whole affair. It meant something to a tyke of a boy to be known among full-grown cowboys as a "hand to ride the river with."

The Treasure is Always There!

by J. Frank Dobie

In a thousand legends of buried treasure and lost mines of the
Southwest, there are ten thousand reasons why hunters have been
baffled in their long and unending searchings. Now and then, as
the tales run, the hidden treasure is discovered—but only to be
again lost and again sought for. The lover pictured on the Grecian
urn is doomed to pursue the pictured maid forever, but never,
never to kiss her. The reason is plain enough, for the picture
cannot change. The reason why the treasure hunter can never
grasp what he reaches for involves circumstances as various as the
things of earth, the laws of nature and the workings of human
imagination.

212

The Treasure is Always There!

One fact, however, is fixed. The treasure (whether money or mine) is always there. The dyed-in-the-wool seeker for it never doubts its existence. History, geology, experience may deny the possibility of every claim asserted by legend; then, history, geology and experience are merely wrong. The treasure hunter may admit that the directions he works by are in error, but he is much more likely to claim that he has made an error in interpreting or in following those directions.

When pirates buried a chest of doubloons, they buried a dead man over it to guard it, a trick they learned—some say—from the Spanish. At any rate half the Spanish treasures of the Southwest are kept by a dead guard. The Mexicans call that guard the *patron*. And a *patron* of some sort, a destiny, a force from gods or devils, a fatal obstacle, which may assume infinite shapes, guards every treasure that has ever been long sought for in this world.

The obstacle may lie in the elements. Unrelenting sands and thirsts have protected the Lost Adams Diggings of New Mexico, the Lost Mine of Death Valley in New Mexico, the Apache Mine in Sonora and many another golden secret of the desert lands.

Years ago a Mexican shepherd girl was lost in a sandstorm in Death Valley, Arizona. For three days the wind blew high and the blinding sand cut deep. Then the girl found herself in a depression that had been swept bare of all sand. And the clean bottom of that depression was covered with gold nuggets—heaps, piles, sacks of them!

By now the girl was perishing with thirst and was utterly lost. Then far away she saw a thin line of smoke. She knew that it was on the railroad crossing Death Valley. She gathered what nuggets she could carry and started across the sands. At length, in a fainting condition, she reached the railroad.

The next train that came along picked her up. Sight of the nuggets set the train crew wild. The girl was cared for, and at the first division point, the crew deserted their work and returned with the restored girl to guide them to the gold.

There were no tracks left in the running sand, no landmarks.

There was only a glaring, mocking waste. The search was fruitless. The winds had come again, and the shifting sands had covered the nuggets. The shepherd girl never saw again the golden rocks that she had stumbled upon. It is said that three of the five trainmen who set out with her on the search continued until they perished.

Years passed. Then a cowboy, a stranger in those parts who was trying to cross Death Valley, rode upon the golden pavement that the winds in their play had once more uncovered. He gathered a great amount of the gold, filling his saddle pockets and even removing his saddle blanket so that he could roll the precious ore up in it. He did not know what a price one might pay for gold— or a horse—in Death Valley. Had he taken the right direction, he might have ridden to water or the railroad. But he did not know directions in Death Valley. His horse at length sank exhausted, and he shot him to drink his blood. Then the cowboy staggered on. He threw away everything that he had, even to the last nugget. Finally he dragged his perishing frame to a water hole and to human aid.

He told his story, but he never returned to seek the mine or the booty left behind. In Death Valley the hot winds shift the sand forever, and there is never a traveler's track but is shifted away. The tale is an old tale, and they say that many a desert rat has been lured by its promise. I do not know what they found. The skeletons out there, buried so deep one day and exposed so bare and naked the next, tell no stories, write no epilogues.

Only be sure of this: what the sands uncover one day they will cover again the next. Tomorrow the mine may be found again, but fate has written that it shall be forever lost.

Sometimes instead of the parchings of nature, the fatal obstacle to treasure may be water. One time a man named Welch discovered the location of priest's gold hidden near a Spanish mission site on the San Gabriel River in Texas. He was going to dig for it the next day, but that night a great flood came and swept away all marks and locating points. Out in New Mexico, somewhere in the vicinity of old Fort Bayard, two miners located a traditional lead of gold that they estimated to be worth $5,000,000. They secured a sackful of the ore, but while they were making arrangements to work the mine, a cloudburst and a resultant mountain slide twisted the geography of the country out of recognition.

Instead of lying in the elements of nature, the obstacle may be some kind of recurring accident. On the Frio River in South Texas, tradition since the eighteenth century has placed a ledge of silver. Late in the last century an ancient Mexican, who in boyhood had been captured by the Comanches and allowed to see the ledge, was getting ready to guide a party of white men to its site. On the eve of departure he died, leaving, however, specific directions. With these directions a man named Whitley struck out to find the ledge. He took his dogs with him. When he got up into the Frio Canyon, he became absorbed in hunting bear, and before he knew it his time was up and he had to go home. He told his brother-in-law about the ledge. A year later the brother-in-law found it and was on his way down the country to tell Whitley of the location when he was murdered. Thus the natural death of an old Mexican, a bear hunt and a murder preserved in succession the secret of the silver ledge.

On the Nueces three men were digging for a muleload of gold doubloons. They had found the charcoal, the mule bones, and then the human bones, all according to the chart, buried directly over the gold. They had one hand on the doubloons, as it were, when their wagon burned up with all the provisions in it and the only decent spade they possessed. They were far from any habitation and had to leave. When they came back later to finish the hole, the doubloons were not there.

No man ever hunts treasure very long without coming to expect these thwartings. The mixture of hope and resignation to fate in the make-up of the treasure hunter is a psychological paradox.

A curious old character named Warner, who lived below San Antonio, had been telling me of some Spanish silver buried on the Medina River. He kept promising that he would take me to look for it sometime. He never understood that I was just after the story and more insight into the storyteller. I could never get him to set a date. One day he flatly said that it would not be of any use for us to go. "The spirits" were against him, he said.

"Spirits? What do you mean spirits?" I asked. "How can they work against you?"

"Oh, they work all right," he replied. "They always find a way to work. Maybe I might get all ready to go and would come home to find my horse lame, or my saddle borrowed by a neighbor or maybe cows broke into my field so I'd have to stay and fix up the fence. Always there's something."

One day, however, we actually started to the Medina. We were in an automobile with wornout casings, and when we turned off the main road, we got into the stumpiest road I have ever traveled. We had one puncture and blowout after another until we were thoroughly disgusted. Warner refused to go any farther.

"Don't you see how the spirits are working against us?" he said in a resigned tone. "It's just like I told you."

Not all treasure hunters are so superstitious. Many old-timers in the Southwest who have taken a dish in some buried treasure or lost mine at one time or another are remarkably free from superstition. But the professional treasure hunter has to become a fatalist, has to believe in supernatural control in order to maintain faith in the existence of what he seeks. Let him get to doubting the treasure instead of himself or the facts of nature, and then the treasure could no longer attract him.

A good deal of the superstition comes from the same people that the legends come from—the Mexicans. I used to know an old-time Negro named Pete Staples. He had been brought to Texas from Mississippi before the Civil War, had been raised in the border country with Mexicans, had married a Mexican woman and had lived for years in Mexico. During the seventies and eighties he drove cattle up the trail to Kansas and beyond, working alongside white cowhands. He combined a mixture of Mexican, Negro and frontier character. In order to bring out his psychology, I am borrowing his story from my *Coronado's Children.*

At the time he told me this story, Pete was cooking for a cow outfit in Live Oak County. The other hands had unrolled their blankets early, and Pete's tones were confidential as we talked by the burnt-out fire.

"One time there was a white man who had got wind of a lot of Mexican dollars buried down below Roma, close to the Rio Grande. He had the place all located and was so sure of hisself that he brung in an outfit of mules and scrapers to dig away the dirt. He was making a reg'lar tank digging down to that money when a Mexican what I've knowed all my life comed along.

"This Mexican moseyed along clost to the tank and stopped a minute under a mesquite tree to sorter cool off. He saw a hoe laying on the ground half covered up in the dirt. He reached down to pick it up and then he saw a whole *maleta* of coins. A *maleta*, you know, is a kind of bag made out of hide. This *maleta* was old and rotten, and when he turned it over with the hoe, it broke open and the gold money jest rolled out in the dirt.

"D'reckly the Mexican went over to where the white man was bossing the teams, and he asked him what he was doing. The white man told him he was digging up some buried money.

"'Well, you's digging where it ain't no use to dig,' the Mexican said. 'The money ain't there; hit's over here. If you want to see it, come along and I'll show it to you.'

"The white man laughed like he didn't believe what the Mexican was telling him, but he comed along. When they got to the mesquite there wa'nt no money in sight, but there was a hole down at the root of the tree kinder like a badger hole, and bumble bees were going in and out, making a roaring sound, and the dirt was fairly alive with great big bugs, maybe tumble bugs, only they were humming and making a sizzling noise and working around awful-like.

"'Huh, this what you call money?' says the white man, stamping down on the tumble bugs. 'I'd hate to offer a banker the kind of gold they roll up into marbles.'

" 'That's all right,' says the Mexican. 'There ain't no dollars here now, I'll admit, but there shore was. They was of gold and silver too. Them dollars is not intinded fer you. White man didn't hide the money; tain't meant fer white man to find it. White man jest as well quit looking. No matter how much he dig or where he dig, white man not going to find nothing.'

"Shore 'nough, the white man kept on digging, and he didn't get nothing. One time I asked the Mexican why he didn't take out the money fer hisself.

" 'I didn't want none of it,' he said. 'I never put it in the ground. 'Twa'nt mine any more'n that white man's.'

"It 'pears, though, that a little while after he seen the money he kinder drapped 'round the place jest fer curiosity's sake and went to scratching about in the sand. And shore 'nough he picked up an old Mexican square dollar. He brung it to Roma and bought some flour and some coffee and some candy, and he give some of that candy to my wife. She was living down there and knowed the man well and she's told me many a time how she et some of the candy that the Mexican bought with the old-time square dollar. I always have thought that money was intinded fer him, but you know how some folks are; and I can't say as I blame him fer not teching what he hadn't no right to.

"If buried money like that is intinded fer a human, he'll come by it nach'ral and easy. If it ain't intinded, he won't come by it no matter how much he hunts. Then even if he did find it and it wa'nt intinded fer him, it ud prove a curse. I'd be afraid of it myself."

One of the profoundest believers in fate and fortunetelling that I have encountered among treasure hunters was "Old Man" Sloan of Oklahoma. For thirty-odd years when I knew him he had been on the trail of a treasure in the Wichita Mountains of his state.

"It was this a'way," he began after I had ribbed him up to tell the story. "When that Wichita country was opened for settlement,

The Treasure is Always There!

I took up a half-section that enclosed a good part of Twin Mountains. A few years later—it must have been about '95—an old Indian woman came in there with some of her people and began looking 'round. She claimed to be one hundred and five years old, and she looked every day of it. After she had poked over the country for a while she told her story, and it run something like this.

"When she was a girl, her people had a big fight with Spaniards and killed off the whole band. As I understood, the Spanish were bringing a pack train out of Devil's Canyon, seven and a half miles to the northwest. Anyhow, after the battle, she and two warriors captured three Spanish burros loaded with gold ore. They took the burros to the western side of Twin Mountains and there buried the cargoes.

"Later on one of the Indian bucks went to Texas and never came back. The other one died. The old woman was gone out of the country for a long, long time, seventy or eighty years. She had never had much use for money, but now that she was back in the Wichitas and knew that her days were about ended, she decided she'd better dig up the gold. Well, she projecked around for a week or two, then left, and that was all I ever heard of her.

"She got me interested, though. I had heard of the buried gold before, but there had never been any definite details. Now I began to investigate. There was plenty of evidence, like pieces of human skulls and lead bullets, that a big battle had been fought. It stood to reason that gold had been carried off the battlefield.

"Now, there was a young woman fortuneteller in Snyder named Dolly, who'd been successful in finding a good many things, and I took the matter up with her. She looked down at the ground a while with her eyes shet, like she always done when she was a-studying, and then she says, 'Yes, the gold is there.' Then she went on to say that I ought to look on the east side of Twin Mountains instead of the west side. This didn't surprise me, for the old Indian woman had been gone so long and the country had changed so much that she could easy of got directions twisted.

"Dolly wasn't very definite, though, and she seemed afraid all along that somebody would prosecute her for telling fortunes. She asked me if there wasn't three hardwood trees close to my fence. I told her yes. Next she asked me if there wasn't a big flat rock nearby. I told her yes. Then to test her, I asked if there was anything on the rock.

"She kept her eyes shet a long time. 'Yes,' she finally replied, 'there's some letters on it, but I can't make out what they are.'

"That satisfied me, for there were letters on the rock which I'd put there myself in white paint—No Hunting Allowed—and they'd been weathered off.

"She ended up by saying that if I expected to find anything, I'd have to keep the search absolutely secret and not reveal her part in it. I told her I just had to have somebody to help dig.

" 'Well,' says she, 'Fay can help you, can't he?'

"Fay's my son, you know, and I said: 'That's exactly who I was figgering on getting to help me.'

"I was so anxious about the matter that I couldn't think about anything else. I lit out and told Fay, even before I'd settled on a place to dig. About this time a nephew came out to visit us. Before I knowed it Fay had told him, and both boys went to deviling me to start the search.

"Well, I went back to Dolly to get more specific directions. As soon as I saw her, I knowed something had happened. The first thing she said was: 'Certain people has been told what you're doing.'

"I couldn't deny it.

" 'Mr. Sloan,' says she, 'I can't tell you another thing now.'

"I argued, but it didn't do no good.

"Of course, I dug. I dug a-plenty—and never found a thing. Nevertheless the gold's there all right, I guess. There's certainly been plenty of proof as to Dolly's power in finding things.

"For instance, one time a merchant there in Snyder was busy with a customer when a man came in, in a big hurry to buy something. I ferget now what it was. He helped himself, laid a silver dollar down on the counter, and rushed out. The merchant was occupied for a few minutes. Then, when he recollected the matter and went to get the dollar, it had disappeared. That night he went to consult Dolly.

" 'Dolly,' says he, 'I've suffered a business loss, and I wish you'd help me. I want to know who it was took my dollar.'

"Dolly looked down in her way for a little while. 'I know who it is,' she says. 'Go to your store in the morning and the third man that comes in, look him square in the eye and say to him, 'I guess you've carried my dollar about long enough.'

"Sure enough the next morning when the third man came into the store, the merchant looks him in the eye and says, 'I guess you've carried my dollar about long enough.'

"The man kinder coon-grinned and pulled out a dollar and said he'd took it off just for fun.

"I could go on with other instances. You see what sort of vision this woman has. She's moved now and getting along in years, but I understand she still tells fortunes on the quiet. I've been thinking about trying her out again on the Twin Mountains gold.

"However, I may not need to consult anybody. In two or three days now a party will be here with a complete chart to the treasure. I'm not free to tell you his name, but his chart's been tested. It calls for a starting point, and this man found that starting point as described. It led him then from one marker to another until he came to a bob-wire fence, every marker called for proving out to a T. When he was about to crawl through the fence, a man on the other side with a shotgun in his hand ordered him not to cross the line. The party I'm speaking of is a peaceable sort of man, and he stopped right there.

"Of course, the three loads at Twin Mountains is just a fraction of the original store. The chief of the Lone Wolf Indians—Kiowas, you know—told some people down at Hobart that he knew where the gold in Devil's Canyon was and would find it if he was given the proper help and security. According to his claim, he got his information from the chief before him. Secrets like that, you know, are handed down from chief to chief and nobody else in the tribe knows about them.

"Don't ask me what'll come of all the chart following and hunting without charts. Like as not, some farmer will just accidentally plow up a fortune some day, or some rabbit chaser will stumble into an old hole with the gold at the bottom of it, while fellows like me who have sweated ourselves half to death digging pits and tunnels won't get a thing. That's the way it generally turns out with this treasure business. You might say that's life.

"Anyhow if it hadn't of been for my blabbing too soon when Dolly told me not to, or if it hadn't of been for that testy feller with a shotgun, the gold might be doing somebody some good now, instead of laying out there idle and maybe rusting to dust."

Two Against
Three Hundred

by Norman B. Wiltsey

The missing homesteader was found at the bottom of a deep ravine, shot through the head. He had not been scalped, his clothing was intact, his rifle rested at his side. At first glance it appeared that young Tim Boyle had accidentally killed himself while hunting, but closer inspection ruled out that possibility. Lieutenant Robertson, leader of the cavalry search party discovering the body, quickly noted that an undischarged cartridge remained in the chamber of Boyle's Winchester. Robertson's Indian scouts reported moccasin tracks on the ridge at the head of the ravine, blood on the leaves where a body had been dragged along the ground. Empty cartridge shells were found in a clump of brush fifty feet from the blood-splashed leaves. The evidence clearly indicated that Tim Boyle had been ambushed and murdered by Indians from the nearby Northern Cheyenne reservation.

At the army post of the First U.S. Cavalry on Lame Deer Creek, Montana, CO Major Carroll listened frowningly to Lieutenant Robertson's report. "This is a hell of a mess, Lieutenant! Must be the young bucks—the older men would never be so stupid."

Robertson nodded. "That's the way I figure it, sir. Boys who got sick of hearing their fathers brag about killing white men in the old days. We'd best sit tight and let the Indian Police do the investigating."

"Right, Lieutenant—but get 'em at the job right away. We've got to clear up this thing promptly. Once these wild young devils get the idea they can kill white men with impunity, we'll be in for serious trouble. As a safety measure we'll bring the Indians in off the reservation until we catch the killers. Camp them around the agency—only way to keep an eye on 'em until this mischief is settled."

One week later two members of the Indian Police reported to the agent. "Young Mule and Head Swift ride off in hills—gone five, six days. Paint for war, take guns and plenty shells. Look bad."

It did look bad. Young Mule and Head Swift were each eighteen years old; each as a child had lived through the Cheyenne imprisonment and subsequent desperate outbreak at Fort Robinson in 1879. The ruthless massacre of their families by the soldiers had branded the minds of these boys with a searing hatred of all whites. It seemed pretty certain that this hatred had finally exploded in the murder of Tim Boyle. Operating on this grim theory, it was vitally imperative that the fugitives be caught before they could kill again. Lieutenant Robertson, leading a squad of Indian scouts, began the hunt immediately.

Four days Robertson scoured the hills without results; the elusive Cheyennes could not be found. On the fifth day a break came. Brave Wolf, grizzled veteran of many battles against the whites, showed up at the agent's office and signed that he wanted tobacco and an interpreter—in that order. Brave Wolf, it seemed, had important information to impart—information he considered worth a pound of tobacco. The agent produced the tobacco on the chance that the old warrior was right.

"Head Swift and Young Mule come last night to lodge of parents," announced Brave Wolf between leisurely puffs on his long-stemmed pipe. "Make big talk—boast of killing Boyle and say they never surrender to be strung up on white man's gallows. Send challenge to soldier-chief and all his men to fight 'em in Gut Valley noon today. If soldiers no come, they raid agency to-morrow and kill heap white people."

The alarmed agent saddled a horse and started off for the army post with this astounding news. Brave Wolf, pleased at the excitement he had created, trotted along clutching his precious can of tobacco. The agitated interpreter ran ahead.

"What is this—a joke?" demanded Major Carroll of the agent. "Two fool Indian kids challenging three hundred soldiers . . . you must be crazy!"

Through the interpreter, Brave Wolf emphatically assured the Major that it was no joke. "Boys Cheyenne braves—no surrender to be choked by white man's rope. Fight all soldiers, like warriors!"

"Well, I'll be damned!" muttered Carroll. He turned to a white scout, an old-timer who had fought with Custer against the Cheyennes at the Battle of the Washita. "Joe, what do *you* make of this nonsense?"

Joe Moore shrugged. "I don't figure it nonsense, Major. These young Cheyennes aim to 'throw themselves away,' as they call it. I've seen it happen—at the Washita and later at Summit Springs. These Injun kids know they're good as dead right now, so they plan to cheat the rope and maybe take along a few white men with them to the Shadow Land. To them it makes sense."

Major Carroll snorted—but arose promptly from his desk and buckled on his gunbelt. "Orderly, have Boots and Saddles sounded at once. We'll accommodate these glory-hunting kids with bullets, if that's what they want."

The bugler blared the call, and the troopers piled out of barracks and rushed for their horses. "Prepare to mount—*mount!*" sang out Lieutenant Robertson. "Forward *ho!*" And the three troops of the First were off for Gut Valley on the strangest mission of its career. The death rendezvous named by Young Mule and Head Swift lay less than a mile from the post, and the appointed hour of noon was drawing near.

The road ran straight through the narrow valley. On both sides rocky pine-clad hills rose, ridge on ridge, at the spot selected by the Indian youths as a last battleground.

At a signal from Brave Wolf, Major Carroll lifted his right hand and ordered "Halt!" The CO remarked disgustedly, "Not a sign of our heroes anywhere. This is a wild goose chase—those two boys have made fools of us!"

The scout pointed to the hills and spoke one word: "Look!"

Through the dark pine forest the Cheyennes were coming to watch the show, scores of them; almost the entire population of the village camped about the agency. The men moved in close to stand silently on the lower ridges; women and children stationed themselves farther back, out of range of stray or ricocheting bullets. Significantly a trail leading to the top of the highest ridge was left open—and toward this ridge the eyes of every Indian were turned expectantly. The squaws began a low, rhythmic keening— and the red scouts in Major Carroll's command stiffened at the familiar, barbaric sound. The CO focused his field glasses on the ridge.

The time was now five minutes of noon. The troopers were deployed along the road, some dismounted, others mounted, in order to fire over the heads of kneeling comrades. Here in the high country on this sunlit September day in 1890, the hardwoods scattered among the pines already had turned to scarlet and gold. The thought of violent death occurring in this peaceful autumnal setting depressed even the hardbitten cavalrymen, who talked in lowered tones as they watched and waited.

Two Against Three Hundred

Noon arrived—and passed. Major Carroll lowered his field glasses, exclaiming: "Well, that's it! They've lost their nerve."

"You're dead wrong, Major," corrected Joe Moore. "There they are!"

Out of the pines midway up the trail, Head Swift and Young Mule suddenly appeared on horseback. Both youths were decorated in full ceremonial regalia; beaded buckskin jackets and leggings, eagle-plume war bonnets, glittering metal ornaments on wrist and arm. Slowly, horses at a walk, the young braves ascended the trail to the top of the highest ridge. Their intention was obvious to charge the troops from the top of the hill. Soldiers murmured in awe and admiration; only Major Carroll remained skeptical.

"Lieutenant Pitcher!" snapped the Major. "Take your troop and block off the road below the trail. Don't let them escape through the southern end of the valley."

"Now that move is plumb unnecessary, Major," drawled Joe as Pitcher's troops clattered off. "These boys are fixin' to die, not run away."

"I didn't ask your opinion, Mr. Moore!" replied Carroll frostily. The CO was getting a bit exercised about the whole fantastic affair.

At the crest of the ridge, the two Cheyennes wheeled their ponies and sat motionless looking back down the trail. No sound broke the tense stillness; even the keening squaws were silent. The youths began to sing in unison their death song. The eerie, high-pitched chant was unintelligible to the soldiers, but Joe Moore unconsciously repeated aloud and in English the opening words:

"Man dies . . . the mighty buffalo dies. Only the earth and the mountains live forever. . . ."

"*Ai-ee!*" wailed the women watching on the ridges, mournfully echoing: "Only the earth and the mountains live forever!"

Lieutenant Robertson, who had not lowered his field glasses

for an instant since the two braves emerged from the pines, spoke quietly: "Here they come!"

Yelling the Cheyenne war cry, Head Swift and Young Mule heeled their ponies into a dead run down the steep trail straight at Pitcher's detachment. Halfway down the hillside the doomed braves opened fire, pouring lead from their Winchesters as fast as they could work the levers. Not a bullet scored; the Indians were shooting high. Fifty carbines blazed a murderous welcome as the wild riders bore down on the troops. Young Mule's pony screamed and went down at the first burst of fire, throwing Young Mule twenty feet. The boy landed hard on the rocky trail and lay still.

Head Swift charged on alone, pumping the last three shots in his rifle at Lieutenant Pitcher and missing all three. He got within yards of the troops before the excited marksmen dropped both horse and rider with a final volley.

Now Young Mule jumped to his feet and charged Major Carroll's command. A hundred carbines blasted at him, and yet he futilely emptied his Winchester before he caught a slug. He fell and dragged himself painfully on hands and knees into a dry wash to seek cover in the scant brush. After him raced the cheering troopers, Lieutenant Robertson leading.

"We crawled through the brush toward him," related Robertson in his official report, "not aware that he was yet dead, and suddenly stumbled upon his body. I was startled, awe-struck, by the weird beauty of the picture he made, as he lay in his vivid color of costume and painted face, his red blood crimsoning the yellow of the autumn leaves upon which he lay."

Ghosts of Gold and Glory

by Nell Murbarger

Empty streets, wrapped in sage and silence; weary old buildings, drowsing in the sun. Crumbling walls and nameless graves, and a lone wind whispering through the night.

This is a ghost town—a mining camp that has had its day, has sung its song.

Every land on earth, every period of time, has known its deserted villages, but only the western United States has propagated them like mushrooms in a meadow. Dream cities, sired by hope and suckled on honest labor, they flourished for a day and faded and were forgotten. From the beaches of Oregon to far above timber line in Colorado, from the Canadian border to the Rio Grande, they drowse in the midst of their mine dumps and memories, no smoke curling from their chimneys, no commerce stirring the dust of their lonely streets.

How many such ghost towns there are in the West is something no man can say, but it's my guess their number is far greater than most persons realize. Since I became interested in these old camps about thirty years ago, I have personally visited and photographed more than four hundred of them and have mapped the locations and collected historical backgrounds of nearly twice that many; yet even now scarcely a week passes that I don't learn of other boom camps previously unknown to me.

Maybe you've wondered how ghost towns come into being and what sort of folks lived in them and why they were started, only to be abandoned in the end.

It's really very simple.

Their pattern was cut in California, as an aftermath of the gold rush of 1849. For every Argonaut made wealthy by that mad stampede, ten others failed to connect with pay dirt, and by the middle 1850's hordes of disappointed gold-seekers were turning away from California's overcrowded diggings. Still seeking the Golden Fleece, they forged north into Oregon and south to Mexico and streamed back over the Sierra Nevada into the Great Basin and on to the Rockies.

Using their burro's tail for a compass, pitting their wits against hostile savages and heat and cold and thirst and starvation, these legions pressed always deeper into the Great Unmapped. As they moved forward they panned the gravel of streams and sampled quartz ledges; and if they found "color," they staked claims and worked the ground until dwindling supplies at last forced their return to civilization.

Back at the nearest settlement—possible 100 or 150 miles from their strike—our prospecting partners exhibited their samples and talked. They were proud of their discovery and wanted everybody to know about it and share in it.

"Hell's fire, pardner—there's gold enough in that mountain for every man in Idaho! Come on—grab yourself a claim!"

It wasn't necessary to twist anyone's arm—they came!

If the ore proved to be rich and fairly plentiful and a few glowing reports percolated to the outside world, there might even be a "rush" to the new strike.

We mid-Twentieth Centurians, piddling around with Geiger counters and black lights and "strategic minerals" that look more like road-building material than anything else, can have little conception of the feverish excitement that attended every major mining stampede of seventy-five to one hundred years ago.

Into remote lands that weeks before had known only sagebrush and jackrabbits suddenly would be flooding a tidal wave of madly hurrying humanity—strings of heavily laden packmules and burros, footpackers, handcarts, men pushing wheelbarrows, every conveyance loaded to capacity, every Pilgrim bound for the same destination, the same poor man's paradise.

Converging from all directions, by every mode of travel, would-be prospectors, mining engineers, surveyors, opportunists, long-line skinners, faro dealers, tradesmen, painted women of the night, bullwhackers with whips a dozen feet in length, saloonkeepers, assayists, Chinese, Indians, Cousin Jacks, Yankees, Chileans, Mexicans . . . a rolling tide of frontier humanity from every mining camp between British Columbia and Sonora, all drawn to one spot like steel filings to a magnet . . . all jostling, shoving, cursing, quarreling, laughing, showing ore samples and assay certificates, buying and selling "mines" without ever laying eyes on the property, fighting to purchase flour at seventy-five dollars a sack and bacon at three dollars a pound . . . fighting for a chance to pay a dollar a night for a pair of dirty blankets and space on the ground to roll them.

That was a mining stampede, a typically western extravaganza, repeated over and over again for a period of more than sixty years.

No one knew, of course, whether a new district would peter out in two months or would go on producing for two centuries. The only means of determining this little item was to dig the ore out of the ground and mill it and sell the bullion.

While that digging and milling was being accomplished, these hungry hordes could scarcely be expected to jackass their way across country every time one of them ran low on plug-cut or blasting powder. Furthermore our frontier miner was distressingly human. He wanted to belly up to a bar now and then and h'ist a few. He wanted to break the killing grind of his labor with an occasional fling at faro or blackjack, and he had a strange hankering for naughty, painted women—maybe because they reminded him of nice, unpainted women he had left behind in Kansas and Ohio. What was more important our miner had hard money in his jeans—likely more money than he had ever before known—and he was willing to pay double what his "stateside" brother would have given for the same stock in trade.

The only practical solution was to start a new town at the scene of discovery.

It was easily done. Pitching his tent, the saloonkeeper turned a wagon box on its side to serve as a bar and installed as stock and equipment a barrel of rot-gut whiskey and half a dozen tin cups. Assayists and Chinese laundrymen hung out their shingles. Someone else began serving meals; someone started a livery stable.

Many such towns never progressed beyond the tent stage—"rag towns" they were called. But if the district held up encouragingly, the tents would be succeeded by wooden buildings; eventually, by brick and stone. The population of the camp would grow to several thousand persons—women and children, as well as men. Hotels and banks, possibly even a stock exchange and opera house, would be built. Newspapers and volunteer fire companies would be founded, lodges chartered, schools and churches organized.

Everything would zip along beautifully for two years, or ten years, maybe even for thirty years. And then would come a day when more astute citizens could sense that the old camp was losing her one-time bounce. Her ledges were petering out, her mills were closing. More miners were leaving town than were arriving. . . .

When the handwriting appeared on the wall, the wise ones got out—but quick!

Some camps died slowly, grudgingly. Others went "Pouf!" like a candle flame in the wind.

But what the hell! Over on Indian Creek, up at Thunder Mountain, Somebody knew Somebody Else who had found gold nuggets big as cabbage heads and seams of native silver so pure you could cut it with a hatchet! Sure she'd been a good camp, but this new camp, pard—this new camp'll beat her forty ways from Sunday!

The king was dead. Long live the king!

Business houses were abandoned, their heavier merchandise still on the shelves. Fancy pianos and solid-oak furniture were left behind as homes were deserted. Pack rats set up shop in grocery stores; birds began nesting in mahogany bars and crystal chandeliers. Sage and greasewood crept back into streets where ribaldry had briefly reigned, and a lonely wind came to whistle through broken windows and run its gaunt fingers over cold chimneys and silent graves.

One more mining camp had run its cycle from sagebrush to sage.

Another ghost town had been born. . . .

With the last major gold strike nearly fifty years in the past, it is almost impossible for any person living today to realize the abundance of precious metal that existed in certain sections of the West, a century and less ago. In the face of that glittering Golconda, man ceases to wonder that those early Argonauts should have offered up a string of boom camps as sacrifice to Midas. The only wonder becomes that any one of those teeming thousands should have escaped with his sanity intact, his honor undefiled!

Which district produced the richest ore or the best placer ground is difficult to say. The history of California's gold rush is interwoven with reports of streams that yielded a pound of gold per man, per day, and other streams that yielded $1,000 in gold to every lineal foot of creek bed. James H. Carson, working near the present ghost town of Carson Hill, panned 180 ounces of gold in ten days, and from the Morgan mine nearby came the largest nugget ever found in the United States—a solid mass of gold weighing 195 pounds and valued at $43,534!

California was rich in gold—there's no arguing that point!—but so were other sections, as well.

When placer miners in central Idaho found gravel running $100 to the pan in gold, they founded the town of Florence, in 1861, and one of the wildest stampedes in the history of the Northwest soon brought ten thousand persons to throng those newborn streets.

At Leesburg, another Idaho town of fabulous richness, a single wheelbarrow load of earth yielded $1,000 in gold dust and nuggets! The discovery had been made by a group of Southern miners, who had named the new camp for their hero of the hour. Northerners, learning of the new district, were fairly eating their hearts out to get in on that rich gravel, yet they couldn't quite stomach the idea of living in a town named for Robert E. Lee. The solution, of course, was the founding of Grantsville, a mile away.

But the Southern gentlemen had the last laugh. Their town of Leesburg grew so fast it absorbed Grantsville and continued to spread over the landscape until it boasted seven thousand inhabitants, one hundred houses, and a main street a mile long! In the course of its productive years, the Leesburg mine put forth $16,000,000 in gold—but Grantsville and Leesburg alike are ghost towns today.

Even spectacular as they were, these golden harvests from Idaho falter and grow pale in the light of stories from several of Montana's placer fields—particularly Diamond City, once a frontier metropolis of ten thousand persons, where early miners working on bedrock reportedly washed $1,000 in gold from *each pan of gravel,* and seven pans of concentrates taken from the sluices in one cleanup are said to have yielded $114,800!

In the category of lode gold, the Oscar surely must go to Nevada, where one carload of ore from Goldfield returned to its shippers the staggering sum of $574,958.39, and ore from the National Mine in Humboldt County assertedly assayed as high as

$200 a pound. According to old-timers, even the material used in surfacing National's streets carried $4,000 in gold to every ton of rock!

Nevada also may have produced the country's richest silver ore. At the Eberhardt mine, near the present ghost town of Treasure City, an open cut excavation seventy feet long, forty feet wide, and nowhere more than twenty-eight feet deep, produced more than $3,000,000 worth of silver! One piece of ore taken from this glory hole weighed close to four tons, assayed $8 and $10 to each pound, and was so pure its metal could be hammered into sheets without the necessity of smelting!

Another rich silver mine was the Pine Spring, located at Turkey Creek, Arizona. While sinking a small diameter shaft to a depth of twenty feet, the owners removed more than $50,000 in ore, including several chunks of hornsilver weighing around sixty pounds each and assaying $14 to the pound! Other ore in the mine, according to U.S. Government mint reports, ran as high as $26,000 to the ton!

But these spectacular dips into the Purse of Fortunatus should not be taken to mean that life in the early mining camps was all beer and skittles and gravel that carried $1,000 in gold to the pan. For every prospect that developed into bonanza proportions, there were a hundred others that paid off only lightly or not at all. And there was hard, hand labor, labor whose like and extent is almost inconceivable to miners of today.

There was the everlasting hand drilling through hard rock with doublejack and steel—the ultimate in this regard possibly being reached in the Murphy mine at Ophir City, Nevada, where 18,000 drill steels were sharpened monthly for a crew of forty men, and more than twenty-five hundred manhours of labor were required to sink only ten feet of shaft!

Prodigious labor also was occasioned by water—either too much of it or not enough.

There was good placer ground at Malheur City, Oregon, but no water for separating the gold from the sand. To remedy this situation miners of the camp dug "The Eldorado Ditch," whereby the water of Last Chance Creek on the south fork of the Burnt River might be carried to the desert settlement. The ditch was excavated entirely by pick-and-shovel labor—much of it through solid rock—and at the time of its completion (1873) it was the largest canal in the West. It cost $250,000, was wide and deep enough to float rafts of logs down from the mountains, and it *was 120 miles in length!*

As soon as water began flowing through the ditch, several other towns were established, and millions of dollars worth of gold dust was washed from the sands. But the ditch is now dry and abandoned—and so are the camps it served.

Incidentally, I never read or hear about hard work that it doesn't call to mind my friend, Maury Stromer. His achievement, I'll admit, doesn't rank with digging the Eldorado Ditch, but I still think it's worthy of mention.

Maury, when I knew him, was past seventy years of age, and the last survivor of Broken Hills, Nevada, where he had come with the first boom, thirty-seven years before. He was working a small mine called The Badger—stoping on a 4-foot vein that carried a couple of dollars in gold and 40 ounces of silver to the ton. Working alone, the old man would descend his 140-foot shaft by vertical ladder, shovel 350 pounds of ore into a bucket, reclimb that man-killing ladder to the surface—a distance about equal to the height of a fourteen-story building—start his gasoline engine, hoist the ore and dump it. Then he would relower the bucket, climb back down the ladder and fill 'er up again!

"Judas Priest, Maury," I said one time, "doesn't that program get terribly tiresome?"

"Oh, I don't know," replied my old ghost-town friend. "I reckon it might if a man was to carry it to extremes . . . but I only make about a dozen trips a day!"

Along with hard labor another terribly present partner in the early boom camps was Death. It rode in the form of "widow-makers" in the mines, accidents in the mills, quarrels over boundary rights; it came in the guise of diphtheria, drowning, scarlet fever, smallpox, typhoid, pneumonia, childbirth.

The spreading cemetery at DeLamar, Nevada, forms a ghastly indictment of early-day methods, when too many mines were improperly ventilated and ore mills in desert regions were too often operated with dry-battery boxes. Only three months in the mines or mills at DeLamar were enough to produce the fatal silicosis—"Miner's con." Even women and children, who never went near the mines, died from effects of Cambrian quartzite dust that forever drifted through the streets. Many of the smaller camps had neither doctors nor dentists. Arms and legs, mangled and threatened by gangrene, were amputated by means of butcher knives and carpenter's saws, with only whiskey as anesthetic. Aching molars were yanked out with blacksmith tongs or were knocked loose with hammer and cold chisel.

As Time goes about smoothing the scars and obliterating visual evidence of these former boom camps, one of the last remaining clues to man's transient presence is that lonely plot of ground inhabited by the "permanent settlers" of the camp—those *bons vivants* who were too slow on the draw or who otherwise terminated their temporal lease.

Anyone looking for drama will go a long way before he finds a better source than these old ghost-town graveyards—when they're the real McCoy. Although thousands of tourists thrill yearly to epitaphs in the boothill cemeteries at Tombstone, Arizona, and Dodge City, Kansas, these places—in my estimation—don't qualify as bona fide ghost towns, and I find their boothills a bit too synthetic.

The graveyard of a good, honest ghost town, on the other hand, doesn't need any fictitious inscriptions or catchpenny devices. Drama is as much a part of it as its weathered crosses and narrow mounds heaped with rocks and overgrown with cactus and sagebrush.

In many boom-camp cemeteries of the hotter desert regions are gravestone inscriptions bearing the phrase, "Succumbed to the

Elements," or "Died of Thirst." An epitaph in the old graveyard at San Andreas, California, reads, "Cruelly Murdered for the Sake of Gold," and numerous ones of the older cemeteries have gravestones bearing the succinct phrase, "Killed by Indians." Of the seventeen white men buried at Mowry Mine, Arizona, fifteen are known to have died violent deaths—mainly at the hands of Apache raiders.

Pioneer women and children who helped people the early boom camps bore no charmed lives, as inspection of any ghost-town cemetery will reveal. Markers in the old graveyard at Aurora, Nevada, show that women in this camp lived to an average age of *only twenty-eight years.* I particularly noticed one crumbly headstone marking the grave of a nineteen-year-old wife who died in childbirth. Its inscription closes with the desolate phrase:

She Hath Done What She Could

Other ghost-town graveyards harbor the remains of notable characters—particularly desperados. In the burying ground at South Pass City, Wyoming, lie "Mountain Jack" Alvese and twenty other gunfighters; and at Bothwell, another Wyoming ghost town, are planted the remains of notorious Jim Averill, and "Cattle Kate" Maxwell Watson, both lynched for cattle rustling. After robbing and killing more than one hundred persons, Montana's ex-sheriff, Henry Plummer, and two of his cohorts were hanged at the present ghost town of Bannack, Montana, where they are buried. (When founded in 1862, incidentally, this town of Bannack was in Oregon Territory. The next year placed it briefly in Idaho Territory, and with the creation of Montana Territory, in 1864, Bannack became its Territorial capital. The red brick building where Montana's first legislature met is still standing, deserted and forlorn.)

But getting back to our marble orchards, it would never do to overlook the famous graveyard in the ghost town of Bodie, California—possibly the only western mining camp to erect a gravestone to a martyred president.

Eighty years ago a lusty settlement of twelve thousand persons and reputedly the most lawless town in the United States, Bodie is now shrunken to a couple of old men. But its streets are still lined with buildings dating from the boom days—some of them partially furnished—and out in the spreading graveyard stands a tall marble obelisk erected to the memory of President Garfield!

The marker originally was purchased by public subscription as a means of paying proper respect to the town's founder, who had frozen to death in his cabin during the winter of 1880–81. Following considerable delay the imposing tombstone arrived from the East on the same stage that brought word of Garfield's assassination. In the several months elapsed since the demise of her fellow townsman, Bodie's enthusiasm for him had cooled so appreciably that her citizens now held a hasty election and voted to engrave and erect the stone to Garfield's memory instead!

Speaking of graveyards brings to mind the subject of resurrection, and resurrection recalls Alta, Utah, where the city council refused to have anyone resurrected and Skidoo, California, where one man was resurrected twice!

As combined results of her death-dealing avalanches and the fact that 110 men are said to have been killed in brawls at her twenty-six saloons, Alta's graveyard at the foot of Rustler Mountain was a large and flourishing institution, when into that mountain mining camp in 1873 came a mysterious stranger who for a small fee offered to resurrect all the dead in the cemetery.

The matter was laid before the town council, which gave the proposal considerable thought and heard recommendations of all interested persons. By and large the idea wasn't popular. Widows and widowers who had since remarried, folks who had inherited property, and other survivors, for their own personal reasons, seemed to think that those who were planted should remain planted.

The town council accordingly turned thumbs down on the proposal, but still the mysterious stranger hung around town. Possibly fearing that he might decide to give a free demonstration of his powers of resurrecting, the townspeople of Alta at last made up a purse of $2,500, which they presented to the stranger on the condition that he blow camp immediately.

He did . . . and Alta again breathed easy.

The affair at Skidoo was an altogether different matter, which had its beginning on the day Joe Simpson, owner of the Gold Seal Saloon, shot and killed Jim Arnold and was promptly lynched for his indiscretion. Immediately following the murder and lynching, county-seat newspapermen got wind of the proceedings and hotfooted it over to Skidoo in quest of photos. Both Simpson and Arnold already had been buried, but the obliging townsmen hastened to dig up Simpson's corpse, which they dusted off and hung all over again while flash powder flashed and local dignitaries posed importantly. With the newsmen happily returned to Inyo, Simpson was reburied.

Sometime later a doctor visiting in Skidoo chanced to mention his need of a nice human skull. Someone remembered Good Ol' Joe, whose corpse was obligingly dug up a second time, decapitated for the visiting sawbones and again reinterred beneath the thorny sod. The doctor was a little abashed by such proceedings, but Skidoo assured him it was quite all right.

Joe wouldn't mind, they said. Joe always had been an accommodating cuss. . . .

In addition to those notables who ended their mining-camp experiences six feet underground, practically all the larger boom camps had their budding celebrities who went on to bigger and better things, like Joaquin Miller, later famous as a California poet, who rode a pony mail route between Lewiston and Pierce City, Idaho; and Sam Clemens (Mark Twain) who swung a pick and worked in a silver mill at Aurora, Nevada.

In the present-day ghost town of Hornitos, California, stands the crumbling store building in which Dominico Ghiridelli sold beans and hardtack and thereby accumulated the stake that launched him in the chocolate business and made his name a household word around the world. At Hangtown, in the same state, Philip D. Armour operated a one-man butcher shop; Mark Hopkins (later of the "Big Four") sold groceries; and John Studebaker, future wagon and automobile tycoon, worked eighteen hours a day building wheelbarrows for the miners. Captain Robert Dollar, who would later found the Dollar Steamship Line, ran a general store at Usal, California, and Darius Ogden Mills, builder of the great Mills fortune, operated an assay office and bought gold in a tent "bank" in the old Forty-Niner camp of Columbia. (This town of Columbia, incidentally, once tried to wrest the California state capital from Sacramento and among its various qualifications cited thirty saloons, a stadium for bull and bear fights, a brewery, and "143 faro banks with a capital of over $1,500,000.")

Why the moldering bones of a dead boom camp should exert such terrific appeal is a little hard to understand, but theirs is a fascination that is perennial and almost universal.

The average cross-country traveler, unfortunately, seldom sees any but the highly touted ghost towns along the paved highways— the "tourist traps" I call them.

Armed with his WPA guidebook and battery of cameras, he is shown half a dozen different Hangmen's Trees where the same outlaw assertedly paid his final obligation to society and makes the acquaintance of Mark Twain cabins in towns Mark never saw. He downs a brace of highballs in the original Bucket-of-Guts Saloon (built in 1927) and tramps the hallowed stage of a theatre where Jenny Lind sang in legend, though not in fact. Having done and seen everything the guidebook says he should do and see, he speeds on his shorts-clad way, terrifically titillated by his firsthand brush with the Days of Gore and Glory.

But he still hasn't seen a good, honest, 180-proof ghost town, and five'll get you ten he never will see one! Folks of his sort just don't take kindly to dusty, high-centered roads and steep grades and places that are terribly far from electric refrigeration and innerspring mattresses and daily stock-market reports. . . .

Stangely enough it's places like this where the best ghost towns are found.

241

Folks sometimes ask which of the old camps I consider the most interesting; but that's a hard question to answer. Not only hard, but about as dangerous as judging a baby contest. Personally I like 'em all!

Most of Wyoming's early-day mining camps are completely deserted, and little remains to show that they ever existed. Montana's ghost towns lie mostly in the western section of the state. There are many of them, and some, such as Elkhorn, are highly explorable.

The state of Washington has a number of boom camps killed by depletion of coal mines and saw timber. The camp of Ruby in the early 1880's was considered the Babylon of Washington Territory, and four miles distant was a second fleshpot that rejoiced in the fantastic name of Loop Loop. Another Washington ghost town with an unusual history is Fidalgo City. To secure land grants offered as bonus for railroad construction, the Anacortes and Fidalgo City Electric Railway was built in 1891. After two trips over the line to insure title to the land grants, the tracks were torn up . . . and that ended the Anacortes and Fidalgo City!

Only the ghost towns of California are older than those of coastal Oregon, where camps such as Althouse, Kerbyville, Sailor's Diggings, Browntown, French Flat and Allentown date from 1851–55, when the first gold discoveries were made in the Northwestern part of the state. Most of these earlier camps have disappeared so completely it is almost impossible to locate their former sites, but many of the later founded boom towns in eastern Oregon (1860–80) have considerable to offer in the line of picturesque ruins.

Colorado's ghost towns—which could scarcely be more numerous if they had been shot into the mountains with a scattergun—are the highest in the nation, many of them being situated at more than 11,000 feet above sea level.

The town of Boughton, Colorado (later Oro City), was born in 1860 when prospectors dug through four feet of snow to pan the frozen sand. By the close of that season, five thousand persons had gathered there, and in less than eight years the camp produced $5,000,000. The richest ore taken from the Cresson mine, at Elkton, assayed $100,000 to the ton ($50 a pound) and was shipped to Colorado Springs with armed guards riding the ore cars. Three railroads once maintained stations at Goldfield, and so numerous were the shootings in Altman that the undertaker advertised "party rates" if all killings were scheduled on Saturdays.

At the present ghost town of Sunshine, also in Colorado, a prospector took $17,500 in gold from a cut only ten feet deep and twenty feet long. Fearing he had stumbled on something "too good to last," he made haste to sell the mine for another $17,500 . . . whereupon the new owners took out $196,000 in only twenty months' time.

Following discovery of hornsilver at Silver Cliff in 1879, the town rose in prominence until it was the third largest city in Colorado Territory and aspired to be the capital. Tarryall had its "Whiskey Pit," a deep hole worked by the placer method. The pit had originally received its name when a group of 150 miners worked it throughout one winter and spent most of their earnings for whiskey. Later any miner who was down on his luck was welcome to pan enough gold to pay for his drinks and lodging. Buckskin Joe, which has been reduced to what can be described only as "the approximate site," was founded following discoveries in 1859. For a time it was the seat of Park County and served its one thousand residents with three dance halls, a theater, newspaper, band, numerous gin mills and several quartz mills. By 1865, however, the camp was almost deserted; three years later the courthouse was moved to Fairplay, and Buckskin Joe became the ghostliest of ghost towns.

Something I've never been able to understand is how the old-time prospectors ever *found* some of the places where they built towns—like Moose City, Idaho, for example. When gold was discovered on Moose Creek in 1862, nine thousand persons swarmed into the new district, and a town of considerable proportions was built. Yet when I visited the ruins of that town in 1940, it still could be reached only by three days' packtrain journey from the nearest road and must be approached over the Bitterroot Mountains from Montana!

Idaho, incidentally, possesses a great wealth of historic and interesting ghost towns. When I last visited the camp of Dewey, the old Dewey hotel was still its showplace—a position it had held since days of the boom. Standing three stories in height with a cupola and double portico, it had been steam-heated and electrically lighted. Pierce City, oldest placer gold camp in the state, was also the first seat of Shoshone County, and the old two-story log courthouse still standing is said to be the oldest public building in Idaho. Another of Idaho's more interesting ghost towns is Silver City, dating from the 1860's. Silver, in her prime, was an up-and-coming center, whose newspaper—*The Owyhee Avalanche*—was the first daily in the state and boasted the first telegraphic wire service in Idaho.

Arizona too has her ghost towns. There's a whole flock of them in the vicinity of Prescott, in Yavapai County—Blue Bell, Congress, Crown King, Gillette, Humboldt, Jerome, Stanton, Tip Top, Turkey, Walker, Weaver and others—and down in Cochise County there's another covey, including Tombstone, which is altogether too lively and tourist-conscious to qualify as a true ghost town. Cochise County camps that are ghostly enough for anyone's taste include Charleston, Contention City, Galeyville, Paradise, Pearce and sundry more.

If you go prowling around the adobe ruins of Pearce, some old-timer's almost sure to come sauntering over with stories of this one-time city whence $30,000,000 in gold was shipped in only eight years' time. The original strike here was made in 1894 by James Pearce, whose wife operated a miners' boardinghouse at Tombstone. According to the Pine Bench Brigade, Pearce immediately sold his property for $250,000, but his helpmate refused to sign the deed until she had exacted a written contract giving her exclusive boardinghouse rights in the new camp!

One of my favorite old-timers was Uncle Billy Newton, last

survivor of Arizona's ghost town of McMillen, in Gila County. Sitting in his homemade rocking chair on the porch of his little adobe cabin, Uncle Billy would puff his pipe and look out over the ruins and spin endless yarns of that once-great camp which he had known since the lush days of the 1870's.

He often told about Charlie McMillen and Rory Harris, discoverers of the rich Stonewall Jackson mine that had launched the camp. Like many prospectors before them and since, McMillen and Harris realized little good from their sudden windfall. After taking out $60,000, they sold the mine for $160,000 more and to all appearances were sitting pretty for life.

"But poor ol' Charlie drank himself to death in a few months' time," Uncle Billy would reminisce. "Harris played it smart. He used his share to buy a seat on the San Francisco Stock Exchange. Ninety days later he was broke and back in Globe washing dishes in a cheap hash-house. . . ."

After Uncle Billy's death I was prowling through his cabin and found the insides of his cupboards all lined with yellowed and brittle pages of the *Arizona Silver Belt,* published at "Globe City, Arizona Territory," in 1878.

Over in Mohave County lie the twin ghost camps of Oatman and Gold Road, where a fast-diminishing retinue of graybeards tell of the mighty Tom Reed mine and of close to $100,000,000 in gold taken from these dry, burned hills. They tell, too, of Oatman's momentous boxing and wrestling matches, held in the pavilion on Main Street, and of championship drilling contests when a man's public esteem depended on the depth of a hole he could sink in a piece of granite in fifteen minutes with jackhammer and steel.

"Back in the old days any man was proud to say he worked at Oatman," declared veteran miner John Voynich, as we sat on a sunny beach in front of the silent and abandoned Honolulu Club. "It was a good town to tie to . . ."

Also in Mohave County sleep the ghost towns of Mineral Park, Cerbat and White Hills.

When I first made the acquaintance of White Hills, that once-lively silver camp still numbered a few old-timers, who liked to tell a certain story on Jimmy Twiggs, former operator of a livery stable. Main kingpins in the development of White Hills, it seems, were the Denver mining tycoons R. T. Root and D. H. Moffatt, and whenever Jimmy had taken on a few too many nips he would stagger down Main Street shouting, "Hooray for Jesus Christ, George Washington and R. T. Root—the three best damned men in Mohave County!"

Utah hasn't too many good ghost towns. Some of her early boom camps, such as Park City and Eureka, are still operating; others have survived the painful metamorphosis from mining camps into farming centers, and the great old camp of Alta has been completely reborn as one of the leading ski resorts in the West. So far as I have been able to learn, not one of her original buildings is still standing.

Keeping these several angles in mind, the most interesting true ghost towns in the state are probably Silver Reef, first place in the West where silver was discovered in sandstone; the neighboring towns of Newhouse and Frisco, where the Hornsilver mine was once valued at $46,000,000—then more than the assessed valuation of all the other real and personal property in the Territory of Utah—and Iron City, where a number of old stone buildings dating from the 1860's recall the days when this place was site of the second iron smelter west of the Mississippi River.

Gold Hill, in western Tooele County, has had three booms—silver, 1892; tungsten, 1917; and arsenic, 1945—but as of now she's a quiet old ghost. Possibly her most colorful era were those years when her efforts were directed toward the mining of tungsten.

One of the more spectacular properties in the district was the Reaper No. 3, owned by the Seminole Copper Company. The Reaper was terrifically rich—some of its scheelite ore carrying as much as 78 per cent tungsten. From a glory hole forty-five feet long, fifty feet deep and nowhere more than fifteen feet wide, more than $80,000 worth of tungsten was mined during the summer of 1917 alone! As a protest against the exorbitant freight rates then prevailing, every pound of this ore was sent to Salt Lake City *by parcel post!* Packaged in small quantities to comply with postal weight limits, tons of the concentrate poured through the Gold Hill post office. Mail stages were swamped, financial ruin faced the contract carrier and postal facilities at both ends of the line were strained to the breaking point. But the mail—and the Reaper's tungsten—still went through.

As New Mexico's more interesting ghost towns, I would choose Bland, Chloride, Cerrillos, Elizabethtown, Georgetown, Golden, Kingston, Mogollon, San Pedro, Shakespeare and White Oaks.

When silver, assaying 12,000 ounces to the ton, was discovered near the present site of Shakespeare in the 1860's, William Ralston, San Francisco financier, immediately acquired a flock of claims which he incorporated in London for 6,000,000 pounds sterling, and the rush was on.

Shakespeare was a rough, spectacular camp. In the dining room of the Stratford Hotel, Ross Woods—son of the proprietress—was killed by Bean Belly Smith in a quarrel over an egg; and from the rafters of the Grant House, another of Shakespeare's leading hostelries, the Law and Order League hanged Sandy King and Russian Bill. Sandy had shot up the town twice in one week, which in Shakespeare's opinion constituted "a damned nuisance" and a capital offense.

When the Law and Order Committee stormed the jail to remove Sandy from custody, they found there a second prisoner, a young Russian who had been nabbed while in possession of a fancy horse which looked as if it might belong to someone else. As the leaguers didn't cotton to horsethieves any more than they did to "damned nuisances," they took the stranger along with Sandy. In the space of ten minutes both men were tried, found guilty and hanged.

A few days after the double lynching, inquiry was received from the Russian Embassy in Washington, D.C concerning Lieutenant William Tannenbaum of the Imperial White Hussars, the

wealthy son of Countess Telfrin of the Czarina's court. The Lieutenant, it was set forth, had been traveling through the American
West, incognito, and when last heard from had been starting east
from a place called Tombstone, Arizona.

The photo enclosed with the letter was that of the yellow-haired
young man who had come to his end on the Grant House rafter.

Yet another of my favorite Shakespeare stories concerns the
hanging of Arkansas Black. Arkansas, it seems, was a handsome
sort of ladies' man, with snapping dark eyes and a little black
mustache. Soon after locating at Shakespeare he had become seriously involved with one of the town's married women, and the
case was referred to the Law and Order League.

Adjusting a hemp noose about the culprit's neck, the committee swung him to the crossbar of the stage company's corral gate.
After giving his neck a good stretching, they let him down, telling
him to take warning and leave town. But Arkansas was stubborn.

"I just got here!" he protested. "I like the place . . . and nobody's gonna run me out till I'm ready to leave!"

Three times they swung him on the rope, each time letting him
hang a little longer; but still Arkansas refused to leave town. The
fourth time they let him swing until he quit kicking, and then
the vigilante chief ordered his release.

"He's too good a man to hang," observed the head leaguer,
wearily. "Tell that other so-and-so to take his damned woman
and get out!"

Many of the old camps still have their "Uncle Jimmies" and
"Uncle Billies" and "Aunt Susans," and to talk with them is to
"shake the hand that shook the hand" of history.

Mrs. Sam Bernard had come to the present ghost town of Kingston, New Mexico, as a bride, sixty-five years before I met her in
1948. As we sat on her porch in the silent old town, she repictured
for me those rousing days when the Apache chief Victorio was
raiding and killing in the surrounding Black Range, when Ed
Doheny, future petroleum king, was getting his start in Kingston
as a hardrock miner and A. B. Fall, later to be U.S. Secretary of the

Interior under President Harding, was teaching the three R's to Kingston's small fry.

"All this flat was covered with houses in those days," said the tiny, frail old lady. "The mines were all running . . . there were twenty-six saloons in the town . . . everybody had lots of money . . . and we were all young . . ."

Another of my favorite old-timers is Dave Jackson, who came to White Oaks, New Mexico, more than sixty years ago and has lived there ever since. In addition to doing a little mining, Dave has set himself up as custodian of the White Oaks cemetery.

"There's no money in the job," he told me, "but shucks! Most of the folks planted here were my friends. . . . Somebody's gotta look after 'em!"

No one would guess it now, but this town of White Oaks was a lively place in its day! One-time frequenters of these streets included Billy the Kid and the frontier sheriff Pat Garrett. Madame Varnish dealt faro in one of the local bistros, and the future Western novelist Emerson Hough practiced law. Another White Oaks lawyer was W. H. McDonald, who was to become the first governor of New Mexico after its admission as a state. Governor McDonald is one of Dave's charges in the weedy old cemetery, as is Susan McSween Barber. After her heroic role in the Lincoln County (New Mexico) War in which her first husband, Alexander McSween, was slain, Susan lived on to become "Cattle Queen of New Mexico." She eventually remarried and spent her declining years at White Oaks, where she was a close personal friend of my friend Dave.

Martha Leonard came to the present ghost town of Unionville, Nevada, eighty-six years ago and has lived there ever since—which gives her a perfect right to call her husband a johnny-come-lately, since he arrived in the town only seventy-three years ago! Mr. and Mrs. Moroni Myers have lived in the old silver-lead camp of Minersville, Utah, for eighty-nine and eighty-three years, respectively—Mrs. Myers having been born there and Moroni arriving with his parents when he was only a few months old. Moroni, incidentally, worked in the old Lincoln mine, whose early lead yield was used principally for making bullets to repel Indian attacks!

Another grand old-timer—now gone on to Better Prospecting—was Aunt Mary Laird, for many years sole inhabitant of the desolate ghost town of Joy, perched on the edge of Utah's Great Salt Desert. How that blizzard-swept, heat-swept little jumping-off place ever acquired such a name is more than I know.

Aunt Mary had worked as barmaid and sporting woman during the boom at Virginia City, and like many who have known the seamier side of life, her heart was as big as all outdoors. When either friend or stranger, Indian or white man, drove into the yard of her drab little wind-battered shack, she would come dashing out the door shouting her stock greeting, "My God, sweetheart—where yuh been all these years? Have you et?"

Still thinking back over the old-timers I've run across in boom camps, I'm reminded of the California gold-rush town of Enterprise—the first ghost town I ever visited. After spending a few days there in 1926, I returned in 1932, rented a miner's shack for $1.50 a month and stayed for a year and a half. Included in the town's white population of twenty-three persons were Johnny Alm and Old Lady Rollins, who had lived directly across the street from one another for more than seventy-five years. They didn't like each other any too much, and when they'd start arguing ancient history it was better than any TV show ever filmed.

"Why you old she-goat!" Johnny sputtered one time. "What do you know about the *early days* in Enterprise? Dammit, I was five years old before you were even born!"

Ghost towns follow no stereotyped pattern. Some of them still possess lengthy streets flanked by scores of abandoned but well-preserved buildings. Other towns, generally as a result of fire, have been leveled to their bare foundations, and still others have vanished from the face of the earth. No road leads to them, no visible evidence remains. These are the towns buried by landslides, towns whose sites have been dredged away in subsequent developments and towns that have drowned.

Ghosts of Gold and Glory

The copper-mining camp of Kennet, California, which I knew twenty-five years ago as a pleasant old ghost with tree-shaded streets and many historic stone buildings, now lies under four hundred feet of water on the bottom of Lake Shasta, part of California's Central Valley project. St. Thomas and Callville, Nevada, were drowned by Lake Mead (Hoover Dam); Bonita Lake, in New Mexico, lies seventy-five feet deep over the former mining camp of Bonita City; and up in northeast Washington the towns of Fort Colville, Kettle Falls, Daisy and Inchelium were drowned by the rising waters of Grand Coulee Dam.

But it remained for Roosevelt, Idaho, to dunk itself without man's assistance.

Founded when Teddy and his Rough Riders were making history, the town soon boasted a population of one thousand persons, numerous stores and five saloons, each of the latter being equipped with a piano which had been packed over the mountains on mule back. Everything was going merrily until a landslide thundered into the canyon at the lower end of town, where it damned Monumental Creek. Attempts to blast the stream bed open were to no avail, and the impounded water began creeping into the business section. Improvising crude boats and rafts, all residents of the camp managed to escape with their lives, but every building in the town—as well as all the pianos—were lost. When the nature-made lake struck its permanent level, water lay one hundred feet over Roosevelt's principal intersection—and there it has remained!

Threat of destruction by avalanche hovered over the northern mountain camps like a cloud of doom. All the buildings in Edgemount, Nevada, including a twenty-stamp mill, were destroyed by a single snowslide in 1917, and during the same week the town of Jarbidge, also in Nevada, experienced more than one hundred slides in only twenty-four hours! Most of the slides stopped just short of the camp, but one penetrated into the residential area, scooped up a five-room dwelling, carried it two hundred feet and slammed it into another house, which was knocked from its foundation by the impact.

But in the matter of disastrous avalanches, no other western mining camp suffered so drastically as Alta, Utah—the town of the unresurrected dead.

One great slide that thundered down the mountain in 1874 claimed sixty known lives and destroyed many buildings. Several smaller slides took their human toll, and in 1885 another giant avalanche killed fifteen men and caused a fire which leveled nearly all the town not already buried under snow and rock.

But minor incidentals like blizzards, avalanches and sudden death couldn't intimidate those rugged individualists of the nineteenth century—not when the payoff was gold and silver!

Contemplating our western ghost towns, where the wheels of business no longer turn, too many observers are prone to interpret their silence in terms of failure and defeat.

But the ghost town does not represent a lost cause, nor should it be regarded as a symbol of greed or disillusionment or dead hope. To so consider it is to repudiate the pioneers who were responsible for these towns—the men who blazed new trails into far places and wrested treasure from desert hills and remained to fill unmarked graves.

Rather than damning them as "a lame and impotent conclusion," I prefer to regard these ephemeral camps as labor pangs in the birth of an empire. Their hour of glory was brief, but in their brief passing they helped break down the barriers of time and distance and served as stepping stones on the road to permanency and stability.

After the last man to have lived in these towns has staked his last claim on earth and the last weary wall and foundation has crumbled back to dust, still these camps must endure in memory as symbols of a vanished era—a glorious, free-wheeling, high-rolling, never-to-come-again era—when giants strode the land with man's greatest dream cradled in their hearts.

Golden Sands of
Whiskey Run

by Francis E. Sell

The southwestern coast of Oregon was a fairyland in 1851. Ever-green forests came down to the beaches, and the blue rollers of the Pacific creamed endlessly on the white sands. It was a beauti-fully uninhabited country save for a few Indian villages at the mouth of the salmon rivers. No wonder Joe Groulois and Jean Baptiste were in no hurry as they journeyed south from Fort Vancouver.

They paused for days with the Umpqua Indians, lolling about the bark lodges—eating, resting, making love to the doe-eyed, dusky-complexioned young squaws who served them in the guest lodge.

"But one must go on, *non?*" Baptiste grunted, half a question, half a statement of fact. His eyes turned toward the flowering

dogwood on the hillside above the Umpqua River Indian encampment; they followed the long blue curve of sky south along
the beach.

They were many miles from Fort Vancouver to the north, and
the gold fields of California, their destination, still lay many
miles to the south.

They saddled their horses and packed their mules with a fresh
supply of dried elk meat which they had purchased with two Hudson's Bay Company hunting knives. Midmorning of a beautiful
early May day, they turned away while impassive, friendly faces
watched them plow south along the white sand beaches.

They swam their pack string across Coos Bay, while they ferried
their saddles and provisions across in an Indian dugout, paying
their fare with a yard of red cloth. Then again they were on a
broad coastal Indian trail just above high-tide mark.

Hot, sultry weather lay like a benediction on the coast. Jean
Baptiste, heading the pack string, pulled up at a small stream a
short day's travel south of Coos Bay where a sparkling shimmer of
fresh water poured over an expanse of jet-black sand. Dismount-
ing, he walked inland to be above the salt chuck, then knelt to
drink. Joe Groulois waited with the horses, absently watching a
white gull drift by on silent wings above the blue curl of the
breakers.

"Joe! Joe! Come quickly! *Mon Dieu,* what a snail you are!"

Groulois slid from his saddle horse, ground-hitching the pack
string, and ran toward the sound of Jean Baptiste's voice in the
low, screening willows.

"Gold!" Baptiste shouted, thrusting a handful of dripping yellow sand toward him. "Gold!" His black eyes snapped. "Gold of a
surety. We have made the rich strike."

That last was probably the understatement of the century. They
were literally standing on the greatest "flour gold" strike Pacific
beaches were to produce. True, some mining had already taken
place at Gold Beach, Oregon. The sands of Cape Blanco had

yielded a fair amount of dust, but this strike was destined to top them all.

The sands were literally golden, shimmering yellow in the May sunshine. *"Mon Dieu!"* Joe Groulois exclaimed. "This is impossible. This cannot be!" They scrambled through the low beach willows, following the course of the brook. As they advanced the richness of their strike became more and more evident. Flour gold could be scooped up in their hands.

Not only gold but the silver color of platinum was mixed with the black sands. Later the tailing sumps of mines were to be silver-colored with platinum, because it was at the time worthless. A miner held a quart pickle jar under a tailing screen and obtained a quart of platinum to send home to his small daughter. Generations later this jar was found in the attic and its contents were worth $2,350.

Jean Baptiste and Joe Groulois rushed back to their pack string. With trembling hands they pulled the burdens off their mules, unsaddled their horses and turned them out to graze on the bench above the beach.

They labored prodigiously until they had diverted the small stream, sending it alongside a ditch, the better to work the golden sands. Stars blossomed over the broad sweep of the Pacific. The trade winds died in the dark forest behind them. They only had time to pan a few shovelfuls of sand before nightfall but they got an ounce of flour gold to each shovelful.

The men talked while they ate a supper consisting of dried elk meat and black, unsweetened coffee. Their driftwood fire made a pinpoint of light against the dark, star-studded backdrop of the Pacific.

"This must be kept secret," said Joe Groulois. "We will work this carefully, but not one word—not even to our Indian friends—must we speak of this. *Mon Dieu,* what a strike! No more trapping for Hudson's Bay Company."

Daylight came, and they were working the bed of the small stream, sweating, slapping at sand flies; and their golden hoard increased at a fabulous rate. The tightly woven Indian baskets in which they had purchased dried venison were used as containers. Buckskin bullet bags, powder cans—anything which would hold gold—was pressed into service. But still there was no end.

That night when their campfire blazed up against the gloom, three Indians appeared. They talked Chinook with the French Canadians.

"Why you stay here?" the squat, greasy-fingered leader asked, eating a piece of the dried venison.

Jean Baptiste shrugged his shoulders. "We rest our pack string for a few days before continuing south."

The Indian stood up, thrust his hand over the heart of Baptiste. "*Ni-ka tum-tum hyui wa-wa!* (Your heart speaks loud otherwise)." He turned and walked off in the darkness, followed by his two companions.

Provisions ran low during the following days. They were down to dried elk meat alone. No sugar. No coffee. Their meager supply of flour was but a memory.

An Indian traveling up the beach trail from the south told them a company of Uncle Sam's Boston Men, as they called the soldiers, had landed at Port Orford, about forty miles to the south. There was plenty of Hyui Scopum fire water and white-man chuck to be had for a price.

Joe Groulois finally drew the job of journeying south to see about the possibilities of getting provisions. Baptiste, it was decided, should stay and work the claim.

"How much gold should be taken? Of a surety things will be high. A mule-load, perhaps?" Groulois looked at his partner.

"What is a mule-load of gold?" Baptiste shrugged. "Do we not stand on gold? Poof!"

If they had known the misadventure this trip south was to set in motion, they would have avoided Port Orford like a plague. But Groulois saddled of an early morning and headed south, trailing a mule with a load of gold. It was perhaps two hundred pounds, the usual standard pack load for mules in the west.

Blue combers were breaking along the beach. At the mouth of the Coquille River he had to wait for low tide before fording. The second day, earlier in the afternoon, he arrived at the blockhouse in Port Orford.

Soldiers loafed about the open gate of the stockade. Others were doing sentry duty on the beach trails, keeping an eye on a sullen encampment of Rogue River Indians, for this was on the eve of a general uprising. Already miners had been killed, a few isolated settlers murdered.

The raw seaport was a teeming city to Joe Groulois, used to the solitude of the northern beaches, a place where one would pick up news, talk to strangers.

He tied his saddle horse and pack mule in front of a log house which had a slab sign with "Saloon" burned in it. Inside, two whiskey barrels were propped up on a crude platform. A tin cup was chained to each one, and the bartender, rifle leaning against the rough board counter, waited on customers. A drink cost as much gold dust as the bartender could take from a miner's poke between thumb and forefinger—a universal custom in the gold fields, where actual currency was very scarce or totally absent.

Groulois drew a tin cup of whiskey, tossed it down, then extended a small Indian basket full of flour gold for the "pinch."

The bartender reached over, took his pay and eyed Groulois speculatively.

"Mining hereabouts? Don't remember seeing you before."

"Came up from the south just now, monsieur."

"Must have a way with those Rogue River Indians. They have been knocking off miners down that way the past month."

"I get along, monsieur. You see, I, too, am half Indian."

There was a tinkle of laughter in the doorway. "Señor, you could also get along with me."

Groulois turned. She was beautiful—she was smiling at him! Indifferent history doesn't record her name. Miners and soldiers called her the "Spanish Lady." A camp follower, she had come with the gold strike at Port Orford. She had it and to spare. Almost

257

immediately she showed concern about the large amount of gold Groulois carried.

It would be best, she suggested, reasonably enough, to leave that mule-load with her. "One can never tell, *señor*. A lot of evil people are here. One cannot be too careful."

Three days later Groulois turned north, his gold carefully cached at the Spanish Lady's cabin. She had outfitted him with a slab of bacon, some coffee and flour. The romance had moved fast. He was to get plenty of gold, as much as two mules could carry this time, then they would move away to a far country, build *"la casa grande."*

"But now one must work, for the season is short."

Within a week, there was a second trip and more smiles from the Spanish Lady, as Groulois unpacked his mules. With a scant load of provisions he turned north again to his inexhaustible treasure trove, the golden sands along the tiny rivulet which poured into the blue-curving waves a short ways north of Coquille River in Southwestern Oregon.

If Jean Baptiste protested these frequent trips to Port Orford or if he felt that Joe Groulois took more than his share of the gold, he showed no signs. "Things come high in the settlement, monsieur," Joe explained.

When Groulois reached Port Orford on his third trip, the Spanish Lady was gone. The miners said she had made her stake and caught a sailing vessel for San Francisco. History records the rather startling fact that a platoon of soldiers were assigned to take her gold aboard at the sailing.

When Joe Groulois turned north to his "diggins," he had a mule-load of whiskey. He unburdened himself to Baptiste, passing a jug back and forth as they lolled about their evening driftwood fire. "Of a certainty, you cannot trust a woman—unless she is Indian and you can take a lodge pole to her now and then!"

They drank far into the night. Groulois talked maudlin about his unrequited love. Baptiste tried to comfort him between drinks.

It was a prodigious bender. How long it lasted is not recorded.

But eventually both came down with the "Blue Devils." They imagined that the forest was full of voices, that they could see campfires to the south. How much was real, how much was whiskey-soaked imagination, is pure speculation.

Early one morning they had their pack string in motion, fleeing north. Within a short distance, they decided they could further their flight by caching their two mule-loads of gold. So they turned aside from the Indian trail they traveled, between their diggings and Empire, Oregon. Beside a huge red cedar, scarcely a hundred yards from the trail, they buried their four hundred pounds of gold dust.

This tree had an odd, twisted root system on the seaward side.

After burying their gold, the men continued on until they reached Fort Vancouver, where they eventually sobered up. Then they realized that their wild flight was scarcely justified. Now they must return at once, for their gold and to work their claim.

But now it was autumn. They were indebted to the Hudson's Bay Company, and the factor placed little confidence in reports of mule-loads of gold when the tale was told by drunken French Canadians. You don't walk out on a Hudson's Bay obligation, either. Indians were paid to bring back trappers who thought they might beat the company. You paid up by trapping and delivering your furs at the fort.

Jean Baptiste and Joe Groulois trapped. With the return of spring they delivered their bundles of beaver pelts to Fort Vancouver, saw their account marked paid. Then they turned south toward their treasure buried beside the Indian trail. There was no tarrying with the friendly Impquas this time, even though the Indian girls were just as attractive, their reception just as friendly.

At Coos Bay, Oregon, Baptiste and Groulois noticed a change in the appearance of the country. Where green forests had pressed down to the blue waters of the bay, nothing remained but charred snags and fallen trees.

Soon they came to the section where they had turned aside to bury their gold. But even the big red cedar with the odd-shaped roots was gone. They searched carefully till nightfall. Tired, discouraged, they lay beside their campfire. Next day they searched again. But it was no use. The fire had so changed the appearance of the country they never did find their buried gold.

Only one thing to do—return to the little rivulet where the golden sands were. "Poof! What are two mule-loads of gold when one knows where there are many more?"

They rode along the beach, the breakers creaming about their horses' feet, both preoccupied with thoughts of the small, tinkling brook with the golden sands.

When they arrived, long shanties greeted them where the beach willows once made an impassable thicket. Smoke curled from at least two score log cabins. The beach and creek were staked tight. Not only was their small brook claimed, but miners had discoveries older and higher beach beds, fabulously rich—discoveries which later were to be developed into the Eagle Mine, the Pioneer Mine, and produce millions of dollars.

"Get out, you damn half-breeds!" they were greeted.

Joe Groulois fingered his long skinning knife at his belt. But they were too many.

"How, monsieurs, did you find this place?"

"That's easy." It was the bartender from Port Orford who answered. "Three Indians put us onto this for a jug of Hyui Scopum fire water. Those three Indians got drunk and touched off the damnedest forest fire you ever did see. Go on up the beach, maybe you can find another claim. You are not getting in here."

"Yeah," added another miner, "you drank your whiskey and run. So we called these diggin's Whiskey Run."

Jean Baptiste and Joe Groulois got nothing more out of their discovery than the questionable honor of naming the fabulous strike.

They turned north again to search for their buried treasure. Winter came, and they trapped again for Hudson's Bay Company. Next summer they returned again to search. But they never found their two mule-loads of gold.

Golden Sands of Whiskey Run

New forest has covered the scars of the great fire which raged uncontrolled through this primitive area of a hundred years ago. The gulls still glide just above the blue curve of the breakers, necks outstretched, watching for sea bounty. But the brooding forests still keep the secret of their buried treasure trove.

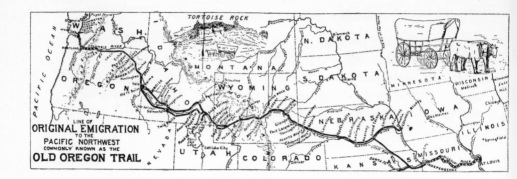

ORIGINAL EMIGRATION
LINE OF
TO THE
PACIFIC NORTHWEST
COMMONLY KNOWN AS THE
OLD OREGON TRAIL

The Indomitable
Francis Parkman

by Tom Bailey

The range of his vision was less than ten yards; the only things in front of him that he could distinguish clearly at the moment were his horse's ears and the trail in the immediate foreground. Beyond that everything was blurred, and he didn't know that he had just passed a war party of Sioux braves who had watched him from a hill.

He had a bad case of dysentery, and his head, "overcrowded with book learning," as his doctor had recently diagnosed, was throbbing with pain, yet he pushed on, relentlessly seeking knowledge of the West that would enable him to write about it firsthand and portray it as it was in that year of 1846. No man with so many physical handicaps to overcome ever sought to fulfill a more ambitious dream.

His name was Francis Parkman and he was to become one of America's greatest historians. Only by his iron will could he hope to forge the links of a chain welding together all his plans of a successful career with a pen, yet today, more than ever, Parkman's achievements stand out as an example of what the physically

262

handicapped may do if they have the courage to pursue their
ambitions.

It can literally be said that Parkman conquered a wilderness
with his pen, for his first book, *The Oregon Trail,* coming as it
did just before gold was discovered in California, lifted from the
minds of many would-be emigrants the bugaboos about overland
travel that otherwise might have kept them from making the long
and perilous journey. Parkman made it quite clear that well-
organized and sizable wagon trains could cross the continent without fear of annihilation. If the hardships could be endured, they
would arrive safe and sound at their destinations.

The book, though not intended for that purpose, did more to
stimulate travel westward during 1849 than any other single factor
except the lure of gold itself. Thousands who made the journey
that year said Parkman's book helped them make up their minds.
For several years thereafter copies of it were to be found in two
out of every three wagons that put in at Fort Laramie. One of the
first books to be written about the West, its widely recognized
authenticity, founded on the author's own personal experiences
as a traveler of that route, gave America a shot in the arm, a stimu-
lant that set in motion countless caravans wheeling toward a
westering sun.

Although it dealt in greater part with the Indians along the
way, it is nevertheless something of a "Bible" to those students of
western history who like their facts hard and cold. For the past
one hundred years it has served as a textbook on the American
Indian and his old way of life.

Parkman was riding alone that morning when his eyesight was
so bad, having taken a short cut to Fort Laramie while his traveling companions sought out a herd of buffaloes reported to be in
the vicinity. Only his apparent cool disregard of the Sioux saved
his life. The war party, already under observation by a Fort Laramie scout, was seen soon after fleeing south as if pursued by evil
spirits.

Shortly after he unknowingly passed the Indians, Parkman was joined in his ride to Fort Laramie by John Hathaway, the trail scout who had him under observation. (For the record I would like the privilege of stating here that John Hathaway, some forty-seven years later, was to become my great-grandfather. Handed down to me over the years were tales of their lasting friendship, so that now as I take up the Parkman saga, 115 years and four and a half generations later, I feel a certain affinity for the man, almost as if we were old, old friends.)

John Hathaway was characteristically immodest, yet honest, when he said of Parkman years later, "He was the most interesting man I ever met on the trail; for one who had been in the West but a few months, he knew the American Indian better than I did, and I thought I knew everything about Indians."

Both men were the same age, twenty-three, hardly adults under today's human timetable, but already they were standouts in their chosen professions.

Although in his book Parkman made few references to his illness, he was so sick at Fort Laramie that his friend and traveling companion, Quincy A. Shaw, urged him to turn back. Of that time he later wrote:

> I had been slightly ill for several weeks, but on the third night after reaching Fort Laramie a violent pain woke me, and I found myself attacked by the same disorder that occasioned such heavy losses to the Army of the Rio Grande [dysentery]. In a day-and-a-half I was reduced to extreme weakness, so that I could not walk without pain and effort. . . . I resolved to throw myself upon Providence for recovery, using, without regard to the disorder, any portion of strength that might remain to me.

He made no mention of the attacks of blindness which were plaguing him at the time, apparently preferring to ignore them as something that would quickly pass.

Francis Parkman was born September 26, 1823, in Boston, the son of the Reverend and Caroline Parkman. His grandfather

The Indomitable Francis Parkman

Samuel Parkman had become one of the richest merchants of that era, and it was Francis' share of this fortune, said to have been about $150,000, that enabled him to finance so many of his writing enterprises.

At the time of his graduation from Harvard, he was far from robust. He tried in the Harvard gym and on numerous hiking trips to build up his physique so that he might endure the hardships of wilderness travel. But he overdid it and went to Europe for a rest. The trip did not help him.

When he came home he decided to study law and give up his western trip; but the fever of exploration burned within him, and after receiving his law degree he set about making his plans, hopeful that the venture would restore his health.

Long before he and Shaw reached St. Louis, Francis realized that he was in no physical condition to endure hard travel, yet he would not give up. Symptoms of some of the ailments that would plague him for the rest of his life manifested themselves from day to day, one attack seeming to bring on another. One day partly blind, the next day suffering stomach pains and hampered by a throbbing headache, he had only a few days during the entire trip when he actually felt well.

His first really serious affliction was temporary blindness. He discovered one morning while in St. Louis that he could not see his hands before him.

"It must be something you ate," Shaw told him. "Lie down for a while. It'll pass."

When hours later his sight returned to almost normal, he was deliriously happy.

It was on April 28, 1846, that Parkman and Shaw, who had been roommates at Harvard, set out on the journey west. Parkman financed the expedition from his inheritance.

Two days out there was a recurrent surge of the "blind staggers" as Shaw called them. "Hadn't we better turn back," he urged, "before it's too late? There are no doctors where we're going."

"It will pass," Parkman insisted. "Man, do you realize this is the fulfillment of my dreams. How can I turn back now?"

They went by boat along the Missouri River as far as the border between Missouri and Kansas, where they hired a French-Canadian guide named Henry Chatillon, whom Parkman never tired of praising. They crossed a corner of Kansas and the whole of Nebraska without serious incident and arrived in Wyoming in about two months. Parkman described this portion of the trip in his book, reciting many amusing incidents that make good reading, yet at no time were there any real problems.

Fort Laramie was a post of the American Fur Company, for whom my great-grandfather, mentioned earlier, served as guide and trapper. Parkman insisted that he accompany them on west but Hathaway declined, fearful that if he accepted he would not be able to return to Illinois that fall for his wedding, scheduled for late November. It was a decision he was long to regret, for had he gone with Parkman, he still would have been back in time for the wedding and he would have earned enduring fame as one of the writer's companions.

Although Parkman did not mention Hathaway by name in his book, referring to him only as "R" for Rusty, the name by which travelers knew him best, they did exchange letters over a period of four or five years, about twenty in all, which are now owned by various private collectors.

The illness which beset the author at Fort Laramie was to plague him for weeks, yet it did not prevent him from moving in with the Oglala tribe to learn how Indians lived. The heart of his *Oregon Trail* is concerned with the arduous time he spent in an endeavor to achieve this experience. He gave to the Indians all the presents he had brought with him and so earned their admiration that the chief urged him to take the prettiest girl of the tribe as his own.

"You can't insult a chief," Parkman later told Shaw, who during this interval remained in Fort Laramie, "so I shared the same buffalo robe with her at night and bribed her to say that I had performed my duties as a husband; though I assure you, my skeptical friend, I did nothing of the sort."

During this sojourn with the Indians, Parkman ate the flesh of dogs and rode with the Oglalas after buffalo, although at times he could scarcely stay in the saddle. He joined in their rough games of skill, doing all the things that no man in his weakened condition should have done, for to reveal his illness to the Indians would no doubt have resulted in his quick expulsion from the tribe.

The net result of Parkman's observations was far from being a romantic description of Indian life. Had he remained with them for a shorter time, he told Shaw, he perhaps would have seen less of the filth and ugliness that was so prevalent. However, when they moved camp, as they frequently did to keep up with the constantly shifting buffalo herds, he moved with them. He watched their love-making, listened to their family bickerings, observed them in idleness and studied their daily habits, becoming the first white man ever to write so intimately about the mysteries of the American Indian.

What were the Plains Indians like before they were herded together on reservations? This question he answered so thoroughly that today high schools and colleges everywhere use his books for reference. Every public library carries a card reference in its "Par" file bearing the name Parkman.

But all was not filth and ugliness in the Indian camps. Parkman found the Indians to be honest within the framework of their established society. They might steal mules from their enemies, but anything of value left around an Indian camp was safe. Each respected the other's rights, unwritten laws were observed to the fullest and there was no adultery. All of this made the Indian, in spite of his lack of education, a more acceptable human being than his white brothers, some of whom if not restrained by authority would rape, steal and kill their own kind.

Customs and habits of the red man in his primitive state composed the bulk of Parkman's writings. After more than one hundred years no one has come up with more answers to the enigma of the American Indian than he did. He so understood the savage mind that he could walk into any strange camp without fear of losing his hair. There was something about his way of approaching them that won their friendship and admiration. At that early date most tribes were still friendly to the whites, who had not yet begun the great migration westward. Hostilities had already developed, however, among the Pawnees and Comanches and a few Crows who resented the white man's invasion of their lands.

On one occasion Parkman rode boldly into a Pawnee village and in a few minutes had established friendly relations with the chief. This so amazed Chatillon, the guide, that he suspected Parkman of possessing supernatural powers.

The nights spent in smoke-filled tepees did nothing for Parkman's eyes except to make them worse, and the kind of food he had to eat did something to his stomach that upset his entire nervous system. Yet he insisted on continuing his journey.

One day when a stray Indian dog joined the Parkman party, Parkman heaved up his breakfast. "Get that animal out of my sight" he told Chatillon. "I've eaten the flesh of so many dogs I can't stand the sight of them." For the rest of his life he was to shun dogs. If he saw one coming his way, he would detour round it. But nowhere in his writings did he ever mention his aversion to dogs. Neither did he inject much levity into his books, although he had a strong sense of humor and was constantly making tart remarks to his fellow travelers. His writings were all in a serious vein, and had it not been for the retentive capacities of Shaw's brain, much of Parkman's ready wit would have been lost to posterity.

At the foot of the Rockies, when they came to an emigrant camp, Parkman gave up. He was too weak to go on. But he made the best of it by talking all day long with a group of guides returning to St. Louis. From them he learned all he could about the rest of the trail, which he now believed he would never see. Like the good reporter he was, he obtained enough firsthand information from the experienced guides to fill his requirements and then turned back, but not over the same route. Parkman wanted to go back by way of Pueblo and Bent's Fort, then along the Arkansas River to the Westport cutoff.

"That's a tough journey," Shaw told him. "I wouldn't advise it. It would be much easier returning the way we came."

"There is just as much ground to bury me in one way as another," Parkman retorted, "and I'm not at all particular, my good friend. Any old spot will do just as long as you select one with a good view."

At this point Chatillon was ready to turn back, for he was unfamiliar with the route Parkman had selected and could be of no further use to them.

"No," Parkman said, "if I'm to be scalped, I can think of no person I'd rather be scalped with than you, Chatillon. In fact I would consider it quite an honor."

They skirted the Rockies, arriving in Pueblo in mid-August, where Parkman was confined to his bed for several days, too weak to stand on his feet. For the first time on the trip he found a doctor, or at least a man who claimed to be a doctor. After looking the patient over the pronouncement came, "I have to warn you, sir, that you're going blind and you may die at any moment from heart failure."

Despite his misery Parkman laughed. "But isn't there something else you can think of that's wrong with me? Surely you're not going to charge me a fee for so simple a diagnosis?"

As soon as he could travel, although he could make out objects at no greater distance than fifty yards, Parkman agreed to accept the company of four others heading for Bent's Fort. It appeared advisable now to travel in numbers. Hostile Pawnees and Comanches were reported to have gathered along the route following the passage of General Kearny's army to Santa Fe. Shaw also heard that due to the increasing danger of attack, the fort itself was all but deserted, and he urged Parkman to lay over a few days until conditions were more favorable.

"We'll do nothing of the sort," Parkman said angrily. "I've a book to write and I want to get back to Boston with all possible haste. So far Providence has been good to us. Let's hope this favor continues."

The first day out, along the valley of the Arkansas River, the party ran into a dense belt of fog and passed within fifty yards of a large Comanche war party without being sighted. For the rest of the few miles to the fort, Parkman's luck held, but they arrived to find it occupied by only a few invalid officers and men who had been unable to leave when the rest of the force pulled out with General Kearny's army. Indians had been seen scouting the layout, and an attack was expected momentarily.

The hot August sun beat down relentlessly, and the rest of Parkman's party wanted to pull out; but the author wouldn't hear of it. "Here is a fort," he said, "that some day will become a historic landmark. How can I pass up this opportunity to acquaint myself with what goes on here?" He was right. Bent's Fort did become a landmark, a place where history was written, and if you drive over U.S. Highway 50 through La Junta, Colorado, you have but to turn north on State 109 for a couple of miles to visit the old site.

The anticipated attack did not come, and after a few days Parkman was ready to go on; but on the eve of their departure he came down with another siege of "the shakes" and sufferd from dizzy spells which necessitated a further delay.

From his bed he quipped to Chatillon, "If this trouble of mine lasts long enough, my good friend, we might still have the honor of losing our scalps together."

Finally Parkman was ready to leave. "Get me into a saddle and I'll make it," he told Shaw.

Late that afternoon the party rode into a little clearing across which they could see the tops of tepees. It was too late to try and avoid the Indian camp, for already they had been seen by two squaws who quickly waddled toward the tepees to spread the alarm.

"I'll handle this," Parkman said. "You fellows wait here."

"Surely you're not going to ride into the camp," Chatillon said.

"Why not?" Parkman retorted. "I can be scalped there as handily as here."

Shaw then engaged in a bit of humor himself. "It's been nice knowing you, Parkman. See you when 'the roll is called up yonder.'"

Parkman was gone so long that his companions thought he was being held against his will, but presently they saw him riding toward them, accompanied by an Arapahoe chief.

Parkman announced that he had smoked the pipe of peace with the chief, who had extended his courtesy by offering bed companions for the night. How many of Parkman's party, if any, accepted the invitation Shaw did not disclose when he related the incident some years later, nor did Parkman mention it in *The Oregon Trail*.

The chapter of his book devoted to that portion of the journey deals almost exclusively with the friendly Arapahoes they met along the Arkansas, and they tarried several days while the author visited with the Indians and studied their living habits, which were about the same, he found, as those of the Oglalas and the Pawnees. It is interesting to note that Parkman made few references to his own physical handicaps; reading his account one somehow forms the notion that he was just as active as the others, especially in the buffalo hunts of which there were many along the trail. Shaw said later that Parkman actually shot some of the animals himself, but only at extremely close range when they were driven past him.

It soon became obvious to Shaw why Parkman had elected to return by way of Bent's Fort and the Arkansas: he had wanted to see the Santa Fe Trail. Soon they were seeing much of it, for they were constantly meeting the fast freight outfits and lines of covered wagons heading southwest. At every opportunity he tarried to speak with the experience-hardened freighters, learning all he could about them and their work. In his book he tells of meeting several companies of Missouri volunteers en route to join General Kearny's army in its conquest of Santa Fe and then of El Paso. Not only was he gaining a firm basis of fact, but he knew how to treat those facts with great literary skill.

As an example of his style, he wrote of this leg of the journey:

> At noon on the fourteenth of September, a very large Santa Fe caravan came up. The plain was covered with the long files of their white-topped wagons, the closed black carriages in which the traders travel and sleep, large droves of mules and horses, and men on horseback and on foot. They all stopped on the meadow near us. Our diminutive cart and handful of men made but an insignificant figure by the side of their wide and bustling camp.

There in a few lines Parkman gives the reader only a quick glimpse of the camp, but one immediately feels its bigness and its importance at the moment. And then one finds something of the good fellowship and camaraderie that might be expected between lighthearted travelers meeting on the trail.

When the Arkansas turned southwest, the party headed across Kansas to Westport, now a part of Kansas City, Missouri, and proceeded by river steamer to St. Louis, arriving early in October. They said good-by to the other travelers, including Chatillon, the guide, and returned to Boston by way of Chicago and the Great Lakes.

Anxious to begin his book he assembled his notes and writing materials only to find that he could not see a word he wrote. Undaunted he summoned Shaw and arranged for him to take dictation. "I shall write that book one way or another if it kills me," he told his friend.

"Now we go to work."

Six months later the book was completed in a hotel room in Brattleboro, Vermont, and appeared serially in the *Knickerbocker*, a New York magazine. The book itself made its appearance early in 1849 and became tremendously popular almost overnight. Re-

viewers in the East proclaimed it a masterpiece of factual reporting combined with the inimitable style of a master craftsman.

During these times Parkman's health made no appreciable improvement, and he remained in a highly nervous state, sometimes
refusing for days at a time to see his closest friends.

"I can't go on like this," he told Shaw one day. "I've got to
keep my mind occupied or I *will* go insane!"

No sooner had he finished *The Oregon Trail* than he began
planning a much more complicated work to be called the *History
of the Conspiracy of Pontiac,* which was to be part of several
volumes dealing with the struggle of the French and English for
possession of the North American continent.

For a man almost blind, and suffering from various other
maladies, this undertaking would seem to have been foolhardy,
for the time schedule Parkman had set for the endeavor would
require many work-crowded years. Though he was only twenty-
five and would finish the entire series at sixty-nine, it seemed
unlikely at the time that he could hold out physically for very
long. His doctor advised against the project.

"You advised me not to go west, too, and look what I accomplished," Parkman retorted. "If I listen to you I'll never get anything done."

"If you don't listen to me," the physician replied, "you'll not
be around to quarrel with me long."

Parkman found that his book had made him popular with
editors, who were clamoring for more material, and he devoted
much of his time to accounts of his life among the Indians and
on the trail, most of which appeared in magazines, and for which
he received top price. So popular were those articles that when
the *Knickerbocker* neglected to run the second installment of a
Parkman story, many of its readers threatened to cancel their
subscriptions.

Parkman found that indeed he had to keep his mind occupied
if he licked his maladies; the magazine stories he turned out
whetted his desire to live, and he gained back some of his eye-

sight, enough to enable him to work alone. Characteristically he overdid it, and the nervous condition returned to plague him.

Since he needed to do much research for his *History of the Conspiracy of Pontiac,* he decided to go to Paris, where much of the reference material was available. While there, he promised his doctor, he would take a long rest.

His first call in Paris was on an eminent specialist, Henri Coulet.

After a lengthy examination Coulet said, "Your symptoms are those of a man slowly going insane. I would recommend a long rest and that you do no work for at least a year."

"I know of no better place to go insane than in Paris," Parkman retorted. "At least you and I will have plenty of company."

In spite of the warning he frantically gathered volumes of reference material and hurried back to New York, anxious to get to work. Moving in with friends on Staten Island who had offered him a quiet place to work, he felt greatly encouraged.

He hired a girl to read to him from the reference volumes while he made copious notes. At first she read for an hour, then the time was cut to half an hour and finally to fifteen minutes, at the end of which time Parkman would find himself pacing the floor, ready to heave an inkwell at the girl. Not only were his nerves getting him down but his eyesight was fading again. It was now quite a common occurrence not to be able to see his hands in front of him.

In order to keep himself busy, he had a frame built in which parallel wires were stretched across his writing paper so that he could write in longhand and not run his words together. It also enabled him to keep on a straight line so that others could read what he wrote. To favor his eyes the room was kept darkened.

In this manner he managed to write as many as fifty painstaking words per day, but some days he wrote less than a dozen. If ever a man worked under a handicap, Parkman did.

In the same year that he was putting down only a few words a day, he developed what his doctors called "effusion of the knee" which confined him indoors for better than two years, permanently weakening the joint and hindering his exercise for the remainder of his life.

Somehow Parkman managed to finish the Pontiac history in 1851, and before the volumes were published, he married Catherine Bigelow of Boston, daughter of a socially prominent family.

The two volumes, twenty years' work accomplished in three, of *History of the Conspiracy of Pontiac* were loudly acclaimed in America and abroad as the only complete history of that affair.

Retaining enough of his eyesight to get around and to work, Parkman sought escape from factual writing by producing his only novel, *Vassall Morton,* which had no great success. The author regarded it lightly from the outset, saying that his one wish had been to get away from serious writing. He was not disappointed when it did not attain a high rating at bookstores, although many people bought it because of his name.

And then came tragedy. His child, a son, died a few months after birth and was followed in death by Mrs. Parkman, or Cathy, as he called her.

"I can stand blindness, dysentery and being a little off in the head," Parkman told his old friend Shaw "but I can't stand this."

Plunged into mourning, he tore up some of his work and vowed he would never write again. His friends became so concerned over his condition that a bodyguard was employed to watch over him. Frequently he would walk along the Mystic River, with the bodyguard trailing him by only a few feet. One morning he turned on the man and said, "Come walk beside me. Being as far back of me as you are, I am afraid that if I did try to jump, you'd not be able to prevent it. You see, my good man, I'm thinking of your interests, for if you let me jump, you'd surely lose your job."

Red-faced, the bodyguard hurriedly caught up and fell in step.

"Now that's more like it," Parkman said. "If I do decide to jump, I can pull you in with me."

Even in deepest gloom, Parkman could appreciate the irony

of any situation. One time an undertaker called at the Parkman home by mistake and apologized effusively.

"Oh, don't apologize," Parkman said. "Now I know what it'll be like when you eventually do call."

For a long time after the death of his loved ones, Parkman's existence was a drab and lonely one, spent in the confines of his own yard. He saw few persons during those times, but eventually he became interested in growing roses, and when he became interested in a thing he had to write about it. The result was *The Book of Roses,* which rose lovers and horticulturists everywhere hailed as the most informative book of its kind ever published. When Parkman wrote about a subject, he wrote about it well. By sheer nerve he drove himself thereafter to write more on his history of the French and English in America. In 1865 came *Pioneers of France in the New World.*

Two years later he finished *The Jesuits of North America,* and in the fall of 1869 *Discovery of the Great West* (later changed to *La Salle and the Discovery of the Great West*). For the past ninety years the latter has been one of the top textbooks on the early West.

There seemed no end of the flow of ink from Parkman's pen. In 1874 he published *The Old Regime in Canada,* and in 1877 *Count Frontenac and New France Under Louis XIV.*

"That doctor in Pueblo told me I was going blind," Parkman remarked to a Boston newspaper reporter one day, "but I still see well enough to read the inscription on his tombstone."

In 1884 came the book *Montcalm and Wolfe,* in two volumes, and in 1892, as he was approaching his seventieth birthday, Parkman published *A Half-Century of Conflict,* also in two volumes. Even then, forty-six years after his return from the Rockies, editors were clamoring for Parkman pieces. The *Atlantic Monthly* and *North American Review* published much of his output.

In a preface for a new edition of *The Oregon Trail* published in 1892, he wrote:

The Indomitable Francis Parkman

For Indian tepees, with their trophies of bow, lance, shield, and dangling scalp-locks, we have towns and cities, resorts of health and pleasure-seekers, with an agreeable society, Paris fashions, the magazines, the latest poem, and the last new novel. . . . The buffalo is gone, and of all his millions nothing is left but bones. Tame cattle and fences of barbed wire have supplanted his vast herds and boundless grazing grounds. . . . The wild Indian is turned into an ugly caricature of his conqueror; and that which made him romantic, terrible and hateful is in large measure scourged out of him. The slow cavalcade of horsemen armed to the teeth has disappeared before parlor cars and the effeminate comforts of modern travel. . . . The wild West is tamed.

It was a fitting eulogy for the stalwart and noble characters Parkman had met on the long trail—and outlived for the most part—and it was the final tribute of a man who had spent more time fighting disease than he had writing, yet wrote more in his day than any man then living.

In spite of his many illnesses, Parkman lived to be almost seventy-one, and when he died November 8, 1893, he was beloved and recognized the world over as an authority on anything he chose to write about.

Buckskin to the Bone

by C. M. Beeler

Danger was known to be lurking in the forest wilderness on this September evening, 1779, but the two keelboats stood well in toward the Kentucky shore and drove their blunt bows through the waters of the Ohio. By avoiding the current in this manner, they were able to make ten to twelve miles daily. Naked to the waist, brawny men rammed their long setting poles against the bottom and tramped the running boards that extended fore and aft upon either side, thus literally walking the boats up river. Meanwhile others searched with keen eyes the Kentucky and Ohio shorelines, for this was war.

The Colonies were slowly winning the Revolutionary War in the East, while Americans in homespun and buckskin were

278

locked in a sanguinary struggle with the enemy on the frontiers of the West. Out here they fought—not so much to win a war for a government of which they knew little and cared less; rather, they fought to protect their homes and win more land from their traditional enemy, the Indian. Many homeless frontiersmen fought for the pure joy of fighting.

Colonel David Rodgers was in command of the two boats and a company of seventy men, which included Captain Robert Benham. They were returning from New Orleans with ammunition and supplies for the far-flung posts west of the Alleghenies and hoped to spend the night at the mouth of Licking River, directly across the Ohio from the point where Cincinnati would be born ten years later. Rodgers was in the lead boat, Benham following close behind in the other.

Pointing at the Ohio shore a rifleman on the Colonel's boat exclaimed cautiously, "Three Injuns on a sandbar over thar!"

And another called out softly, "Canoe with two Injuns puttin' off from the Kaintuck side! Now they've sighted us and are turnin' back."

Colonel Rodgers leaped to the top of the cabin and took in the situation at a glance. "That canoe was going across to pick up those on the other side. Probably a small party heading south to hunt or raid the settlements. We'll try to stop them. To shore and tie up!"

The command was quietly but quickly passed to the rear boat and all hands were soon ashore. Two disgruntled men were sent back as guards. Even the most impetuous and undisciplined of these frontier fighters paused to wipe dry the flint and pan of his rifle and to gaze hard at the inscrutable forest of mighty trees and almost impenetrable greenery that glowered down upon him in unfriendly welcome. The two officers said a scout should be made before they ventured into the woods, but a majority of the men ridiculed the idea and defied their superiors.

Taking the lead was a lean and hawk-faced hunter with hatred of Indians in his soul and the smell of fresh scalps in his nostrils. He stepped out, growling, "I crave hair!"

A lanky boy laughed and followed. "That's the talk, Kaintuck! Who in hell wants to live till he's old and wicked? Me—I want to die young and innocent. Whet your horns, boys, and let's go!"

Rodgers turned to Benham. "What d'you think, Bob?"

The young Captain shrugged. "They're spoiling for a fight, Colonel. We can't hold 'em, so we'd better lead them."

Rodgers nodded. "I'll lead. You guard our rear."

They moved in single file a few yards apart, hard brown men in hunting shirts, buckskin leggings and moccasins, knives and tomahawks at their belts, carrying their long rifles so as carefully to protect flints and primed flash pans from the dew that had already accumulated on the dense vegetation through which they crept like ghosts. Even at midday, sunlight had difficulty reaching the floor of the forest, and so late in the evening a deep twilight prevailed. From time to time the column halted while some suspicious sight, sound or scent was investigated, for these were woodsmen whose craft equaled that of the Indian and whose senses were keenly developed by the necessities and dangers of everyday life in the wilderness.

Colonel Rodgers led the company along an animal trail toward the Licking, several hundred yards inland from the point on the Ohio where the canoe was sighted, obviously hoping to cut off the Indians. At the rear of the line Captain Bob Benham grew more alert with every step away from their boats, realizing that the men were behaving recklessly because of their numbers.

Life was good to Bob. He had spent most of it on the frontier, dodging and fighting Indians. He knew that in such cover a man might remain hidden while you passed within six feet of him, provided his body odors didn't betray him. The noses of frontiersmen were keen and never forgot a scent. The moist air encouraged smells, and through the perfume of growing things, there crept the unmistakable odor of Indians. Benham halted and tested the air. The scent of Red Death came from all directions!

Bob quickly overtook the man next ahead and whispered, "Pass the word to the Colonel—I smell Indians!"

"Huh!" grunted the man. "Now that you name it—so do I!"

A few moments later the line halted. Men half crouched in the path, fingering their weapons, straining their eyes for a glimpse of the foe which all now sensed to be near. Suddenly the whiplash crack of a Kentucky rifle split the silence.

"*Tree!*" bellowed Rodgers, the frontier signal to take cover.

A blast of gunfire echoed his command. Hundreds of rifles and muskets hurled lead at the little band of white men. Tricked by some wily chief the Colonel had led his men into ambush.

The attack drove home with ferocity from all sides. After the first devastating volley, gunfire largely gave way to savage yells mingled with cries of the wounded and dying. Having emptied their guns, Indians sprang to the slaughter with knives and tomahawks. White men had no time to reload. They met their fate in hand-to-hand combat. Colonel Rodgers was one of the first to fall, and in a matter of minutes only ten remained alive!

Captain Bob Benham was one of these. At the first shot he had taken cover behind a down-log and killed an Indian who sprang into the path to block retreat. Crouched in underbrush there, he reloaded quickly. Other Indians appeared in the path, running toward the butchery ahead. Bob shot the leader, jumped over the log and tomahawked another, then narrowly escaped death from the ax of the third. He caught the blow on the barrel of the rifle in his left hand and brained the savage with the tomahawk in his right.

"To the boats!" yelled Benham.

The surviving white men broke loose from the conflict and ran toward him, leaping over and around their own dead and wounded. Indian blood lust saved them momentarily. The savages fell to scalping the dead, killing and scalping the wounded. Captain Benham raced with his men down the path. He coolly reminded them to reload as they ran. Once on a boat they could shove off into the current and escape. Victorious yells behind them and thoughts of safety ahead gave wings to their feet. But before they reached the river the battlefield fell silent. Having completed their butchery back there, the savages would be coming to finish it down here.

More than one of the fleeing men muttered an exultant cry when, through trees, he caught a glimpse of the broad Ohio. They dashed suddenly from the forest—halted in consternation. One of the boats was in midstream, the two guards poling away. The other swarmed with Indians!

Captain Benham acted swiftly. "Don't try to get the boat. The others will be on us before we can do it. Take to the woods or they'll have us surrounded. Scatter! Every man for himself. Good luck, boys!"

A few precious moments were lost while some hotheads argued, eager to attack the boat. Benham blocked their path, knowingly risking his own life by delay in making his escape. When it appeared they'd charge the boat in spite of anything he could do, a British musket roared in the woods behind them, and a man fell dead. That ended the argument. Eight men followed Bob Benham in a desperate assault on the enemy now in their rear.

This proved to be a thin screen of swift-footed Indians, thrown out in an attempt to cut off the whites. Nine Kentucky rifles did execution. Their guns empty, the frontier fighters attacked with knives and tomahawks. Captain Benham saw four of his men killed outright. Four escaped into the woods, some wounded. Attempting to cover their retreat, he was last to fight his way free. He turned to run. A heavy ball tore his legs from beneath him. Both were broken above the knees!

Bob fell in bushes near the top of a giant old tree that recently had been blown down by the weight of its massive crown. It was almost full dark in the forest now. He lay perfectly still, clenching his teeth in an effort to stifle his hard breathing. Indians beat the brush behind him for a few minutes but didn't venture far into the woods. Presently the forest was silent, and a savage celebration broke loose at the boat as they looted it.

Benham examined his wounds. No major blood vessels were severed, for bleeding was moderate. Grimly he resolved to make a fight to live. After reloading he managed to drag himself and his rifle deep into the top of the fallen tree. Arranging his crippled legs as comfortably as possible, Bob settled down to wait for morning.

Benham slept or passed into a coma. He awoke at dawn, tortured by a burning thirst and pain that coursed through his body and pounded inside his skull. At times it blinded him, and the pounding was all he could hear. Cautiously he gathered in what leaves he could reach and licked the dew from them. He shook his head in an effort to clear it. He listened. The nocturnal song of the forest was waning normally and night was reluctantly making its departure in peace. Had the Indians gone?

Bob thought of the men who were with him, wondering whether they got away. One or more might be hiding nearby, like himself unable to go farther, waiting—just waiting. And he took stock of the recent action: two on the boat, the four men and himself were all that escaped—seven out of seventy!

What consternation the news would cause in the settlements: *The Rodgers company massacred by Shawnees at the mouth of Licking. Sixty-three dead!*

Indian voices suddenly jerked Benham's thoughts back to his own situation. Apparently they had spent the night near where the boat was moored, and now their camp was waking up—a large party feeling safe from attack and making no effort to be quiet. The odor of wood fires and the aroma of broiling meat soon came up from the river. Maybe they'd leave after breakfast. Even so what could he do? His legs were swollen and feverish. He couldn't move them independently and the very thought of dragging them made him sick. But he'd simply have to get water somehow.

Daylight crept into the forest and with it came the sounds of approaching Indians. After listening a few minutes Bob surmised this was a group of young warriors scouting the battlefields to make certain no scalps had been overlooked. For the space of seconds stark fear gripped the captain. Pain from his wounds was enough to make a man want to die, so why not shoot an Indian and get it over with? What the hell! He'd die anyhow.

Thinking of death, Bob thought of home. He thought of that great morning when his pioneer father had placed in his boyish hands a new rifle—his first. "She's a good gun, son. Throws where you hold her and she won't quit on you. And no matter how tough things look, don't you ever give up. Just recollect—you're buckskin to the bone."

That boast of the frontiersman who might be killed but couldn't be licked, *buckskin to the bone,* fired Bob Benham with the courage to stick it out. Metal on his long rifle would reflect a beam of light. He quickly hid the weapon beneath his hunting shirt and leaves. His knife was sheathed, and the blade of his tomahawk dulled by dried blood. Bob had held onto his summer hat, a thing woven of tough grass and smoked dark in sulphur. He pulled it low to hide his face and waited.

The Indians rapidly came nearer; then one cried out, and they halted a short distance away. A heated argument ensued. Benham understood a few Shawnee words. They had discovered an un-scalped body and were quarreling over who should take the prized trophy. That would be Charley Weston's body. Bob had seen him fall there. Pretty soon the triumphant scalp cry went ringing through the woods, silencing all other sounds. Benham held his breath. In a moment he again heard Indians moving through the brush, going away! Bob passed out then.

Benham judged it to be midafternoon when he awoke. His thirst was almost unbearable, and the pain from his wounds was, if possible, even more intense. He looked at his legs, swollen tightly now in the buckskin leggings and almost wished that he had died while unconscious. He lay back and gazed at a patch of sky visible through the roof of the forest. Buzzards were circling up there. Seemed like hundreds of the things. Suddenly he realized that the voice of the woods was normal again. The Indians had gone!

Benham stared at the buzzards. He thought of his men—his friends lying out there. At least they had died fighting. He cursed the buzzards and sat up. He'd make a fight to live. First, he had to have water. The blood of fresh-killed game would help. Bob renewed the priming of his rifle, and his inflamed eyes eagerly searched the forest for a shot. Squirrels everywhere, but he needed something larger—deer, elk or a wandering buffalo adrift from its herd in some nearby canebrake. Presently he saw a raccoon coming down a tree and shot the animal. The crack of his rifle again struck silence to the woods. He listened intently.

A hoarse and unintelligible cry came from a point deeper in the forest. Benham kept still. Someone moved out there, coming this way. In a moment a man cried out, "If you're white, for God's sake answer me! If you're Injun, come and finish me!"

Bob's heart leaped. "Over here, Kaintuck! It's Benham in the top of a down-tree!"

The gaunt and hawk-faced man who had led the revolt was a sorry sight now. His long arms hung straight down in sleeves caked with dried blood, and he staggered. "Both arms busted in the fight, one right after t'other'n' and I cain't wiggle a finger. How're you fixed, Cap'n?"

Bob told him.

Kaintuck sat on the tree trunk. His long body slumped hopelessly, and his head sunk forward. "I ain't got no arms. You ain't got no legs. We're both nigh dead, many a mile from help. We cain't cut 'er, Cap'n. Ain't but one thing left for us to do. You shoot me, then shoot yo'self. That white patch over my ear is a good mark. Draw a bead and put a ball dead center. . . . So 'long, Cap'n. See you in hell, afightin' Injuns!"

"Are you a damned coward?" inquired Benham scornfully.

The haggard frontiersman lifted his head. Fire of battle flashed in his dull eyes. "Nobody ain't never called Old Kaintuck a coward and lived to brag about it."

Bob forced a grin. "That's what I figured. Why man—we ain't licked. We're buckskin to the bone!"

Kaintuck fixed a fierce gaze on the young officer. The fire flamed higher in his sunken eyes. "Who says I ain't buckskin to the bone?"

"You just the same as said it when you tucked your tail and begged me to shoot you."

The woodsman looked down at his puffed and useless hands. "Maybe so," he admitted sheepishly, "but I got me a burnin' fever and hardly know what I'm sayin'. Been a-skeered to go to the river, crippled down this way. Cain't you spare a man nary a drap of water, Cap'n?"

"Haven't got a drop, but a fat 'coon is full of blood. I just shot one. He's there under that big sycamore. Go and roll him over here with your feet before he leaks himself dry, then I'll feed you juicy hunks of 'coon meat."

With an example to set and responsibility to shoulder, Captain Benham undertook something he had dreaded. He dragged himself from the fallen treetop to a small opening beside the huge trunk. Twice during the ordeal he almost fainted, hanging onto consciousness by sheer will power. At length he leaned back against the tree, gasping and streaming sweat.

"Buckskin to the bone!" muttered Kaintuck.

The warm, raw meat helped to relieve thirst and renew hope. When each had eaten all he wanted, Bob wiped his knife on the raccoon's fur and declared, "Now we've got to get water. In a few days you'll be strong enough to walk with me hanging to your shoulders, but you can't do it now. So—"

"Maybe not, but I'll shore give 'er a try."

"No—you've lost a lot of blood and you're running a high fever and it's all you can do to carry your own weight. We've simply got to have water, though, and I've got an idea. This straw hat of mine is light, but it leaks. I'll line it with the big leaves on that sycamore sprout over there if you'll go and pull off some with your teeth."

"You betcha. I've got grinders like a mule."

Bob fastened the leaves shingle-fashion with small splinters and hoped it would be nearly watertight. He then rolled the brim on one side and put it in Kaintuck's mouth. "There's a sloping bank where we tied up. It goes away out. Walk into the river until the water comes to your chin. Suck in a big drink for yourself and fill the hat. I'll bet a jug of Monongahela you can do it and come back with water."

Kaintuck nodded with determination and left. There followed the longest thirty minutes Benham had ever experienced. Having gambled their lives, all manner of doubts tormented him. Neither could survive without the other. But the lanky woodsman came back soaking wet, the hat filled with water!

On that September evening Captain Robert Benham and the man called Kaintuck launched their strange struggle for survival in a hostile wilderness. One supplied the arms, the other the legs. Bob contrived bark splints for their broken bones and bound them with buckskin thongs, but some time elapsed before he could bear to drag his legs or suffer himself to be carried.

Meanwhile Kaintuck brought water from the river with his teeth and walked game to within range of the Captain's rifle, chiefly squirrels and wild turkeys which could be kicked along to the tree when killed. Bob once shot a small fawn. Trying to roll the carcass with his feet Kaintuck got it caught in brush, whereupon he laid hold of a hind leg with his teeth and dragged it to their cooking fire. He sometimes carried dry fuel in like manner. Benham fed the tall woodsman and otherwise cared for him as if he were a helpless infant.

Eventually Bob could hobble a little on crutches and Kaintuck was barely able to feed himself with one of his hands. They managed to move to the mouth of Licking, where they could watch both rivers in the hopes of being rescued before winter came. The prospect of snow and intense cold was fearful for them to contemplate. Finally on November 27, 1779, they hailed a flatboat, and a canoe came to pick them up. The Captain and the hunter silently shook hands. Their throats were too tight for speech.

As the canoe took them away, Benham looked back at the forest and declared, "Some day I'll come and buy that land and clear it and build a home there."

"I ain't a-hankerin' for no home, Cap'n," drawled Kaintuck, "but I'd shore like to trail along with you. You've got good hands and I've got good legs."

They both laughed.

The two hardly frontiersmen were taken to Louisville, where they received medical and surgical treatment. Each recovered completely. They went on to fight through the Indian wars with Harmer, Wilkinson and St. Clair, and they shared the triumph of Mad Anthony Wayne in the final victory at Fallen Timbers, August 19, 1793.

Major Robert Benham lived long and happily at his home near the mouth of Licking. One of his cronies who came unannounced and left without excuse was an old wilderness hunter they called Kaintuck.

Cap Mossman and the Apache Devil

by Glenn Shirley

Cap Mossman, who had already accounted for so many criminals-at-large in Arizona Territory, was determined to wind up his law-enforcement career with the final elimination of Augustin Chacon, the gaunt, whiskered bandit who for years had been terrorizing that section of the Southwest.

Both men had become almost legendary figures. Chacon, a big man with long gorilla arms and huge paws at the ends of them, was the killingest outlaw ever to run loose in the wild border country. He exceeded Billy the Kid in the number to die by his gun. His score totaled twenty-nine. And he shot men down with no more compassion than other people would kill a rattlesnake. He was a half-breed Apache but was inspired by no idealistic drive to avenge the wrongs of his Indian blood brothers. Unlike the great Indian chieftains, he was just a ruthless bandit. Yet for all his admixture of white blood he was as stealthy and deadly as Geronimo himself.

The Mexicans sang of him in their long *canciones* as a man who robbed the rich and gave to the poor, but he was nothing but a thief and murderer. Yet he had a sweetheart in almost every mining camp, and his many Spanish-speaking sympathizers, believing he was persecuted because he had the courage to fight against the conquering *Americanos* who had taken over the land and become wealthy in the process, protected him. With a huge gang of Mexicans, he would cross the border and raid some Arizona ranch house or store, murder the victims and all the witnesses, load his pack animals with plunder and leisurely return to Mexico.

The law had him only once. In 1896 he looted a store at Morenci and butchered the storekeeper. Sheriff Billy Birchfield of Graham County led a posse after him. Deputy Sheriff Davis tracked the bandit, following bloodstains, to the hut of a Mexican named Contreras. Here there ensued a fight in which Chacon, after killing his old friend Salcido, a deputy, while the latter was urging the bandits to surrender, was himself wounded. Finally Chacon was captured in a box canyon and brought to Solomonville, where he was tried and sentenced to be hung. The sentence was appealed, but the higher court refused to change the verdict.

Because the authorities suspected a plot to rescue Chacon, he was removed to Tucson from the Solomonville jail. The date for the hanging was fixed anew, and the convicted man was sent back to Solomonville. A petition was circulated asking for a milder penalty for Chacon, but the governor turned it down. However, with the help of a pretty girl from nearby Morenci who smuggled him some hacksaw blades hidden in a prayer book, he escaped jail, hid out in the Sierra Madres of Mexico and resumed his forays across the border with increased savagery.

He pursued his bloody course for three years, through the cactus and chaparral stretches of the Southwest. He crossed and re-crossed the border so many times he once sent word to Cochise County's famous sheriff John Slaughter that he was coming to Tombstone to get him. Slaughter cut loose on the bandit with a shotgun and might have killed him had not Chacon reached the edge of a gully and ducked from sight in time to miss the hail of lead.

Another time he killed two prospectors in Eagle Canyon, near Solomonville, where he was under sentence of death, stole a horse and with a .45-70 rifle—also a part of the loot—kept his pursuers at a distance as he fled west. At New River, near Phoenix, he raided a sheep camp, killing two Americans; robbed the stage at Agua Fria; then rode south into the Papago country, playing hide-and-seek with sheriffs' posses for two weeks before he vanished.

Eventually he became a fabulous figure in song and story, like Murieta of California, the Younger brothers and James boys of Missouri and the Daltons of Oklahoma and was accused of most of the unsolved crimes in the territory. He grew a bushy black beard to conceal his identity, and the Mexicans called him *Peludo*, The Hairy One. At the zenith of his blood-dripped career, a steely, jut-jawed cowpuncher named Burton C. Mossman rode into Arizona.

Mossman grew up in the rough Territory of New Mexico. He had "cut his teeth on his daddy's six-shooter" fighting cattle rustlers and sheepmen. At an early age he learned to cuss in two languages, tend his own business, read sign like an Apache and play a good game of poker.

At twenty-one he was ramrod of a New Mexico ranch running eight thousand cattle. At twenty-seven he was manager of the Bloody Basin outfit of northern Arizona, where he accomplished the almost impossible feat of gathering ten thousand cattle from a country too rough for a pack animal. Three years later he was called to manage the Hash Knife, the most famous of the cow outfits of old Arizona, with two million acres and sixty thousand head on the Little Colorado River and the reputation of being the biggest bunch of killers and thieves in the Territory. Its own cowboys were stealing it blind before Mossman became superintendent.

Mossman selected a few men he could trust, taught them the rudiments of rangeland detective work and within two years had run the rustler bands out of the country, sent them to prison or extinguished them. He had a reputation as the best man hunter in Arizona when the rangers were organized in 1901.

This organization was the result of lawless conditions in Arizona at the turn of the century. Nervy little John Slaughter had sort of "pacified" things down in the southeastern corner of the Territory. But after he quit the sheriff's office and retired to his San Bernardino ranch near Douglas, the badmen had drifted in again. All along the Mexican line from Yuma to New Mexico, where miles of mesquite were covered with unprotected cattle, rustlers and horse thieves had run their own brand on the range. Up across Grand Canyon to the north stolen stock was run over into Utah and Colorado. No one had made this part of the Territory hot enough to discourage thieves and killers, and it had become a haven for outlaws of every description and color.

It looked like the small cattlemen would have to quit. The big outfits such as Slaughter, the Erie Cattle Company, the CCC and Colonel Bill Greene hired armies of fighting men to protect their interests, but they weren't making the rustlers hard to catch.

The sheriffs and their deputies were practically of no help at all. Many were cattle thieves themselves, or had been. Even when they tried, the rustlers would scatter to the four winds and fade like Apache hostiles.

These were ideal conditions for Augustin Chacon. His depredations and those of men like him were running out capital and settlers. Either something had to be done, or they would be giving the thieves a bill of sale to the Territory. When the legislature met in March, they authorized the governor to create a body of men to bring law and order to the country, and Governor Nathan O. Murphy asked Mossman to form a ranger company.

The job paid only $120 a month, less than some cowboys were making at the Hash Knife. Mossman's head bookkeeper drew $125. But Mossman didn't consider the pay. Six peace officers in six months had been slain, and not one of their killers had been caught. It was a tough country. Someone had to clean it up. Mossman had proved that he was qualified. He felt a duty to Arizona and had to perform it before he could return to horses and cattle —the life he loved.

He was appointed captain and thereafter became known as "Cap" Mossman. They gave him only thirteen men—one sergeant and twelve privates—but they went to work. They ranged the southwestern territory and became as much a part of it as its deserts and hills and valleys. No Northwest Mounted Police, Texas Ranger or other famous crew of hard-riding, straight-shooting, fearless men ever did more for civilization.

There were only fourteen of them, covering an area larger than New England, but they did what hundreds of sheriffs and deputies had failed to do—slam the fear of God into the whole army of the orneriest hombres who ever straddled leather. They worked swiftly, secretly. Mossman himself took Black Jack Christian's trail and ran him and his gang of killers into the White Mountains of New Mexico, and they never came back. He captured scores of others.

Stories of his prowess became legends. But the most dangerous criminal, the one he wanted to account for more than any other, the gaunt, whiskered Augustin Chacon, was still at large. The real test of his career as a law-enforcement officer would be the capture of the Mexican half-breed bandit.

Governor Murphy demanded it. Territorial politicians were making a great deal of talk about it, and Cap's enemies, including sheriff's envious of his reputation, were quick to point out his failure. For every boast about Cap's success in cleaning up the Territory, someone gibed: "What about Chacon?"

This sort of talk touched Cap on the raw. The idea of Chacon still at large hounded him like an obsession. Chacon was hiding in Mexico, and Arizona officers had no legal right to cross the border to kill or capture Mexican citizens. The privilege applied only to Americans chasing Americans and Mexicans chasing their own nationals.

How to lay hands on Chacon under these circumstances? Cap worked out a plan, risky but perhaps feasible, which would require the aid of two former law-enforcement officers who had later turned outlaws, Burt Alvord and Billy Stiles. Mossman, in pursuit of his scheme, passed the word around that he would pay plenty to be put on Chacon's track. Meanwhile he talked his plan over with his friend, Judge Barnes.

The judge had at one time been a friend of Burt Alvord, an early-day Tombstone character. Alvord was short, bald-headed and as dark as a Mexican. He was as tough as Chacon and as notorious, except for a record of brutal murder. His chief interests were guns, horses, pool halls, poker and rustling. He had been a deputy sheriff for John Slaughter off and on and worked on his ranch as a cowboy. He was present the night the little lawman had pumped his shotgun blast at Chacon.

Afterward he had served as marshal in a couple of towns and rode shotgun for Wells Fargo before taking a professional interest in train robbery. He and Bob Downing—whose real name was believed to be Jackson, a former member of the Sam Bass gang in Texas—a ruffian named Matt Burts and a snaky little gunman named Billy Stiles robbed an express car at Cochise Station, ten miles west of Willcox, and hurried back to town to establish alibis.

The amount obtained was about thirty thousand dollars. The gang used the utmost caution and might have gotten away scot-free had they not become so overconfident and staged another robbery at Fairbank, a few miles west of Tombstone. A member of their gang, "Three-Fingered" Jack Dunlap, was filled with buckshot. The posse found him next day lying beside the trail in the desert. He lived just long enough to tell the officers what they wanted to know.

Alvord, Stiles, Burts and Downing were arrested. Stiles turned state's evidence because Alvord had taken all the loot. No one else knew where he had hidden it. Wells Fargo men, anxious to recover the money, made a deal with Stiles and set him free, hoping he could help them find the hidden loot.

Stiles went to see Alvord in jail at Tombstone, but Jailer Bravin wouldn't let him in. So Billy shot Bravin, took the keys off him, turned Alvord loose and fled south with him into Sonora.

With Alvord, Stiles and Chacon all hiding across the border and wanted by the law, they surely had got acquainted. Judge Barnes suggested the possibility of contacting Chacon through Alvord.

"Of course," he added, "you may not come back all in one piece."

Cap realized his danger. But he had no quarrel with Alvord. He wanted Chacon.

Judge Barnes mentioned another point. "I know the Governor. I might be able to get him off with a light sentence if he co-operates with you. I'll give you a letter to that effect."

"All right. Where is he hiding?" asked Cap.

"I couldn't say," the Judge replied. "Maybe his wife can help you. She lives in Willcox."

Cap found Alvord's wife in poor health, almost destitute, and lonely. She was willing to do anything to get her husband to give himself up and let Judge Barnes do what he could to help him. But she had no idea where he was.

She remembered that Billy Stiles had once mentioned a half-brother who was a steam-pump operator in an English smelter at Minas Prietas, on the Nogalas-Guaymas railroad down in Sonora. It would be a long trip and a slim chance that he would know

Alvord. Cap decided to find out and went to Judge Barnes for the letter.

Judge Barnes put it in his own handwriting, stating the facts clearly. Alvord might even be acquitted, since nearly everybody who had seen the crime committed was dead or had disappeared. Besides his wife had consulted him about a divorce. He would agree to get her to postpone the matter for a while.

He gave Cap the letter, shook his hand and wished him luck.

Sheriff Dell Lewis of Cochise County and Sheriff Tom Turner of Santa Cruz told Cap he was a fool.

"We've been down to Sonora after Alvord, but got nowhere," Turner said. "Better watch out. Burt's all steamed up right now. He's liable to kill you without waiting to hear your proposition."

Meanwhile Cap was threatened with a fresh complication. A new administration, that of Theodore Roosevelt, had moved into the White House after McKinley's assassination. Cap realized that the new people who would be appointed to office in Arizona would give him short shrift as captain of the rangers. He would have to work fast.

He slipped down to Nogales that night and the next morning quietly boarded the train a few minutes before it left for Sonora. At Minas Prietas he went straight to the manager of the smelter with his story. The manager thought he was crazy.

"But it ain't my head that's going to get blowed off," he said, and told Cap where to contact the half-brother, who was working twenty miles back in the hills.

Cap found the half-brother skeptical and surly. Cap talked fast and let the man read Judge Barnes' letter. In the end the half-brother came around and fixed Cap up with a horse and saddle and gave him directions where he could find Alvord.

Cap rode for several days. One evening, as he came around a bend, he saw a hut and a stocky-built man waiting with a Winchester handy.

Cap didn't reach for his six-shooter but rode boldly up to the man. When he was still a few yards away, the man's rifle swung level, and Cap halted. Cap had never met Alvord, but he had seen his face on wanted posters and knew for sure that this was the man he had so long been trying to contact.

"You're Burt Alvord," he said.

"Who the hell's asking?"

"Cap Mossman. I guess you know who he is. But don't get riled. I haven't brought anyone with me all this way. I've a letter to you from Judge Barnes and a message from your woman."

The rifle in the outlaw's hands wavered. But the barrels of three others that Cap could see pointed at him from between the gaps in the wall of the hut remained steady.

"Call off your dogs, Alvord. All I have is a revolver. I got more sense than to try to use it."

Alvord barked an order and the rifles disappeared. He now demanded to see the judge's letter.

Cap handed it over; Alvord read it slowly. He wasn't much on reading, and he had to spell out the words to himself. Finally he turned again to Cap and asked how he had been able to find him.

"Billy's half-brother told me," Cap replied.

"What do you want?"

"We'll get to that later," Cap told him. "Right now I'm hungry."

Alvord took him in to a supper of the usual Mexican variety. Afterward they sprawled around the fire and drank mescal. It appears that Cap's silver-and-gold-mounted Colt attracted the interest of a member of the gang.

"Let me see it," he asked.

"If you'll leave me have yours," Cap replied.

When they had traded guns, the Mexican, who had imbibed rather freely of the local juice, hinted: "But it would be a very pleasant thing if the next time I visit my *dulce*, I could show her this fine pistol and tell her it was a gift to me from the captain of the Arizona Rangers."

Cap replied politely: "Yes, but I am sure she would not be

happy to come upon you dead on the trail somewhere. Would she now?"

For a moment murder hung in the air. But Alvord didn't want a fight just then. He had too much at stake. He ordered the bandit to hand over the fancy weapon.

Cap and Alvord had their talk later, when they could be sure no one was overhearing what they said.

Cap told Alvord: "Arrange it so I can get Chacon up near the border. If I get Chacon, you stand the chance of being acquitted, you can be with your wife again and you and Billy Stiles can divide the reward between you, fifty-fifty."

Alvord whistled. But there were obvious risks. Chacon wouldn't fall easily into any trap they might set for him.

"Tell him," Cap suggested, "I'm a chap who's just broke out of jail and is looking for the right connections. Tell him I have a good deal all staked out. Perhaps he already knows about that pasture just across the line where Colonel Greene keeps his race horses. I don't think Chacon (tell him) could pull it off alone. Certainly I couldn't. You might add there's a fine stallion over there Chacon might want for himself. . . . It'd be a cinch for two or three working together."

Alvord thought it might work out. But he couldn't get to Chacon direct himself. Billy Stiles was the man for that. Cap realized that both Alvord and Stiles were first-rate scoundrels. But they offered him his only chance. So he decided to risk it.

Cap left next morning. Back home things had changed as predicted. Already Teddy Roosevelt had appointed a Rough Rider, Major Brodie, territorial governor. Cap promptly submitted his resignation. Brodie wrote back asking him to stay on until he found his replacement.

This gave Cap more time. How much, he dared not even guess. The new governor might make up his mind any day. Cap hoped to get Chacon before he did. Weeks passed with no word from Alvord.

Cap contacted United States Marshal W. H. McCord at Phoenix

and asked for a deputy's commission, claiming that it would allow him to operate outside the Territory. McCord fell for the idea. He issued Cap his papers July 2, 1902. Cap could now fall back on his federal commission if necessary.

He had to capture Chacon. He had sworn to bring in the outlaw and even if relieved of his office he was going to stay on the killer's trail as long as there was even a thin hope. It was his duty to Arizona, and not until he had killed the notorious bandit or captured and brought him in to be legally hanged would he feel it completed.

And his only chance lay with two desperate characters. Stiles was in it for half the rewards offered for Chacon. The other half didn't interest Alvord. He wanted to see his wife again and someday dig up the loot from the Cochise robbery.

Even if they were able to lure Chacon to the border, there was no assurance Cap could take him. Chacon might kill him. But Cap vowed he wouldn't if he got the first shot.

Cap didn't want to kill him. It would be a greater blow to his critics if he could bring in the notorious bandit alive.

Cap received a wire from Governor Brodie. His resignation, tendered in July, would be accepted August 31. On September 1 Tom Rynning, a former sergeant in the famous old Sixth Cavalry and lieutenant of Troop B of the Rough Riders, became the new captain of the rangers.

Cap was through as a ranger. He still had his deputy United States Marshal's commission. But it looked like he wouldn't even need it now.

Then the next evening, just before dark, Billy Stiles brought him word that Alvord had arranged a rendezvous with Chacon!

As Cap and Billy headed south that night and crossed into Mexico at Naco, Cap didn't even consider that he might be riding to his death.

By morning they were a good way south of the line, near Carizzo Springs, wondering where Alvord and Chacon were. Cap was worried. He had not been sure of Stiles' loyalty from the beginning.

But Stiles seemed disturbed over the failure to make connections as Alvord had planned. He decided they had ridden too far.

They kept out of sight in the chaparral most of the day, then started back to the border. About nine o'clock that night, somewhere east of the San Jose Mountains, two figures rode out into plain sight.

Alvord was being very cautious. He mentioned no names. Cap would hardly have recognized Chacon, although he had seen pictures of him, for the five years since his escape from prison had wrought a great change in him. His form was bent, and his beard was tinted with gray. He was now an old man, but Cap wasn't fooled for a minute. The bandit was still as dangerous as a rattler. Alvord spoke to Chacon, who grunted noncommittally. Cap began talking fast, before Chacon's suspicions would lead to a shooting. Over there, beyond the border, he said, were Colonel Greene's horses just waiting to be run off. He threw in a remark about the stallion, too.

"We can cut the international fence," he told the bandit, "grab them tonight, and by morning be away into Mexico again."

Chacon said little. But he remarked in Spanish that it wasn't possible. You couldn't manage unless there was more light to see by. Obviously he suspected a trap and was choosing his own time. Cap saw he couldn't rush matters. So he proposed waiting for daylight.

They camped hidden away in the brush. They stretched out around the fire, and the long night's vigil began.

Cap fought off sleep. He intended to be alive in the morning. He kept double watch on Alvord and Stiles. He couldn't trust either of them, and any moment Chacon might try to kill him.

A dreary drizzle set in about midnight; Cap slipped into his slicker. While so doing he managed, without it being noticed by his companions, to get his revolver where he could use it fast when needed.

As dawn grayed the sky Alvord saddled his horse and said he was going to look for a spring for a drink. As he passed close to Mossman he whispered: "Look out for Billy Stiles. He'll double-cross you." Then he mounted and was gone.

Cap knew Alvord had quit—wouldn't be back. Cap was with Chacon where he could capture him—if he was lucky. It was up to him, Mossman, now. Alvord wanted to be miles away when the showdown came.

Cap moved into position to watch both Chacon and Stiles.

They cooked something over the embers of last night's fire for breakfast. Stiles wielded the frying pan. Alvord's excuse for leaving had not justified Chacon. His eyes never left Mossman's face while the bacon was sizzling.

Chacon squatted by Stiles, and the two men lighted cigarettes. Cap strolled over and asked Chacon for a smoke. Chacon obliged.

Sitting down, the outlaw was at a disadvantage; he couldn't draw quickly, but the light of a sort of intuitive awareness was in his eyes. Cap picked up a burning twig and lighted his cigarette. For a moment, because Cap's hand seemed busy, the bandit relaxed. Cap leaned down as if to shove the glowing twig back into the embers. Then he suddenly came up with his Colt.

"All right, Chacon," he shouted, "get 'em up or I'll cut you in two!"

Chacon hesitated for the fraction of a second, glancing hopefully in Stiles' direction. Cap shifted to cover both men. He had never taken such a chance in his life, and he never knew which side Stiles was on until the little gunman stepped over and disarmed the big outlaw. Had Chacon called Cap's bluff, Stiles would have probably helped him kill the ranger.

Cap pulled a pair of handcuffs from the lining of his coat and ordered Stiles to put them on the outlaw Chacon. Then he backed to where his rifle was leaning against a mesquite tree, jerked the gun open and pushed a cartridge into the chamber and leveled the weapon at his captive. He was ready for any emergency now.

"Now you, Billy, drop your own gun!" he ordered.

Billy played it innocent.

"What the hell, Cap," he protested.

Cap repeated: "Drop it, Billy!"

Billy obeyed. Cap ordered them to back away from their weapons.

"We'll leave them here," he said. "Saddle the horses, Billy; we've a long way to ride."

The little procession started off slowly toward the border, with Stiles leading Chacon's mount. The outlaw rode with his hands cuffed behind so he could not touch the reins. Cap brought up the rear, his rifle and six-shooter ready for action. He didn't breathe easy until he had cut the border fence six miles west of Naco and ridden through. When he saw a train coming, he signaled it. He ordered Stiles to ride over to Bisbee with the horses. Then he boarded the train with his prisoner. This was near Packard, a little station a mile or so above the border, near Colonel Greene's pasture.

"Well, I'll be damned!" exclaimed Jim Parks, the new sheriff of Graham County, when he saw Cap climb off the local with Chacon in handcuffs.

He knew how dangerous the outlaw was, and the first thing he did was hand Cap his pistol before he stooped to clamp leg irons on the prisoner and slip new cuffs on his wrists before removing Cap's old ones.

Chacon was promptly arraigned as an escaped criminal under sentence of death. On November 21, a little more than two months later, he was led out onto the gallows. He delivered himself of a long harangue in which he maintained he was innocent of the crime for which he was being executed. To the end he remained imperturbably cheerful. At the very last moment he rolled a cigarette and smoked it calmly. As the cap was being adjusted, he shouted: *"Adios Todos Amigos!"*

That day Cap was with Colonel Greene at the Waldorf in New York City. He had finished his duty to Arizona, but he had kidnaped a Mexican citizen. He feared international complications.

Colonel Greene had been wanting Cap to pay him a visit, and Cap decided there was no better time to make himself scarce.

But things worked out all right for Cap Mossman. Burt Alvord went to Canada, then to Central America and was never heard from again. Stiles, the only other witness, was killed in a gambling casino in Nevada. Cap had several thousand dollars in the bank at Bisbee. He drew out a thousand, transferred the balance to a bank in Colorado and went back to ranching in New Mexico.

He spent his last days at Roswell in his seven-bedroom home. Eighty-nine and confined to a wheel chair before his death, he enjoyed swapping yarns about the old time, mostly about the humorous happenings in his life.

"I never wanted to kill a man," he said.

Although he early severed all contacts with Arizona, to him belongs the credit for organizing the state's first rangers and the respect of all honest men for carrying the law into the desert and mesquite with a fearlessness unequaled by any officer of the old Southwest.

Juan Cortina –
Hero or Bandit?

by Ruel McDaniel

He commanded and ruled with iron discipline an army of over a thousand outlaws and adventurers of many nationalities.

He stole 900,000 head of cattle and horses, practically decimating the great herds of famed King Ranch.

He was mayor of a city, governor of a state and a close second in a race for the presidency of a republic.

He was hero to thousands of Mexicans along the Rio Grande, who smarted under loss of Texas to the United States. He was admired and respected by important Americans on both sides of the Rio Grande, and his family was among the richest and most powerful between San Antonio and Mexico City.

To Texans he was America's first gang leader, a large-scale bandit and a killer without compassion. He was Juan Nepomuceno Cortina, more Texan than Mexican, because his great-grandfather settled on a ranch in Texas in 1767 and acquired ownership by a grant from the King of Spain—although Cortina actually was born across the Rio Grande in Mexico.

Juan Cortina was an eternal contradiction. Physically he resembled his genteel maternal ancestors. He had sandy hair, light-pigmented skin and the outward gentleness of his mother's family. But his father had been Trinidad Cortina, a commoner, and his father's blood and spirit ruled Juan. He was uncomplex, direct, primitive; a well-built lad of incredible physical endurance. The baby-blue of his eyes hardened into the cold gray-green of his father's eyes as his lithe body matured.

Soon after Juan was born his father died—but the father's indomitable Indian fierceness lived on in the son. His mother moved to Texas and built a permanent home of seasoned ebony and mesquite on her share of the huge family ranch, which she named *Rancho Santa Rita,* about seven miles up the Rio Grande from Brownsville.

Here she lived in the gentle semiseclusion of a cultured widow of that day and quietly reared her children. She employed a family friend of long acquaintance to handle the estate for her and the children, and in this appointment probably lay the first small seeds of rebellion in young Juan Cortina. Gradually it developed that this guardian, a German-American, systematically robbed the family of the ranch's earnings and helped other avaricious Americans later to set up legal machinery whereby many families of Spanish descent were robbed of their properties.

This was possible because the strip of territory between the Nueces River and the Rio Grande was still in dispute. Both Mexico and Texas claimed it, and it was left largely without government by both claimants. To this vast area flocked adventurers, land grabbers, and fugitives from the United States, Mexico, Texas and Europe. Law was by nerve, audacity and the six-gun. The gentle Spanish families were helpless against such hard-bitten sharpsters.

But Juan Cortina inherited the good looks of his artistocratic Spanish forebears, not their gentleness of spirit. He possessed a fierce pride, and the shabby treatment of his people by these ruthless opportunists brought it boiling to the surface. Land belonging to the Cortinas had been seized by these robbers; even the Salt Lakes to the north, which had belonged to the family for many years, had been commandeered by the newcomers.

Leader in the conniving and land grabbing was Charles Stillman, an unscrupulous operator from New England who gained his foothold and influence in the area by selling ammunition to Mexican rebels south of the Rio Grande. For obvious reasons Juan Cortina hated Stillman.

Young Juan killed several men in the course of protecting his family's properties against the opportunists and common thieves. Charlie Stillman, being the political boss of Brownsville, controlled the semiannual grand jury. At his direction Juan Cortina was regularly indicted for murder at each meeting of the grand jury. The warrant was never served; everybody was too busy robbing his neighbor or guarding his own life and property from retaliation.

Looking to the future, Cortina gathered around him a number of reckless young men who either worked for his mother or shared Juan's growing resentment of the treatment the defenseless Spanish families were receiving at the hands of the land grabbers. Before the citizens of Brownsville fully realized what was taking place, Juan Cortina and his hard-riding crew had become a dangerous problem.

When the citizens did realize it, they held a mass meeting for the purpose of raising money to pay a town marshal. They found the man they wanted in Bob Shears, whose first instructions were to arrest and jail Juan Cortina and his followers on various and sundry charges. Once jailed, Stillman's hand-picked judges were prepared to "throw the book" at Cortina and his men.

Marshal Shears wisely waited for Juan to show up in town before acting on the warrants. Cortina, accompanied by half a dozen of his outfit, rode into Brownsville on July 13, 1859. No longer a wild kid, Juan had developed into a tough fighting man of thirty-four.

On the morning of the thirteenth, Marshal Shears observed Cortina and three of his men enter a *cantina* near Market Plaza. At the same moment, he spotted another Cortina man enter a café across the street. Sending word to his deputies to come *muy pronto,* Shears decided to take the lone Cortinista himself. Pedro Juarado, however, saw him approaching the *cantina* and ran out. Shears shoved the muzzle of his six-gun in the man's ribs and ordered him back inside the café.

The marshal's maneuver was quickly executed, but not so quickly that Cortina, from his stool in the *cantina* across the street, did not see it. In a flash he was outside. Mounting his big stallion, Juan headed him straight across the plaza and through the *cantina* door. Bob Shears didn't have a chance. The marshal was in the act of removing his prisoner's gun, when the doors burst open and Cortina charged in. Juan fired twice, and Shears fell, badly wounded. Bartender and customers dived for cover, and the deputies—just answering the marshal's summons—fled through the back door into the patio.

Cortina scooped up Juarado and rode his horse back through the batwing doors. The stud's pounding hoofs kicked up dust in the sleepy plaza. Still holding his man around the waist, Cortina sprayed the plaza with bullets, including a shot at the plate-glass window in the Stillman office.

Whooping defiantly, Juan and his Cortinistos galloped up the street and on toward his ranch.

This was Juan Cortina's first public show of defiance. The citizens of Brownsville were startled and worried at his reckless outburst. Many were in fear of their lives. The wounded marshal's deputies refused to take action. Town officials, by going personally from store to store and house to house, managed to get together thirty men who agreed to help the sheriff arrest Cortina for the shooting of Shears. Brownsville merchants contributed rifles, six-guns and ammunition, and the posse took off under the leadership of Sheriff Brown.

Just before sundown they arrived at a spot outside the corrals of *Rancho Santa Rita*. Sheriff Brown, a longtime friend of Cortina, rode out ahead of the posse and yelled, "I've come to arrest you, *Cheno*. Come out with your hands up."

"*'Sta bueno, amigo!*" laughed Cortina. "Come and get me!"

Sheriff Brown wheeled his horse and faced his thirsty possemen. "You heard what he said. Let's go get him!"

Not a deputy moved.

Brown turned his mount and rode alone up to the gates of the corral. A warning bullet buzzed over his head. The sheriff drew a white handkerchief from his pocket and waved it frantically. The gates opened, and Cortina came out.

"*Cheno*," Brown said plaintively, "not one of my men will lift a hand to help me take you. Surrender to me. I'll see you get a fair trial."

Cortina chuckled. "With *Señor* Stillman picking the jury? No, my frien'."

The parley continued, and in the end Cortina made formal demand on the sheriff to deliver to him a list of men whom the outlaw leader felt had stolen from, wronged, or mistreated his immediate family and friends. He would deal with these men in his own way. The list included names famous or infamous in Nueces Strip history: land lawyers William G. Hald and Francis J. Parker; Charles Stillman; Mifflin Kenedy and Richard King, cattlemen; J. S. Lake and O. Klem, lawyers; Adolphus Gaevecke, politician and guardian of the widow Cortina, and most of those who attended the secret meeting and contributed to the fund to hire Marshal Shears.

With his cowardly posse slinking to the shelter of the mesquites, Sheriff Brown realized he was in a tight spot. Should Cortina, in one of his wild moods, decide to strike Brownsville at that moment, there was no force south of San Antonio that could stop him. Behind those pole corrals, scores of armed men awaited impatiently the word of Cortina to strike—anywhere, any time. The original plan to arrest Cortina now was forgotten, pushed aside by this graver problem.

Smiling, a corn-shuck cigarette hanging from his lips, Cortina waited for Brown to speak.

"I can't deliver these men today, *amigo*," parried the sheriff.

Juan spoke one word. "When?"

"You say when, *Cheno*."

Cortina shrugged. "I give you three days."

To this, Brown agreed. The posse rode back to Brownsville, and the dickering continued. It went on to a week, ten days, finally a month. Messengers rode back and forth almost daily from *Rancho Santa Rita* and Brownsville. As the days passed the apprehensive citizens of Brownsville began to feel better. By now, they had persuaded themselves that the demand of Cortina had been an angry gesture and nothing more. When thirty days slipped by with no sign of the outlaw, everybody relaxed. Another month passed, and still nothing happened. Now Brownsville folks began to crack jokes about Cortina and his list.

Then on September 30 Red Thomas, a Brownsville citizen, went across the river on business to Matamoros. There, on Plaza de Benito Juarez, a boy handed him a printed handbill. He glanced at it and rushed for the ferry to Brownsville. For all practical purposes it was a printed death warrant for many Americans in the Nueces Strip. It read in part:

Fellow Citizens! My part is taken! The voice of Revelations whispers that to me is entrusted the work of breaking the chains of your slavery; that Our Lord will enable me to put our powerful enemies under foot in compliance with that sovereign majesty . . . on my part, I am ready to hold myself in sacrifice.

A society is organized in Texas which devotes itself sleeplessly to exterminating tyrants . . . and driving the invading Americans back across the Nueces . . . The names of members shall be inscribed in a book which shall forevermore remain a secret . . .

Cortina's bold proclamation fanned old hates into flames of vengeance against the usurping Americans, for even the government of Mexico had never relinquished its claim to the area between the Rio Grande and the Nueces, much less the rank-and-file Mexican citizen.

Men flocked to the Cortina banner by the hundreds—some genuine Mexican patriots, many outlaws, and wanted men of American as well as Mexican extraction; adventurers, fortune seekers without loyalty to any government. It was a motley crew, but Cortina ruled every man with an iron will. No leader in history ever had a more loyal army than the men who rode under Juan Cortina.

Red Thomas had learned that the manifesto had been in circulation for some time and that Cortina was ready to strike. His news filled Brownsville with terror and especially those citizens on Cortina's death list. Wild and unorganized plans for defending the city sprang up. Many of the wanted men left town and hid out in the chaparral with rancher friends or relatives.

Cortina, with his new Mexican recruits, crossed over to the Texas side above Brownsville and moved to his ranch headquarters seven miles from that town. Awaiting him there were scores of recruits from the Texas side, ready to ride and die, if called upon, with *Cheno*.

There followed one of the most amazing episodes in American history. Within the week Cortina marched on Brownsville. He captured Fort Brown, held by the U.S. Cavalry; he took the city hall and all other government buildings. His men methodically sacked the city, devoting particular attention to the property of the men on Cortina's death list. The outlaw leader liberated all prisoners, some of whom promptly joined up with him. He had the entire city searched for the men on his list, but to his chagrin found that most of them had fled. Cortina set up headquarters in the commandant's office at Fort Brown and ruthlessly dealt out death to all who had opposed him in the past, wherever his men found them.

By sunup the following morning, after his men had sacked much of the city and got thoroughly drunk on mescal and tequila, Cortina called a halt. He adorned himself in an American colonel's uniform, marched to the center of the city, called a meeting of all citizens who would venture out and handed them a list of men he wanted. "Within one hour," he told a committee he named from the crowd—most of them his former friends—"deliver to me these men, and one hundred thousand dollars, American gold. If you don't—I'll burn the city!"

Americans frantically appealed to General Alejandro Carvajal, *commandante* of the military in Matamoros, across the Rio Grande in Mexico. The General promptly dispatched a formidable army of *rurales*, dragoons and dismounted troops to Brownsville's aid. With them rode a prominent Matamoros banker and merchant, the commander of customs guards, as well as General Carvajal.

The Mexican troops found Cortina in Stillman's store, issuing turpentine balls to his band, with directions to fire every building in town.

General Carvajal, a Cortina kinsman, delivered his ultimatum. Cortina knew his hard-boiled kinsman meant business. Sullenly he rounded up his men and departed from Brownsville.

He marched back to his ranch headquarters, and his army grew by scores as he marched. Fearing reprisals from the powerful Matamoros leaders if he returned immediately to Brownsville, Cortina systematically bottled up the point of Texas leading into Brownsville. He posted his men across the strip above the city and allowed nobody to pass in or out of the beleaguered town without explicit permission. He intercepted all mail. When the postmaster at Brownsville attempted to send mail up the Mexican side of the Rio Grande to Laredo, Cortina's men stopped it. He intercepted steamer traffic to Brazos Santiago and Point Isabel, as well as up the Rio Grande.

Business in Brownsville was completely suspended. The residents abandoned most of the city and huddled with their valuables in the center of town and awaited their doom.

In the meantime Cortina sent his men roaming the back country, robbing ranch homes and driving off cattle and horses.

Finally Red Thomas, veteran of the border country, managed to slip inland up the Rio Grande in Mexico and elude Cortina's patrols. He reached Laredo, 200 miles distant, in six days. He sent out from there urgent appeals for help. He sent messengers to Corpus Christi and San Patricio begging aid, and he himself made a Paul Revere ride to San Antonio, a distance of 150 miles, in three days.

Relief parties began forming. A ranger company under Captain William G. Tobin headed for Brownsville, recruiting as it went. The Army got busy. General Carvajal, of Matamoros, was prevailed upon by Brownsville citizens to send over an army to help break the Cortina siege. Mexican soldiers and American army men, as well as volunteers, were formed into a force called the "Brownsville Tigers." They marched on Cortina in temporary headquarters in a *resaca* a few miles from Brownsville. The cunning outlaw feigned defeat and retreat at the opening of the fight and lured the Tigers into a trap. Slaughter followed—then wild retreat. The surviving Tigers high-tailed it back to Brownsville, except for those who took the occasion to swap sides. Flags, two cannon and many rifles were captured by Cortina. His band suffered only a few casualties while killing twenty of the enemy and wounding an undisclosed number.

Companies of volunteers were formed in several Texas towns. Lieutenant A. L. Walker, at Laredo, was ordered to join Major S. P. Heintzelman, besieged in Brownsville. The U.S. Army ordered Brevet-Colonel Robert E. Lee, at San Antonio, to assume command of all U.S. forces along the border and to proceed against Cortina. The order, however, was countermanded by another, instructing Lee to proceed with all haste to Harpers Ferry, West Virginia, to take command in the John Brown affair.

Rangers, volunteers and army men converged upon Brownsville, many of the outfits fighting among themselves and the officers jealous of power. They assembled near Palo Alto, scene of a Mexican defeat during the Mexican War, on May 8, 1846. Cortina was encamped on the old battlefield, and the confident Americans attacked. Again Cortina whipped the combined American forces. This victory, coming on the site of the ignoble Mexican defeat of thirteen years before, made the outlaw chief still a greater hero among the Mexicans.

Rangers and army men continued to gather, and finally in December a combined attacking force of 300 men surprised a Cortina lieutenant and 350 men at Jackass Prairie and routed them, killing about 20 Cortinistos. Other fighting forces arrived, all quarreling among themselves.

On December 17 Cortina—realizing that he had pillaged this area bare and that the opposing forces were growing too strong for him to capture Brownsville—broke camp at *Rancho Santa Rita* and headed north. As he marched he destroyed by fire the ranch homes of his enemies.

Three days later he captured the town of Edinburg and marched on to Rio Grande City, head of navigation on the Rio Grande 135 miles north of Brownsville.

Cortina captured Rio Grande City on Christmas Eve, 1859, and levied a ransom of $100,000 American gold on the city. In less than three months of action, Juan Cortina had made good his boast with a vengeance. He had captured two U.S. Army forts, two cities, a dozen villages and had taken over $100,000 in gold; he had driven off livestock valued at over a half-million dollars, and he had virtually uprooted all semblance of law and order in an area nearly as large as New England.

On Christmas Day, Cortina ordered a fiesta for his men—and therein made a fatal mistake. By now rangers, soldiers and volunteers were moving in on the area from all over Texas. More than a thousand men were in the field in pursuit of Cortina. Ranger Captains Ford and Tobin, disgusted with the slow-moving tactics of the Army, called for volunteers, formed a fighting force and crept to within hearing distance of the carousing Cortinistos.

After Cortina's men were full of barbecue and mescal and deep in their siestas, the force struck. It was a sound defeat for the surprised Cortinistos. Cortina led the defeated remnant of his band across the Rio Grande into the safety of Mexico.

In Mexico the outlaw chief reorganized his force, set up headquarters and began making raids into Texas. He raided the ranches of King and Kenedy, as well as others whose names still graced his death list. He continued to be a power on both sides of the Rio Grande.

It was claimed that he stole 900,000 head of cattle and horses from Texas ranchers during his raids.

Cortina's raids were finally broken up by Ranger Captain McNelly. The hard-riding rangers hounded and harried the outlaw leader until he withdrew from the border and turned to politics. He was elected mayor of Matamoros, then governor of the Mexican state of Tamaulipas. He fought valiantly against Maximilian when the French set him up as a puppet ruler of Mexico. In a race for the presidency of Mexico, he was beaten out by his first cousin, Porfirio Diaz.

All in all, Juan Nepomuceno Cortina was *mucho hombre* and will long be remembered on both sides of the Rio Grande.

The Quality of Courage

by Walter Prescott Webb

The readers of *True West* must be people who admire courage, whether it is exhibited by the bad man or the good man. The Old West of which so many like to read was filled with brave men. Some of them were good and some were bad; some within the law and some without. But the good man and the bad man by western standards had one quality in common, and that was courage, bravery, intrepidity. It is really this quality that we admire and like to read about whether it was exhibited by Wyatt Earp upholding the law or Jesse James or Sam Bass or some other breaking it.

In writing the history of the Texas Rangers, I had the opportunity of studying the action of as courageous a group of men as ever trod the western plains. Again and again I came upon the record of such Rangers as Jack Hays, Ben McCulloch, L. H. McNelly, John Armstrong, John B. Jones, and Frank Hamer, to mention a few examples of men who had courage in the highest degree. I followed them as they met the Indians, the outlaws, the bandits and the murderers of Texas. Some of their deeds are incredible and difficult for the average person to understand.

After poring over these records, extending back a hundred years and more, I began to ask: What is this quality of courage? What did these men have that I and most others do not? How is it that they could walk into danger with the calm that an ordinary person would enter a drug store? What is the quality these men have that most others do not?

Then I came up with an answer that is as curious as it is unexpected. I decided that these men *lack* a quality that most people have. Instead of having something—in this case courage—that most lack, they lack something that nearly everybody has. They lack fear. It has been, in a few cases, left out of their composition. Their courage is not a positive quality that has been added, but a negative quality that has been omitted. Fear has been given to all animals as a protection, and they survive because they have it. They run away from danger and thereby avoid destruction. So do most people, whether they admit it or not. But there are exceptions, a few men who are *fearless*—utterly without fear.

In the gunfighting days of the Old West such men had a great advantage. They were not bothered by fear when they went into a fight. They did not have to put it down because it was never there. Therefore they could be as cool and collected, as intelligent in a gunbattle as they were in any other transaction. All of their wits were about them, their minds were free to concentrate on the business in hand, and their muscles were relaxed so that they could receive and execute the orders from the brain. Their hands remained steady, they took time to catch the sight before they pulled the trigger, and they had the ability to be alert to everything that was going on around them. This lack of nervousness, this coolness and deliberateness, gave them a big advantage over an opponent who had to fight his fear and his enemy at the same time. The man without fear has nothing to do but fight his enemy. It has been said that some of these men smile when the danger is greatest, and that a smiling fighter is very dangerous. A little thought will show that he who smiles is relaxed, relaxed like an athlete when he knows in advance that his delivery will be right on the mark.

Of all the great Texas Rangers L. H. McNelly had this quality of fearlessness to a greater degree than any other. To him a gunbattle was like a chess game, something to be won first with the mind and then with the body. Many others had the same quality.

It must never be thought that these men were foolhardy. They were too intelligent for that. In the gunfighting of the West the foolhardy did not survive long enough to make a reputation. I do not want to leave the impression, either, that because the men I am talking about were relaxed that they were not alert. They were prepared to act quickly, but they were not strung up until their muscles were tight and out of control.

I have not seen this theory of courage set forth in print, though it may have been. I have discussed it with Texas Rangers and other officials who are frequently in danger, and some of them agree that the theory is sound. I am submitting it to the readers of *True West* to see what light they can throw on the question as to whether courage is a positive or a negative thing.